THE EVERYTHING HOMESELLING BOOK

From open house to closing the deal,
everything you need to know to get the most
money for your house

Ruth Rejnis

Adams Media Corporation
Avon, Massachusetts

An Everything® Series Book.
Everything® is a registered trademark of Adams Media Corporation.

Published by
Adams Media Corporation
57 Littlefield Street, Avon, MA 02322. U.S.A.
www.adamsmedia.com

ISBN: 1-58062-304-2

Printed in the United States of America.

J I H G F E D C

Library of Congress Cataloging-in-Publication Data
Rejnis, Ruth.
The everything homeselling book / Ruth Rejnis.—1st ed.
p.   cm.—(The everything series)
Includes index.
ISBN 1-58062-304-2
1. House selling—United States. 2. Real estate business—United States.
I. Title. II. Series.
HD255.R4432 2000
333.33'83—dc21   99-055560

This publication is designed to provide accurate and authoritative information with regard to the subject matter covered. It is sold with the understanding that the publisher is not engaged in rendering legal, accounting, or other professional advice. If legal advice or other expert assistance is required, the services of a competent professional person should be sought.
—From a *Declaration of Principles* jointly adopted by a Committee of the American
Bar Association and a Committee of Publishers and Associations

Illustrations by Eulala Conner and Barry Littmann.

This book is available at quantity discounts for bulk purchases.
For information, call 1-800-872-5627.

Visit the entire Everything® series at everything.com

Contents

Introduction ix

Part I:
The ABCs of Selling Your Home

Chapter 1: The *Very* Big Picture 3
Real-Estate Agents 7
Buyers and Sellers in This Game 8
How Can a Seller Win? 8
A "House" Is Not a "Home" 9
The Very Bottom Line 9

Chapter 2: Why Are You Selling? 11
The Company Transfer 13
Need a Larger House 15
Trading Down to a Smaller House 16
Purchased Another House 18
A Divorce 19
Protecting My Investment 20
A Death 24

Chapter 3: When Is the Best Time to Sell? 25
When You Have the Freedom to Choose 26
The Home-Selling Calendar 27
What about the National Economy? 32
The Economic Picture Closer to Home 33

Chapter 4: Setting a Sales Price 37
Tax Assessments 41
Replacement Cost 42
Personal Comparison Shopping 43
A Professional Appraisal 44

The Comparative Market Analysis 44
Using Competing Real-Estate Agencies 46

Chapter 5: How Much Will You *Really* Make from This Sale? 49

Your Plans? 55

Chapter 6: Major Buyer Turn-ons— and Turnoffs 57

Exterior Painting 59
Landscaping 60
The Garage 61
The Basement 61
Termites 62
Why Buyers Are So *Nervous* 63
A House Inspection for Sellers 65
    The Inspector's Job 65
    Finding a House Inspector 66
Other Inspection Concerns 66
How about a Warranty? 68

Chapter 7: Smaller Stuff: Minor Repairs and Decorating Fix-ups 69

Eeeeuw—Dirt! 70
    Get Rid of Clutter 71
Sprucing Up the House 71
    Windows and Coverings 71
    Hall Closet 74
    Living Room 74
    Dining Room 74
    Kitchen 75
    Pantry 76
    Stairway and Hallway 76
    Master Bedroom 76
    Bedroom Closets 77
    Children's Rooms 77

CONTENTS

Bathrooms 77
All Around the House 78
Odors 78
What Will All This Cost? 79

Chapter 8: "I'll Sell It Myself, Thank You" 81
Taking the Plunge 83
Companies That Help FSBOs 87

Chapter 9: Ten "Must-Do's" for FSBOs 89
1. Describe the Property 90
2. Locate the Property 93
3. Know the Town 94
4. Qualify the Buyers 95
5. Be Prepared for an Offer 98
6. Advertise 98
7. Answer the Phone 100
8. Show the Property 102
9. Negotiate the Sale 104
10. Know When to Turn to the Pros 105

Chapter 10: Working with a
Real-Estate Agent 107
Who's Who Here? 110
Determining the Right Broker for You 111
Office Location 111
The Nature of the Business 111
Privately Owned or Franchise? 112
Cooperation 112
Training and Competence 113
Financial Savvy 113
Goodwill 113
Commissions 114
Discount Brokers 114
Interviewing Agents 116
Fair Housing 118

What a Listing Contract Should Contain 118
Can You Ever Get Out of a Contract? 121
Preparing Your Listing Sheet 122
Photograph 124
The Lockbox 124

Chapter 11: Disclosure: What to Tell Before You Sell 125

Then 126
What Most States Say You Must Tell 126
   Disclosure of Property Condition Form 127
   Lead-Based Paint Disclosure Form 127
Radon and Asbestos 128
   Radon 128
   Asbestos 128
Other Disclosures: Necessary or Voluntary? 129
"Traumatized" Properties 130
   Airport Noise 130
   Problem Neighbor 130
   Threatening Dog Next Door 130
   Crime Scene 130
   Death from Natural Causes 130
   Near a Cemetery, Jail, or Sewage-Treatment Plant 131
   Handicapped Access 131
Haunted House 131
What about "Fixer Uppers"? 132
If It Bothers You Not to Tell 132

Chapter 12: For Sale by Internet 133

If You're Selling Your House Yourself 134
Working with an Agent 135
A Long Journey 136

Chapter 13: While Your Place Is on the Market   137

The Lockbox 139
A Sign 140

CONTENTS

The Open House 141
    The Realtors' Open House 141
    The Public Open House 142
Well, Look Who's Back 143
The Telephone 144
The No Show 145
Patience, Patience 147
Your Kids and Your Pets 148

Chapter 14: What to Do When It's Not Selling 151

Buyer Response 152
Price Too High 154
The Money Market 155
The Local Marketplace 155
Some Suggestions 155
    Lease/Purchase Option 156
    Seller Financing 158
An Auction 160

Chapter 15: Negotiating: The Art of the Deal . 161

The Browns 162
The Greens 164
The Whites 167
Susan Gray 168
The Paynes 172
The Blacks 175
The Upwards 178

Chapter 16: The Sales Contract 181

Common Additions to a Contract 187
    Termite Inspection Clause 187
    Professional House-Inspection Clause 188
    Disclosure Clause 189
    Walk-Through Clause 189
Take Your Time 190

Chapter 17: Winning at the Waiting Game: The Closing and Taxes 191

Is Your House Still on the Market? 193
Sold Is Sold, Right? 194
The Closing 195
And Then There's Uncle Sam 199

Chapter 18: When You Must Sell One House to Buy Another 201

The Corporate Transfer 202
Changing Jobs 204
Stepping Up 205
Building Your Dream House 206
The Safe Switch 207
The Empty Nest 208
Divorce 210

Chapter 19: Easing Some Particularly Knotty Sell/Buy Problems 211

The Bridge Loan 212
"Time Is of the Essence" 213
Occupancy before Closing 215
Occupancy after Closing 215
Month-to-Month Tenants 216
The Guaranteed Sale 218
Selling the Vacant House 218
  Decorating 219
  Maintenance 220
  Showings 221
Confusing, Isn't It? 221

Chapter 20: Getting a Move On 223

Three Steps to a Successful Move 224
  Your New Community 224
  Take Inventory 225
  Select a Mover 228

The Corporate Move 231
The Role of Relocation Companies 231

Part II:
Special Sales

Chapter 21: Selling a Condominium
or Cooperative 237

All Together Now 238
You Tell 'Em 238
Why Not Rent? 240
Disclosure 240
Inspection: More than Meets the Eye 241
S-P-A-C-E 241
Little Things Mean a Lot 243
Advertising 243
For Condo Sellers 244
For Co-op Sellers 245

Chapter 22: Selling a House You Inherit 247

The "How" of Estate Sales 248
Negotiating 250
Do You Have the Authority to Sell? 252
An Auction 252
Renting the House 254
Ownership Styles for the House You Want to Keep 255

Chapter 23: Selling a Vacation House 257

Get Going, and Sell! 258
Selling by the Season 260
Some Paperwork 261
Clever Marketing 264
Do It Yourself or Use an Agent? 266
  On Your Own 266
  With an Agent 267

Chapter 24: Selling a Resort Time-Share 269

What Time-Sharing Is—and Is Not 270
The Olden Days 271
The Difficulty in Selling 271
Reasons for Holding on to Your Time-Share 272
    Trading 272
    Renting 274
    Your Estate File 274
"No, No, I Really Want to Sell" 276
Is Financing Available? 000

Glossary 277

Index 287

Introduction

So, it looks as if you are going to be moving. You're certainly going to be busy in the next several weeks or months!

Remember when you bought your present home? It might have been two years or thirty years ago, but you no doubt looked at a number of places for sale, so many that at some point you probably couldn't remember whether it was 134 Hyacinth Lane that had the breakfast nook or that ranch on Dumont Circle. It was exciting considering the possibilities of all those homes, but tiring too.

Remember the mountain of paperwork you had to wade through to apply for a mortgage? And how you held your breath waiting for its approval? You left after the closing on your home poorer, but happy with your purchase and excited about moving in.

All or some of that process may have been nerve wracking for you, but especially if you were a first-time homebuyer, it helped you gain important knowledge of the real estate market.

Now you are about to sell. You are all set. You hope to reap the reward for wisely buying your present place and maintaining it over the years. However, you now have "challenges," too, which are quite different from a buyer's. Then you were trying to purchase the best property at the least cost to you. Now, of course, you're on the other side of the front door: You're an owner who wants to sell at the greatest profit and in the shortest time possible.

Perhaps you have sold several homes and just want a refresher course in what's been happening over the last few years in residential real estate. Or maybe you are selling the house you have lived in for the last twenty years and need more than just a brush-up. Should you sell on your own, you wonder, or with an agent? What about capital gains taxes for sellers these days? Should you buy the next place before you sell this one?

Wherever you are on the real estate gameboard—a fairly seasoned seller or a complete neophyte—you are wise to have picked up this book to look for assistance. To win here calls for specific knowledge and skill. In these pages you will find exactly what you need to arm you with the confidence to sell well. So congratulations on your smarts in reading on. You are already a few moves ahead in this game!

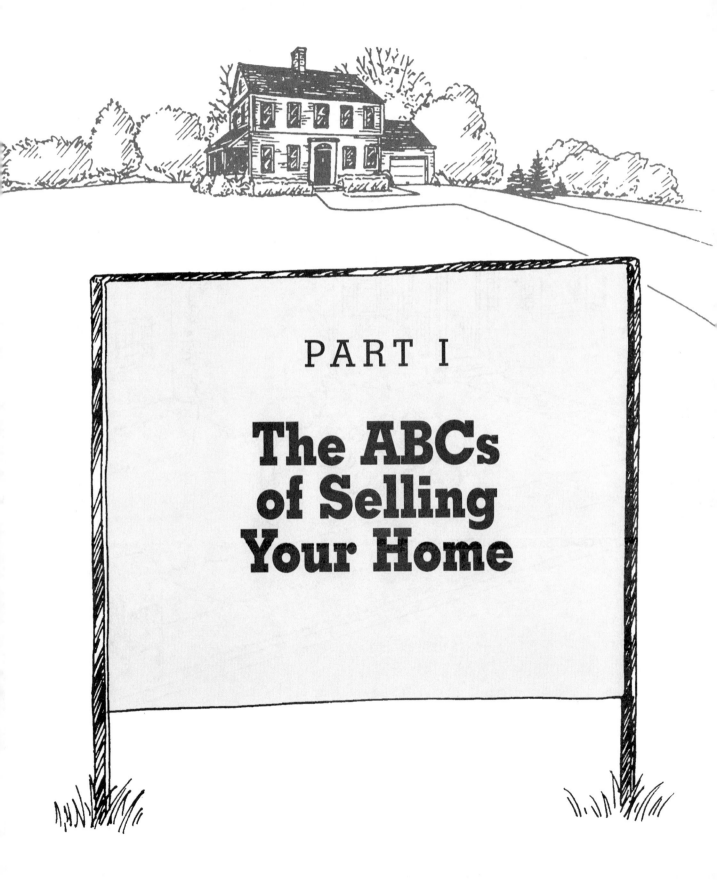

PART I

The ABCs of Selling Your Home

CHAPTER ONE

The Very Big Picture

race and Tim Johnson smiled at the real-estate agent as she reached out to shake their hands; she too was smiling. They had just signed with her to represent them in the sale of their house.

That very weekend the Johnsons seemed to have sold the house. The agent brought through a buyer who offered them the full asking price. Almost unheard of! Good news? Not 100 percent good to the Johnsons. Now they were racked by doubts. Did they sell for too little? Why *did* they ask the price they did? The couple agonized over the dollars they could have made if they had inched a little higher with the sale price.

Or *could* they have made that extra money? Was the sale price fair and they simply lucked out with a buyer who was willing not to quibble? The Johnsons would never know the answer.

On the other side of that pleasant town, Barbara and Greg Lane were selling their home, too. Greg had taken a new job in another part of the country, but his new employer was not helping him sell the house. The Lanes were selling on their own, without an agent, to save a real-estate commission. They composed the advertisement that would run in the local paper. It ran (and for your convenience as you read, this is the normally written version, not one using classified advertising abbreviations):

> Executive colonial with a view, beautiful landscaping, 3 bedrooms, 2 baths, wall-to-wall carpeting, owner moving across country, immediate occupancy. $140,000 firm.

That first week the phone rang off the hook. Unfortunately for the Lanes, most of the calls were from realty agents looking to list their home. Still, there were some queries from prospects who asked any number of questions. What about the kitchen—new or at least remodeled? What color are the bathrooms? What are the dimensions of the living room? What fiber is the carpeting? What's its color? How old is the furnace? What's the address? We'd like to drive by and take a look. At some point in the conversation, after one particular answer to their question, most callers said something like "oh," and found a reason to end the conversation.

Test Your Home Buyer/Seller Savvy

How does your market knowledge measure up?

1. How many properties does a buyer look at in a typical home search?
   _____ 8   _____ 10   _____ 14

2. Home buyers are more likely to learn about the house they bought from friends or family than from newspaper ads.
   _____ True   _____ False

3. What is the number-one problem reported by FSBO (For Sale by Owner) sellers?
   _____ Attracting buyers   _____ Pricing the home
   _____ Holding an open house

4. Approximately one in every _____ buyers is a single male.

5. What percentage of buyers used a mortgage lender recommended by their agent?
   _____ 28%   _____ 57%   _____ 69%

6. What percentage of sellers say they would use their agents again?
   _____ 71%   _____ 84%   _____ 91%

7. What percentage of sellers actually did use the agent again?
   _____ 60%   _____ 32%   _____ 23%

Source: 1998 National Association of Realtors Homebuyers & Sellers Report
Answers: 1. 8; 2. True; 3. Holding an open house; 4. 10; 5. 57%; 6. 71%; 7. 23%

Still, of those callers, about half made an appointment to look at the house. Of those, two-thirds actually showed up, but not one was a buyer.

By the fifth day, calls were down considerably. By the end of two weeks, there was only a trickle of interest. No one was coming to look at the house.

There was one caller the Lanes were hearing from consistently—Vera Eager, a local real-estate agent. Vera was the most persistent of the professionals who called. Indeed, she had even been to see the house, and had left her card. She told the Lanes she could think of three families who might be interested in the property, but she could not show the house without a contract. The house really needed the exposure only a real-estate agency could give, she told the couple, and then it should sell with no trouble. Signing a listing with her would relieve the Lanes of responsibility and worry, and get their house—the magic word—*sold*. The couple finally acquiesced and said fine, bring the listing contract over.

Vera worked her calculator for a few minutes and came up with $148,400 as the price needed to meet the Lanes' asking price and pay a 6 percent commission. Vera suggested they ask for $150,400. "That leaves you with some room to negotiate," she pointed out with a smile. "I'm making this listing out for a six-month term," she added. "That's just the traditional length of time we write in. Of course, it won't take nearly that long with *this* house."

It took five and a half months.

Those were not exactly stress-free and pressure-free days. Greg Lane had to leave to accept his new job 1,500 miles away. He lived in a motel room. Barbara, who would eventually be job hunting in the new locale, stayed behind. The children remained in school, and Barbara straightened up the house daily, waiting for agents and buyers to come.

The Lanes reduced the asking price, and then dropped it again. At $148,900 there were more lookers. The house sold for $146,500, from which they paid $8,790 in commissions, netting them $137,710.

Had $137,710 been a fair price originally? Or had the listing become tired and dog-eared and the Lanes desperate? The couple would never know.

Pricing—and selling—homes is an art, not a science. Although there can be suggested formulas for arriving at both numbers, the truth is that a house sells for what a buyer is willing to pay and what a seller is willing to accept. Indeed, those are the terms for the sale of any item, from a thimble to a nine-room split-level.

There is stress inherent in the process of selling a home, but that process can be focused and rationally controlled, bringing maximum profit and minimum pain. To do that you must toss out some long-held ideas about homes in general and your home in particular, and read the next few hundred pages carefully as you step into a world you may not have known existed.

Real estate is big, big business and is the riskiest, most complex game most of us will ever play. What is more alarming is that amateurs play against professionals, sometimes the most experienced players there are.

Real-Estate Agents

Real-estate agents are the professionals in this field, but they range widely in ability and understanding of the game. Every state in the country has licensing laws for them. Many states require thirty or more hours of classroom study followed by a state-controlled exam. A significant percentage of the applicants fail those exams. Those who pass usually start work with an established realty broker and within a few weeks are confused and disillusioned.

Why? Because the real-estate schools or courses they attended taught the rules, but not the game. Classwork concentrated on the laws governing realty practices. Those laws carefully define the boundaries and procedures of the real-estate marketplace, or the "science," if you will. But they do not mention the "art"—the pushing crowds, blind alleyways, illusions, and pitfalls. That knowledge constitutes the art of playing the game and, as in every game, skillful playing is the essence of success.

You need both experience and skill to win at this game. It takes six months to a year on the job to train a good real-estate agent, and the really good ones keep learning as long as they are working. The more they learn, the more often they play and the more often

INFORMATION

The average American stays in one house for seven years, according to the National Association of Realtors.

Home, as defined by *Merriam Webster's Collegiate Dictionary,* is (1) one's place of residence; (2) the social unit formed by a family living together; (3) a familiar or usual setting: congenial environment; also the focus of one's domestic attention.

they collect their commission checks. They play the game only for money, risking only their time.

Buyers and Sellers in This Game

On the other hand there are those who play for higher stakes. At the end of the game, the buyers bring cash for which they have mortgaged the property they will buy, and the sellers sign over the deeds to their homes and write the commission checks. These are real estate's amateur players, yet they too play "for keeps." They risk tremendous amounts of money and often their happiness.

It may be difficult to be in the position of the realty agent, but it is every bit as hard, and often every bit as risky, to be a playing seller. It is also harder to learn.

Buyers can enter and exit the real-estate field many times with many different agents. They can ask questions, compare notes, be rejected, learn the game, and continue. Sellers must wait—and wait and wait. They have just one house to market. Usually they are committed to just one agent. They do not know what is happening in other houses for sale around them, and the answers to the questions they ask are often vague and along the "everything'll work out" line. Good advice, in this instance, is hard to come by. It's lonely being a seller. Experienced sellers do best at this game, but experience is hard to acquire since most people sell only a few homes in their lifetime.

How Can a Seller Win?

What is "winning," anyway?

- Winning for realty agents is getting that commission.
- Winning for buyers is getting the most house for as little money as possible.
- Winning for sellers is selling quickly, without too much pain, and coming away with as much money as possible.

To win at this game, a seller cannot rely on luck, or simply sit and wait. Although buyers and agents have more freedom of movement in the realty game, the sellers have more control. Using that control effectively is essential to success, but it depends completely on skill and knowledge. As a seller, you must know what you are doing and why.

An important point here: As a seller, you must have at one time been a buyer. That's a totally different mindset from selling. Please forget, or at least suspend in your memory, the dictums and *do's* and *don'ts* you may have learned in your buying experience. Selling is different, very different.

A "House" Is Not a "Home"

Before going any further, here's the first step to success: Stop using the word *home* when you talk about the house that you are going to sell. "Home" is among the most emotionally weighted words in our language. People get involved, they listen more attentively, when you talk about their homes. But what you have for sale is a *house* (if you are selling a condominium or cooperative, see chapter 21 for some other terms you might want to use during this time, although you can certainly use house too). Think of your real estate as an item, a piece of merchandise on the market to be sold to the highest bidder. By all means cherish the memories of the good times you have had in your "home," but stop loving it. Sell a building, a structure. When you do that you can evaluate its worth more accurately, and place it on the market more effectively. Think of *home* as where you will go on to live after you sell this *house*.

To help keep you in the "house" mindset, that word will be used throughout these pages. Yes, this book *is* called *The Everything Homeselling Book*, because that's a recognizable term to those who are selling. The word *home* lasted a few paragraphs into this chapter, too, but now it is gone for the duration. (Well, it's gone until chapters 21 and 23 anyway, when it makes a reappearance. The reason for its use there is given in those chapters.)

The Very Bottom Line

Every seller and buyer knows, or should know, that a real-estate agent works for the seller of a house, not the buyer. It is the seller who pays her commission, although naturally she is interested in seeing buyers purchase a house, and one that they like. Indeed, only by making a successful match can she earn that commission.

TIP

If you think you can remember to switch back and forth between terms without driving yourself loco, you can certainly use the word *home* to buyers, when you refer to their living in your "house." *Home* is a warm term with good connotations for them.

INFORMATION

Women make up the overwhelming majority of residential real-estate agents, so to avoid complicated his/her terminology, agents will be referred to as "she" in these pages.
(Commercial realty agents, on the other hand, are predominantly male.)

So the agent is working for you, yes, and far more than for the buyer. But keep in mind at all times that as good as she is—and a good real-estate agent can be a very valuable ingredient in a successful sale—she is not going to work for you as hard as *you* are going to work for you. You cannot rest and let her take over. For one thing, an agent is not out to help you as much as she is out to make money. If you think she is going to fight for you to get a higher price for your house than the one attached to a specific offer, you are wrong. She wants to make a sale and get her commission. A $10,000 difference in price is $10,000 to you; to her it is just $600 in commission. She would rather see you sign a contract for the house at $10,000 less than fight for more and perhaps see the whole sale go down the drain.

So you must maintain control at all times in this major transaction. You *must* know what you are doing. This book will help you. It will inform you and guide you around potential catastrophes, or just simple mistakes on your way to selling at the best possible price.

If you follow its suggestions you will win at this particular real-estate game. Part of your victory will be cash—from the sale of your home—and part will be peace of mind that comes from knowing that the entire process went as well as it could be expected to go.

Are you revved up about now? Let's get started.

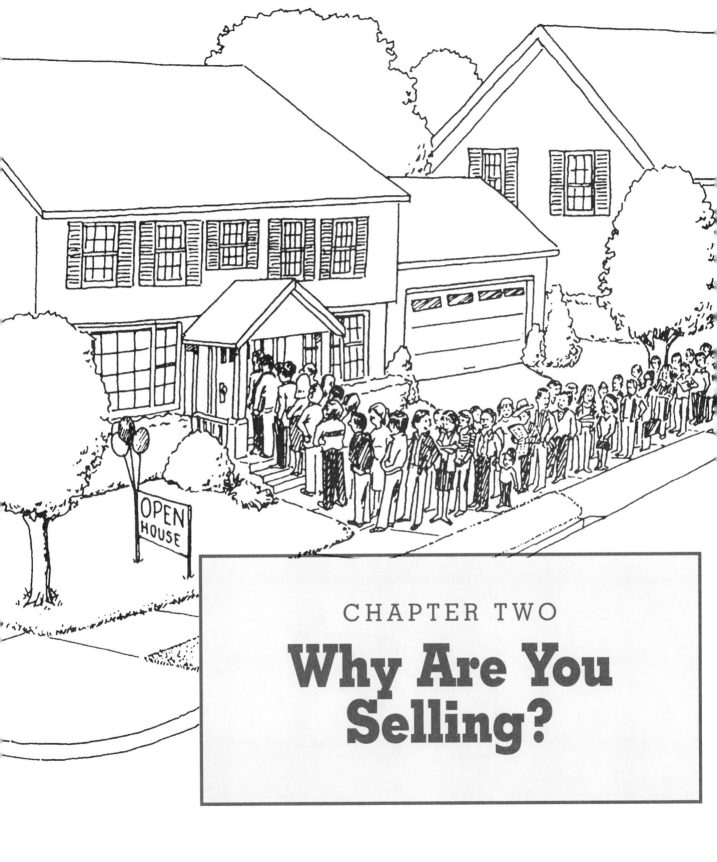

CHAPTER TWO

Why Are You Selling?

All buyers want their own place: first, it makes good financial sense, and second, well, there's that pride of ownership—the "putting your feet under your own table" sort of thing.

Sellers usually have a variety of reasons for setting out the For Sale sign. However, one of those reasons is not that the house is "a lemon." Of course, every house is imperfect. Termites gnaw their way into the structure, faucets drip, windows stick, the wind whistles through a multitude of cracks, toilets don't flush, and a dozen or so other ills assail every house at one time or another (it is hoped not all at the same time!).

But a house is a major investment. Folks don't sell because something or other doesn't work. Houses, unlike cars or computers or television sets, are too valuable for that. The investment of time, money, and emotion in a house is huge; and selling and moving are traumatic, expensive, and time-consuming.

So it takes more than a few problems to get folks to sell. Actually, real-estate agents will tell you it is very difficult, usually impossible, to get an owner to sell if he or she does not want to. (We'll skip the situation where for some reason someone offers the seller $50,000 or more over and above what the house would ordinarily sell for. That's the stuff of dreams.) A real-estate agent must get out there and beat the bushes in an effort to find people who want to sell and persuade them to sign a listing contract with her office. Or she persuades people to sell their old houses by selling them a new one, and isn't that crafty?

This is a very *human* business. In general, people resist change. Sometimes that resistance is a fear of the unknown. People would rather struggle with problems they recognize than risk the possibility of facing new ones—a case of "the devil you know." That same principle often keeps bad marriages together for years of misery for both parties. And that same inertia holds people for years in jobs they cannot stand. It is an inertia born of a desire to avoid pain, or at least any more pain or any new pain.

We have a tendency to set down roots in even the simplest of houses and neighborhoods. Friendships are made, behavior established, and a sense of security built upon. To move is to lose something, even when that move is a step up.

So we don't chuck houses the way we do troublesome cars. Some home owners fix the problem, while others just learn to live with it, fixing only the most serious concerns. For some, *anything* is better than moving.

Therefore, you are not likely to be selling your house because it is falling apart. Although it may well be, your desire for a bigger house in a better neighborhood is more likely to be your motivation than wanting to leave a house that is tumbling down.

It is important to identify your motivations precisely, and early in the selling game, since the motivation for selling affects the marketing and sometimes even the marketability of a house.

Here are a series of seller profiles, each one focusing on a particular motivating situation and explaining how that situation affects the marketing of a house. You will almost surely find yourself among these sketches, but do read them all, even the ones you do not think apply to you. As you read in chapter 1, one of the problems for home sellers is a sense of isolation. You rarely know much about your competition—the other sellers and their houses. These profiles will give you an armchair insight into that competition. Read through all of them, identify your own motivation, and then evaluate the advantages and disadvantages other sellers have in comparison.

The Company Transfer

The company move is very much a part of middle-class America. Giant corporations spend millions of dollars each year transferring their middle management people. Most of those folks own houses that they must sell. Most companies help with the selling and moving, and maybe provide some other aids, too, such as helping "the trailing spouse" with job hunting.

Depending on the amount of company support offered, the transfer can be the easiest, most pleasant way to sell. Consider the Browns. Mr. Brown works for one of the largest, most generous, most employee-moving companies in America. That company offers the Browns several approaches to selling their house. These options are not necessarily offered by every corporation.

INFORMATION

Women make up just one in five (17%) of corporate transferees, according to the Employee Relocation Council, the national trade association for the relocation industry. Most transferees (76%) are married, according to the council, and over half (52%) have working spouses. Sixty-five percent of transferees have dependent children. The transferred employees tend to be in middle management, are on average thirty-eight years old, and earn $59,482.

- The Browns can choose a real-estate firm and list the house at a price they themselves set. When the house is sold the company will pay the real-estate commission and all closing costs.
- Or they might elect to have the house appraised by two professional appraisers of the company's choice, for which the company pays. The two appraisals must come within a certain percentage of each other, maybe 5 percent. If they do not, a third appraisal is made. When two appraisals are within the required percentage of each other, their average is taken as the "fair market value" of the property, and this amount is offered to the Browns. They may then sell to the company and leave. Their house is put on the market after they have moved out.
- Or the Browns could elect to take the appraisals into consideration and then list the house at a price that they determine, usually several thousand dollars higher than the company offer. They then have two months to sell the house at their price, with their real-estate agent, before the offer becomes void. If they sell at a price higher than the company offer, the company still pays all commissions and closing costs. If they do not sell within the two-month period, they can reject the company offer and continue to market the house at their price, or they can take the house off the market and accept that offer. It's a game the seller can't lose!

Besides companies differing in their own specific policies regarding transferees, they sometimes vary according to the state of the national economy.

Still, this may all sound like heaven to the poor soul who's had his house on the market for six months with no buyers in sight. There are some disadvantages, though. In a transfer situation, there is always time pressure. The sellers cannot choose when to move and are sometimes forced to put their house on the market in a slow selling season or at a time of tight mortgage money. Often the employee is sent to his or her new job ahead of the family, leaving little time for sprucing up the house.

All of this does not matter, of course, if the family is satisfied with the company offer. These offers are usually very fair prices, though they are rarely "a killing." However, not all companies will buy the house from their employees. A large number of national corporations simply offer to pay closing costs and commissions. This puts pressure on the family to sell, whatever the market and season.

Still, even with a company that won't buy the house, and even with the time pressure of family separation, people like the Browns are still ahead in the real-estate marketplace. Because the transferring company will reimburse them for the amount of real-estate commissions, they have that dollar figure as a cushion in their negotiating. They can afford to sell at market value and still come out several thousand dollars ahead; they can also sell below market value and come out with the same amount of cash as, or even more than, their next-door neighbor who is selling with a realty agent but without support from "the company."

So if you are like the Browns, consider yourself fortunate. If the Browns of the world are your competition in the house-selling game, however, be aware of how very tough that competition is.

Need a Larger House

This appears on more "why are you selling" lists than any other reason, whether the seller is leaving behind a cottage or a substantial split level or colonial. There seems to be a stage in life—usually from the thirties through early forties—when many people want a larger home. But let's take a look at a typical example of these sellers.

The Greens' house is a two-bedroom Cape Cod. On the front lawn is a tricycle and a large rubber ball. In the living room, a three-year-old boy navigates a motorized dump truck through an assortment of toys. In the kitchen, a fourteen-month-old girl tosses spaghetti from her high chair. Her pregnant mother is at the sink preparing dinner. Dad isn't home from work yet. Upstairs, the bedrooms are overflowing with furniture, scattered toys, and clothing.

The Greens have obviously outgrown their starter home and are ready to move up to more space. They are fortunate in that there is a demand for smaller starter houses. These properties usually sell quickly and well; although disrepair and obvious crowding, such as you find at the Greens', will invariably delay the sale and bring a lower price.

What should the Greens do? First off, they should get as much help as they can at the start of the selling process by moving as much furniture as possible into the basements or garages of their friends. In a small house, even one article of clothing thrown on the floor or tossed on a chair stands out and shrieks "clutter." (There is more about straightening up in chapters 6 and 7.)

The Greens should also try not to be at home when the house is shown. People tend to fill up a house, and the four Greens, the realty agent, and perhaps two would-be buyers is a crowd in this small place. Buyers need to feel a sense of space around them.

The Whites have a different concern. They live in a four-bedroom split-level with a formal living room, a separate dining room, a family room with a fireplace, and a large eat-in kitchen. The physical space is adequate by most standards (the Greens would love it!). But the small business Mr. White opened four years ago has flourished and the family income has almost tripled. The couple dreams of a glass-and-stone contemporary, a separate study for Mr. White, an office for Mrs. White, who works outside the home, and a guest room.

People like the Whites do not really need to sell. Their properties are usually well maintained and well decorated, and show extremely well. Their main problems as sellers are usually time-related: Will the house they are building be ready on time? Will they be able to sell quickly enough once they decide on the new house they are going to buy?

Trading Down to a Smaller House

This phrase appears less frequently on realty listings, probably because to some degree it seems to carry less status, but also because it often appears in variations: "retiring," "moving," or "moving to a condo."

These days the huge number of baby boomers (those born between 1946 and 1964) are at that stage of life when the so-called empty nest looms or has already arrived. With possibly both partners in a household working, there is no need for, or interest in, a large home.

Susan Gray is one of those boomers. She is a widow with two children. Samantha is married and a teacher; Joe is in his last year of college. Susan owns a four-bedroom, two-story colonial home in Connecticut, where property taxes are quite high. In her fifties, she is not ready to retire from her job with a local computer company, but is tired of heating and cleaning the empty rooms. (After graduation, Joe plans to share a Manhattan apartment with some college buddies and is not likely to return to home full time.) Susan suffered a nasty leg fracture a couple of years ago, and on bad days does not look forward to climbing stairs. We won't even get into the expense of having someone care for the front lawn and backyard that comprise her half-acre lot. Susan may look for a one-story ranch house on a small lot, or maybe even a condominium.

Sellers like Susan Gray have both time and space on their side. They are under no pressure to sell and can wait for a good selling season and perhaps even for a "seller's market." (There is a full explanation of a seller's market and a buyer's market in chapter 3.) Their houses show well; they are well maintained and usually uncluttered. Unlike the Greens in their too-tight Cape Cod, Susan Gray's rooms are nearly always presentable and ready to be shown on a few moments' notice.

Does Susan have a selling problem? If she does, it is usually in overpricing her property. Her attachment to her "home" is usually great, and she feels a pride of ownership. With no pressure to sell, it is easy for her to see her property as very valuable, more valuable than the market can tolerate. She may have to wait several months of on-the-market time before she re-evaluates her asking price. Or she might find and purchase the perfect smaller house for her, giving her an incentive—and putting the pressure on her—to price her larger house more realistically.

The "retiring" variation of moving to a smaller house is a story similar to Susan Gray's, except that the very act of retiring is a strong motivator. With less income and more time on their hands, retiring home owners often look forward to a change of scenery and a lessening of responsibility. They, too, may overprice their house, but are usually more open to negotiation and price readjustment. They are eager to get moving, literally, with their new life.

DEFINITION PLEASE

Fair market value is generally accepted as the highest price that a ready, willing, and able buyer will pay and the lowest price a ready, willing, and able seller will accept for the property in question. You will see this phrase frequently in these pages.

Purchased Another House

This is a red flag when it appears on a listing. Every real-estate agent knows immediately that the seller wants to sell and is willing to negotiate. Trouble is, every buyer knows it too.

The Paynes' story is a profile in extreme, but in it are all the ingredients of the typical tale.

Tom and Sarah Payne found a house they really liked through a for-sale-by-owner ad in the local newspaper. They had their lawyer draw up the contract allowing them almost three months until the closing date. The seller agreed and the Paynes were delighted. They felt that they had won a good deal on the house they were buying and had plenty of time to sell their old house at top dollar.

In the course of those three months, mortgage money dried up, putting an especially tight stranglehold on first-time buyers (the most likely candidates for the Paynes' present house). To make matters worse, there was a sudden rash of fights between groups of teenage boys at the town's high school. They were minor incidents, but the local newspaper filled its front pages with highly emotional stories for several weeks. Houses in the town became "undesirable."

The Paynes were trapped. They were legally and financially committed to their purchase and they could not find a buyer for the house they were selling. The bank where they had secured their mortgage commitment on the new house helped them with a "bridge loan." (There is a complete explanation in chapter 19, pages 212–213, of this financing, which allows sellers to borrow on the equity in their old house to make a down payment on the new.) This loan enabled them to close on the new house. They moved in, hoping their old house would sell better empty. (In most cases, this is an inaccurate assumption. Houses usually sell better with people living in them; more about this later, too.)

Now the real squeeze began. The Paynes had to make their new higher mortgage payment each month. They also had to continue to make payments on the mortgage for their old house to protect their credit rating, and they had to pay the interest on the bridge loan. Their savings began to disappear at a terrifying rate.

They reduced the price twice; nothing happened. Finally, desperate for cash, they rented the house to a young unmarried couple on a month-to-month basis. Showings became more difficult; the couple didn't always cooperate and the house, uncared for, showed more and more poorly. The Paynes argued often and became depressed. Neither Tom nor Sarah could see a way out.

It took over a year to sell that house and the final negotiated price was $3,000 below the second reduction price. It had been a nightmare.

Fortunately, few sellers experience horror stories of this intensity, but the commitment to buy another house when you are still responsible for one is difficult to accomplish without considerable financial loss and legal entanglements. Needless to say, it is also the strongest motivator for selling the old house. Home owners who sign up to buy before they have a purchase contract on their old house must be careful to set the selling price within negotiating range of market value. They must also take care to show the house as well as possible, to be aware of the competition and selling conditions in the real-estate market of the town, and to get several months' lead time before closing on the new house.

Why all these precautions? Because most families need the cash from the equity in their old house as a down payment on the new house. If you cannot get the cash out by selling, you must borrow until a sale closes.

If you see Tom or Sarah Payne looking back at you in the mirror, and you have allowed your listing real-estate firm to print "have purchased another home" on your listing sheet, be prepared to negotiate hard. Every buyer who reads the phrase will come in with a low first offer, and every real-estate agent will have an extra trump card in her negotiating game.

When you must sell one house to buy another, and how to finesse your way around that potential financial land mine, is the subject of a whole chapter later in this book, chapter 18.

A Divorce

Calling a home a house separates the cool from the emotionally involved. Add the breakup of a family and a divorce to the picture and you have a selling situation that is white-hot, no matter what you call the property.

TIP

You're reading a book about selling your house, but if you are cramped for space, you might save the time, money, and aggravation of moving by building onto your existing place. For a few years now, Improve, Don't Move has been a slogan of the home-remodeling industry aimed at squeezed-tight home owners. However, don't overimprove to make your house the most expensive on your block or, worse, *far* more expensive than the others.

Dick and Donna Black have separated. Divorce proceedings may or may not have begun, but the marriage is over. He moves out, she stays in the house with the children, and they agree to sell the property and divide the profit. They also agree on the asking price—usually it's high since they each get only half of the proceeds. They also sign a real-estate listing agreement.

Fine so far, but then the trouble begins. Although Donna and Dick both want as much money as possible, *he* wants a quick sale, so time is worth a few thousand off the asking price. *She,* on the other hand, wants time to look for a new place. So why not wait for the best offer? Or *she* wants to get away from the bad memories the house holds now, and will sell for something less. Meanwhile, *he* wants every single dollar the wretched property can bring, no matter how long it takes.

House sales motivated by divorce vary somewhat. In general, however, the selling agent must negotiate each item of the contract twice, usually in two different places, with two people who have different goals and often feel negative, resentful, and even openly hostile toward each other. Sometimes one party will hold up a valid sale just to "spite" the estranged spouse.

If divorce is going to be your selling motivator, please try to come to some rational agreement early. In the presence of your lawyers (but *not* the realty agent), discuss what price you could both accept for the house. You might even want to consider securing a fair market appraisal of the property from a professional appraiser. (It's likely to cost you around $250, but it is a good negotiating tool later and can be a nonpartisan point of agreement in a divorce situation.) When you do agree on your rock-bottom figure, try to agree, too, on what will remain in the house and how soon you would like to close. The relatively brief time you spend working out those details in a lawyer's office can save you many nights of sleeplessness and emotional turmoil.

Protecting My Investment

This phrase does not appear on a real-estate listing, and sellers usually do not mention this exact reason for moving to realty agents either. They fear it would be the kiss of death for their sale. It is,

Why Am I Selling?

You can answer that question in a word or two, can't you? Even if you immediately reply "transfer" or "more space," there may be some secondary pluses you hope to gain through the sale of your house. Maybe it's buying a house that will at last give you a home office. Or perhaps you'll pull out some of the equity from that sale to purchase a second (or third) car for the family. It helps to see all of this in print, so your selling reasons—all of them—are clear to you. So why *are* you selling? Jot your responses here, from the principal one to those other benefits you hope to gain from the sale, and remember your answers as you read the next couple hundred pages.

Major

_____

_____

_____

_____

_____

_____

_____

Others

_____

_____

_____

_____

_____

_____

_____

however, a very real motivator and far more prevalent than anyone would like to admit. It is Joyce and Fred Upwards moving to the next town, or the one beyond that, because it is a "nicer" place to live.

If you visited the Upwards in their lovely home, and sat in their living room munching cheese and fruit and sipping good wine, you would hear them rave about the high quality of the schools in Nextown, where they plan to move, the low taxes and, my goodness, how property has appreciated there. It's going up much faster than the town where they are now.

"In ten years I don't think you'll be able to sell a house in this town," Fred says of the community he plans to leave.

Joyce gushes, "Oh, Nextown is *so* nice. They have a lovely shopping mall and no traffic jams and the best high school football team in the state."

"A wonderful investment," Fred concludes. "We can just watch our money grow there."

Perhaps the Upwards are a bit over the top. But people do move from one town to another because they foresee that the "status," or the desirability, of their town is decreasing, while that of the other is growing. Usually they are right. Towns and cities are living, breathing entities. They are not static. Their fortunes rise and fall, perhaps staying inert for a few years, but not forever. A town's character and reputation does affect the appreciation rate of the houses within its borders.

People who move for this particular reason can be either very rational or very emotional. The rational ones are financially oriented. They look at their homes as an investment, and they want the best return on the dollar—and the best in local schools and services while they are earning that return. The emotional ones want the prestige of the best address. A pretty fair number of people belong to both groups.

These folks don't have to move from one town to another. They can move to a different neighborhood within the same town borders.

The Upwards decided on a move after long consideration of the likely value of Nextown, and a fairly long time spent watching what they felt was a subtle decline of the community in which they presently lived. More often than not, however, the decision to move for investment protection is precipitated by an immediate crisis: a headline in the daily newspaper that scares an owner, a decision of the town planning board, or a series of incidents or changes in the neighborhood.

If you were able to track down and interview "investment protection" sellers, you would probably hear that there are too many apartments being built in the town, or the local taxes are going up yet again, or a new highway is going to be built a short distance from their house, or the zoning has been changed, or students are going to be bused long distances.

Sometimes the threat is real. After all, if a new highway does go up within a few hundred yards of a house, that *is* likely to affect property values. Much higher property taxes one day will mean a smaller pool of home owners who are willing and able to pay those taxes. Still, sometimes the threat is only an emotional response to the owners' fears and prejudices. In either case, the sense of impending doom and of impending loss of profit and salability can drive home owners to list their property, perhaps long before they ever intended to move. Get out while the getting is good, they think.

People like the Upwards, who move with long-term "vision," if you will, tend to price their houses on the high side. After all, as they see it the town is still desirable. It's their estimate of ten years down the road that is motivating their decision to leave. Folks who respond, however, to a real or imagined immediate threat to their property's value often price their houses at market value or lower and are quite open to negotiating downward.

If you are selling because you feel your investment will be safer in another location, be careful to examine your situation as rationally

and thoroughly as possible. Is that other town really as good as you think? How long before significant changes occur in your present town (or neighborhood)? How definite are proposals for a change? Can you fight them? How do your neighbors feel? Are you reacting quickly and emotionally to a situation that will cool down in the near future?

Ask yourself those questions. Then, think carefully about the answers before uprooting yourself from a home and community you like—and certainly before paying the expenses of selling and moving from one place to another.

A Death

Death is an unwelcome visitor. The real-estate marketplace is no exception. Among the most difficult houses to sell are small estate sales. Picture this: a house with overgrown shrubbery and grass; dusty windows; worn, old-fashioned furniture; faded wallpaper and paint; and framed photographs resting on top of the television set and on every tabletop in sight. It is very quiet in these homes. Would-be customers soon become uncomfortable intruding in this obvious backdrop to the interruption of a life. They aren't considering the traffic pattern or the location of schools. They just want *out*.

If you inherit a house and want to sell it, chapter 22 can help you with common estate-sale problems.

That's it, then. All the likely home sellers. If you have not found yourself among these profiles, you may have found at least some elements that seem familiar. Or perhaps you recognize parts of yourself in several profiles. It is not essential that you say "I am just like the Greens," or "Yup, the Blacks—there we are." It *is* important that you look at your own situation, examine your whys for selling and know that those whys will affect your selling procedure and your chances for a good deal. Next comes *when* to sell and then—ta-da—we start on *how*.

CHAPTER THREE

When Is the Best Time to Sell?

The very best time to sell your home is when you have a buyer willing to pay your price, and willing to agree to other requirements you may have, such as a closing date that is convenient for *you.*

That's ideal. Sometimes luck is on your side. Most times real life gets in the way of a quick, slick sale.

In these days of family planning, the corporate transfer has taken the place of an unexpected pregnancy as the most common life-change around, and it can be a mixed blessing. With a transfer there is no question of "when" and no time to plan ahead. You are simply plopped into the situation of the transferred employee. Short of giving up your job or passing up the chance for a promotion, you list your house for sale, begin to close out bank accounts, collect doctor and dentist records, and schedule farewell luncheons with work colleagues and your closest friends. The season of the year, the emotional and physical health of members of your family, the state of the national economy, the availability of mortgage money, the condition of the real-estate market where you are and where you will be heading, the appearance of your house—none of these factors can affect your decision to sell. The decision has been made, and it's time for you to get packing and assume your new responsibilities 100 or 2,500 miles away.

When You Have the Freedom to Choose

Not everyone is part of the corporate world, though, and most people *can* decide when to move. Sometimes that freedom to decide causes problems in itself. For example, a couple may agree that they need or want a different house, but can't agree on exactly when to sell and when to begin house hunting. They put it off for the "right" time.

You know as you examine your own life there is usually never a perfect time. Something is always boiling. You want to wait until Jason finishes grade school. You want to wait until your term on the library board expires. You want to wait until you get the next promotion. You want to wait until you've first bought the new car you need. You want to wait and see if your mom will be moving to town, and maybe you'll buy a two-family house. You are afraid the stock market's blissful ride will come to an end, so you want to wait and see what happens. Life is full of "somethings." The trick is to decide which are important enough to affect the decisions you make and the course you want to set for yourself.

You would be wise to consider all of the "when" factors in this chapter. Knowledge of these factors will help you to understand what is happening while your house is on the market. Later, it will help you accurately determine the market value of your property. It will help you decide your strategies during the negotiation part of the game. It may even nudge you to put your property on the market a little sooner, or maybe a little later, than you originally planned. Generally speaking, however, these time factors should not determine *whether* you should sell your house—just *when*.

Real-estate time factors are external pressures. The spur to move should come from internal pressures, the motivators you read about in chapter 2. Of course, sometimes they all get jumbled together. Protection of your investment may be an internal motivator in your family, yet it is also tied to time, the economy, and the reputation of your town.

Sometimes time itself is a prime family motivator for selling or not selling. For example, impending childbirth will stimulate some families to seek a larger house, others to wait until things settle down a bit for mother and infant. Sometimes a family will delay a move to allow a high school senior to graduate with his class. Sometimes the health of a relative will affect the decision. But these time factors are not related to real-estate time factors and the economy; they are factors internal to the family.

So you must examine your *family time factors* to make an informed decision to sell. This chapter will tell you about *real-estate time factors* and how they will affect your sale. "When to sell" is concerned with the selling season and the weather, with the state of the national economy and the local real-estate market.

The Home-Selling Calendar

Let's start with, instead of the best time to sell, the very worst. We'll get that over with and then work our way up to the best months or season.

TIP

You have probably heard the expression "You only get one chance to make a first impression." Choose the best time—of the year and in your community—to put your house on the market.

December, holiday time for the nation, is also a holiday for the real-estate business. A number of realty conventions take place in late November and December, and they are well attended. This is when real-estate salespeople and brokers tend to their own business with colleagues, since there aren't many sellers or buyers around! In real-estate offices this is the time to take vacations, long lunches, and shopping jaunts; hit the various office parties; total up the year's revenues; and do other paperwork that is not actual sales. The phone does not ring much, except for one person or another calling to wish someone "Happy Holidays."

December is the worst month to put a new listing on the market. The fact that yours will be one of the few trickling in is not an advantage. Real-estate agents are just people, and like all of us they get caught up in the spirit of things. And the spirit of December is holidays, shopping, and "spirits." Few agents will take the time to go out and inspect houses, since they won't have customers for a month or more. And by that time, the new listing that came on the market December 4 is "old."

Newness, whether it's the latest clothing or music style or car, generates curiosity and interest. It's the same with a listing—agents get out to see what's new to sell. And every agent who personally inspects your house remembers that house better than the ones she saw only as a picture and statistics crossing her desk. When that agent answers a phone call with a potential buyer, she may remember your house well enough to describe it, or at least some aspect of it, with enthusiasm. That kind of positive attitude can get that buyer out to see the house with a positive attitude of his own. It's only a possibility, yes, but it does happen, again and again. So if you can avoid it, don't waste the drawing power of a new listing during real estate's dead time. Enjoy your holidays.

Fortunately, in **January** we have a temperature thaw, which is a glimmer of hope that spring will eventually be here, and excitement for work once again builds in realty offices. Holiday time is over, and now it's time to make money. Buyers who gave up house hunting at the end of October are back in full force, looking for listings. Executives who heard about their upcoming transfers in November and begged for a last holiday season at home are now resigned to moving, and eager to get the show on the road. And potential sellers, like you, having enjoyed the holiday season without interruption, are coming out of the woodwork. Business begins humming again.

With the exception of the most northern states, January is a relatively good time to list and is especially good if you live in the southern states. Actually, if you live in the nation's winter or warm-weather vacation areas, it's the best time to list, for that is when the largest number of people are visiting that area, and some of them are bound to be looking to buy, whether it's a retirement home, a vacation home, or an investment property. Snow is good weather in ski towns! Sunshine and heat can't be beat in warm southern resorts!

There is more about selling a vacation house, in a cold- or warm-weather climate, in chapter 23. If, however, you live in a part of the country where winter is just *cold*, without any mountains and resort facilities to pretty up the picture, you should be aware of the disadvantage of winter selling. Sometimes would-be buyers refuse to look at a house because the driveway looks too steep and they are afraid the agent's car isn't going to make it (the agent might be afraid too!).

Sometimes it's just too cold to get out of the car. Sometimes a prospective buyer can't adequately look at a house because it's buried under seven feet of snow. Sometimes a snowstorm forces the buyer to cancel an appointment to go through a house. Some buyers just get weary of the whole business and decide to wait for spring!

February is not usually a pretty month, most of us will agree. Where the weather is harsh, February makes winter seem interminable. Everyone appears to have the midwinter blues. Again, though, the more southern states have a slight advantage. By the end of the month, they will see bags of mulch and fertilizer delivered and stacked outside local supermarkets, nurseries, and home centers, signaling the warming of the earth beneath those residents' feet. And winter ski and sun resorts are still "hot." Everywhere else, people just keep grousing and shoveling.

By **March**, the weather almost everywhere is beginning to ease up. Buyers are not yet out in full force, but listings are beginning to appear in larger numbers, and agents, not yet frantically busy, take more time to do preinspections. Note: This is an *immense* advantage.

Watch your step *literally*. Remember to keep walkways and driveways shoveled in the winter if your house is on the market then. It may be the law to clear snow where you are. Cleared spaces are certainly more welcoming to agents and house hunters than banks of ice.

It is the reason March gets the most votes—by sellers and by those in the profession—as the prime listing month. When an agent preinspects your house, she sees it professionally and the evaluation is rational. She's not trying to sell it and is not on a tight time schedule the way she will be in a few more weeks.

This gives you, the owner, a chance to talk with her, to point out any special features in the house, tell her about the terrific playground for kids just one block over, and rave about your neighbors. The more information you can give to the agent, the more she has to tell would-be buyers, so talk on. One of your comments may attract just the buyer you need.

The downside to March is that it is still pretty dreary looking in much of the country. The sparkling white snow is gone, the trees are barren, winter debris is scattered all over lawns and roads, and the only flowers around are in a florist's window. An early spring often brings a sudden thaw, with home owners faced with flash floods (April has this problem too). This is water-problem time. If your basement has a present or potential water "situation," this is not a good time to put your house on the market.

At this time of year it is difficult for house hunters to visualize your rose garden, your velvet-green lawn, your vegetable garden. If folks can't see it, it doesn't exist for them. This excludes the numbers of home buyers who know all this, and are out to get a head start on the prime selling season.

House sales peak in **April, May,** and **June**. This is when real-estate offices in most of the country are busy, buyers are out in full force, and anyone considering selling is cleaning up and calling a real-estate agent. If you list your house now, there will be plenty of folks to look at it. But you will have fewer preinspections by agents coming alone. They are just too busy.

You will also have maximum competition at this time of year. If there are large numbers of buyers, there is an equally sizable horde of sellers.

It is the prettiest time of year to sell, and the weather is generally conducive to human comfort. Buyers walk around a property. They see the barbecue, wonder if they could put a pool in the backyard, or imagine a pool party in summer if the house already has a pool. All of this is good for you if you have those special features.

Buyers are already putting themselves into your house, seeing themselves as owners.

It all crashes in **July**. The month is not quite as dead as December, but things are still pretty quiet in realty offices. It is vacation time across the land, and sellers and buyers are holidaying. Sometimes agents are too. The serious buyers of summer are generally trying to get into a house before their children start school in September, or they have sold their house and have only a month or two to find another, or they have been transferred.

July and **August** are not impossible times to list your house, but you should be prepared for less activity. Everything moves more slowly. The newness of your listing is lost, too, to all the agents who are also on vacation. By September your house has been around for a while.

Actually that can be both good and bad. The "bad" is that initial loss of enthusiasm. But the "good" is that those summer months may give you a chance to evaluate buyer response to your house (and to the price you have set) and, if necessary, to make some adjustments, either to the house or to the asking price, before things pick up again.

And pick up they will in **September**. Adults are back at work, the kids have headed back to school and the weather is as perfect for house hunting as early spring is (all right, in the Deep South it can still be pretty warm in September).

Early autumn is a very good time to list—if you are careful to price your house accurately. Both activity and sales in September and **October**, even early **November**, are good.

But if you overprice your property, you can have a disaster on your hands. Sellers who emotionally set high prices on their houses need about two months of on-the-market time before they realize that a price reduction is in order. If those two months are September and October, these sellers then face the dead holiday season with a listing that has already become dog-eared.

If there is no time pressure to sell, you'd be wise to withdraw your listing from the market over the holidays. Then, re-list your house in January.

For sellers who have not been able to get their price in September or October, and who must sell for one reason or

DEFINITION PLEASE

A **preinspection** by a realty agent is that agent's personal look at your house, before he or she brings around prospective buyers.

another—a transfer or the purchase of a new house—there is no quick, happy solution. The price reductions that come through the multiple listing sheets in late November and December just do not receive the same attention they might have drawn in June or September. There simply are fewer buyers.

Keep in mind those who are house hunting in December are bargain shoppers. They know some sellers will be biting their nails by then, and so they hope to take that property off the seller's hands for several thousand dollars under its market value.

What about the National Economy?

Season is only one factor affecting real estate. There is also, for example, the national economy. Is it good? Is it slipping? Is it in the cellar? The national economy affects every single sale in the real-estate market.

A powerful factor in the economy is the availability of mortgage money. No mortgage money means essentially no buyers. That happened in the mid-1970s, when money dried up for home loans. How many buyers can afford to pay cash? So no buyers meant no business. Real-estate offices everywhere were struggling to stay afloat. If your house was listed for sale then, you were caught, a victim of time and circumstance. Some sellers sold at low prices to investors with money, some rented their properties on a month-to-month basis trying to make ends meet, some just had to wait. When mortgage money did become available, rates were sky-high. But people paid the price, and the market boomed. The same slump hit again in the late 1980s, when mortgage interest rates again climbed.

As this book is being written, we have been enjoying a marvelous economy and practically fantastic real-estate market, with plentiful, low-cost mortgage money. Will things be the same when you *read* this book? One fervently hopes so.

If times remain good, you should have no trouble finding buyers, and they should be able to secure financing at good rates. Good times mean *a seller's market:* there are plenty of buyers, with easy access to lending—but a scarcity of properties. Goody for you! However, there are two important things to remember here:

1. Unless you are retiring and/or moving to a rental apartment, or unless you already own another house to which you are moving, you will have to face this same seller's market (where the seller rules) *as a buyer*!
2. Nothing is ever constant in real estate. The seller's market that now has you rubbing your hands together with glee could be turned around by a reversal in the economy. Then mortgages will become scarce, buyers few. Or some local crisis could throw a wet blanket on the local economy.

The gloom and doom of huge changes that are both rapid and radical are rare. Just keep in mind that when unemployment is high, new jobs are scarce, working hours are cut, and money is tight everywhere. People become more cautious. They tend to save rather than spend, and they are far more likely to stay put. The number of serious house buyers decreases (although there can be more "lookers" at this time), houses stay on the market longer, and negotiation brings the prices down further than the thousand or two "play" the sellers had built into the asking figure.

That is *a buyer's market*, where the buyer can call the shots.

The Economic Picture Closer to Home

The local economy is no more controllable and no less important in real estate than the national economy. In an area where business is growing and companies are establishing new plants and offices or enlarging existing ones, house sales will be good and prices will continue to rise, even if the national economy is somewhat depressed. And if the national economy is good, a booming local economy can send the real-estate market into orbit.

On the other hand, the local real-estate market can be depressed even when the national economy is on the upswing. This can occur for a variety of reasons, but the most common cause is the large corporation. If the employer of hundreds, perhaps thousands, of people closes down or moves out of an area, the effect on property values is lethal. Suddenly there are a glut of houses on the market—many more houses than buyers—and a local buyer's market is created even though nationwide a seller's market may prevail.

DEFINITION PLEASE

Multiple listing is an agreement between sellers and real-estate brokers that allows brokers to distribute information on the properties they have listed for sale to other members of a local real-estate organization or board, in order to provide the widest possible marketing of those properties. A *multiple listing service (MLS)* is the office that supervises the distribution of listings shared by members of the local Board of Realtors.

Changes in commuting patterns, rising taxes, poor schools, or simply public whim can cause a buyer's market "pocket." Even a single town can be one of these pockets in an area experiencing a seller's market. The character or reputation of a town always colors its real-estate marketplace, and this is a real-estate time factor that is difficult to handle. A change in reputation is generally a long-term, gradual process.

Consider, for instance, a revival neighborhood near where you live, or in an adjoining town. These can be found all over the country, from inner-city enclaves to small suburban towns. At one time this community was for the wealthy, although perhaps that was as long ago as the turn of the century (the nineteenth into the twentieth!). Then over the years it fell from public favor, becoming shabby and then downright seedy. But lo, along about the 1970s, 1980s, or even as late as the 1990s, housing renovators, or just young people with little to pay for houses, discovered these towns or neighborhoods and began to revive them. Soon they were back in favor, zooming up up up in price until bingo! Now they are too expensive for the original settlers of twenty or thirty years ago, and that community again has the prestige its name brought when it was in its prime a century ago.

You will remember reading that nothing is permanent in real estate. Hooray for suburbia, but when gasoline and commuting costs become too steep, people look for houses close to where they work, which is usually the city. Sometimes they just want more free time, hours not spent commuting or maintaining a lawn. A move by a fair number of house hunters back to the city in the late 1990s has helped some urban areas become more desirable than outlying suburbs.

Round and round it goes. This is part of the real-estate game. Those buyers who correctly foresee coming change from an unfavorable reputation to a favorable one can buy low and wait to win when the prices go up. That is if their crystal-ball gazing is accurate! Sellers sometimes become concerned that a reputation is falling and sell for investment protection—remember the Upwards from chapter 2?—when in actuality there is no such change in the air. On the other hand, sometimes sellers think everything is stable in their community or neighborhood, when in reality it is not. A gradual change in reputation is taking place, and the question is "Which way is it going?"

Fine, you say, but where does that leave me as a seller in my town today? Only you can make that evaluation. Try to judge the character and desirability of your town as if you were a buyer from another part of the country. That may be almost as difficult for you as evaluating your own personality, for emotional ties to "home-town" are almost as strong as those to "home," and color perceptions accordingly. Talk with people—with real-estate agents, other sellers, bankers, lawyers, educators. Watch the local newspapers for information on growth patterns, new developments, roads and highways, zoning changes, shopping centers, proposed corporate moves or expansions, and, of course, the schools. All the information you can gather will help you make a realistic evaluation of the selling potential of your property. Read your local paper, not just as a resident of your town, but as an investor carefully looking after his or her investment.

When deciding to sell, try also to tap into the climate of the local real-estate market and the availability of mortgage money. Obviously, that is going to be important to buyers.

You have just read quite a few generalizations, and there is a saying that generalizations are dangerous. It is quite true that the possible exceptions to every rule are infinite, and as long as there are possibilities, things will happen. For example, more than one realty agent has sold a home on December 24. More than one has made a cash sale in two days. A house that is far overpriced has sold for the asking price within six days. All things *can* happen, any agent will tell you. But the more you know about "timing" in real estate, the better you will play the game.

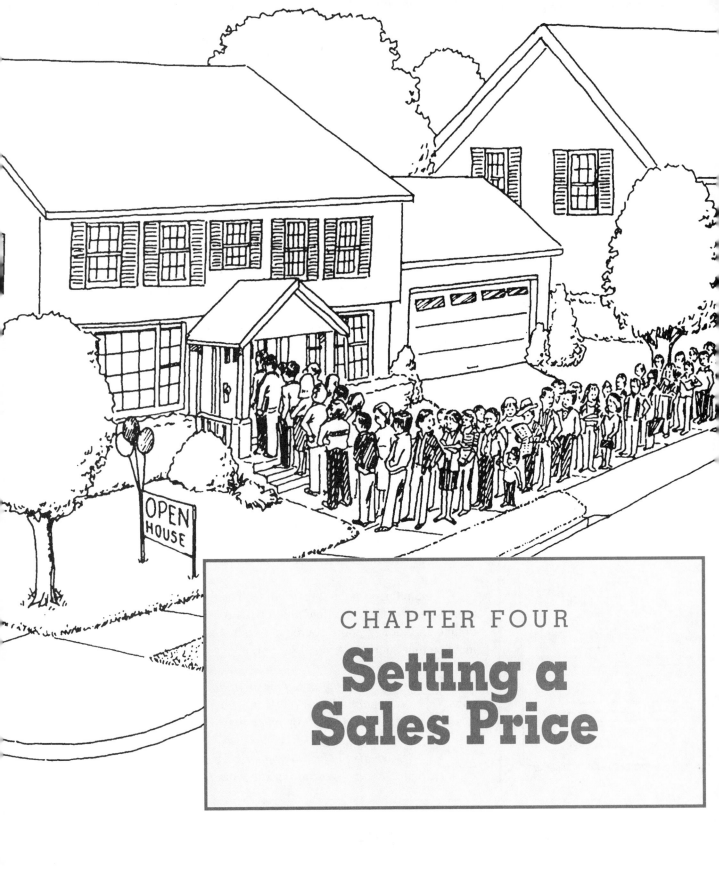

CHAPTER FOUR

Setting a Sales Price

Now we are closing in on the nitty-gritty of selling. What price tag should your home carry? This is one of the most important chapters in this book.

The original price you set on your property will affect the length of time it takes to sell that house. It will affect the number of headaches, arguments, junk food binges, harried phone calls, and sleepless nights in your whole selling experience. And it will affect the final outcome of your negotiating.

With so much riding on this decision, you would think sellers would agonize over it, changing their mind a few dozen times, filling a lined pad with notes and computations and talking about it seemingly every free moment.

Alas, that's not so. Sellers may agonize over *whether* to sell and *when* to sell, but the price to set? That may go something like this scenario:

Scene: A barbecue at the Smiths', with a few relatives and friends.

Mr. Smith: *We're thinking of selling our house.*
Friend Joe: *Really? What for? You have such a nice place here.*
Mr. Smith: *Well, we saw this wonderful lot at Euphoria Acres and we always wanted to build so we could have just the place we want.*
Mrs. Smith: *Yes, and the home we want has this marvelous family room/kitchen combination, with a fireplace and an indoor grill and insulating windows across the entire back of the house. It's gorgeous!*

(The Smiths do not tell their guests that repair problems in the twenty-five-year-old home they now own are becoming a burden in terms of time and money, and a source of frequent arguments. They also don't mention that Euphoria Acres is located in Status Township.)

Cousin Ed: *Well, congratulations, Beth and Al. Euphoria is a beautiful area all right, and you'll probably make a bundle on this place here. You know, my sister-in-law, Alice, is in real estate and she says the market is just jumping right now.*
Mr. Smith: *Really? Who does she work for?*

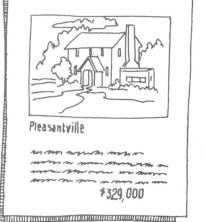

Pleasantville

$329,000

Cousin Ed: *She's with the Friendly and Quick Agency.*

Mr. Smith: *Yeah, they're big around here. And she's doing really well, huh? What do you think they get for a house like this?*

Cousin Ed: *Gee, Al, I don't know. But there was a house down the street from us that's a colonial like yours, and I heard it went for $125,000.*

Wife of
Cousin Ed: *Come on, Ed, that was nine months ago. This house is worth more than that. Besides, I think the Jeffersons' house only had three bedrooms. This place has four, doesn't it, Al?*

Mrs. Smith
(interrupting): *Yes, it does, and besides, we spent $7,800 last year remodeling our kitchen.*

Mr. Smith: *Yeah, and how about the $3,600 we paid for the carpeting, and you paid a pretty price for all those custom-made draperies, didn't you? Wasn't it around $1,000?*

Mrs. Smith: *Yes, but we'll get all that back when we sell, honey.*

Friend Joe: *Oh sure, all that and more. Good decorating is worth money, you know.*

Cousin Ed: *It certainly is. Alice always says a clean, well-decorated house is worth thousands more.*

Mrs. Smith: *And besides, we have a whole triangle of land behind us. It's the biggest lot in the whole neighborhood.*

Mr. Smith: *We figure that ought to be worth plenty for the privacy alone. You know the Riley house on the next block is listed for $127,900.*

Joe's Wife: *You're kidding! I've been in there. Why in comparison to your home that's really . . . Well, a dump.*

Mr. Smith: *You think so? I've always thought it looked kind of nice from the outside, but I've never been inside.*

Joe's Wife: *Oh, it's nothing like this, Al. You can do much better than their price.*

INFORMATION

Opinions vary on the value of using a rounded-off figure in setting a sales price (such as $160,000) or one with $900 added (like $160,900). Adding the $900 (or $500, for that matter) does give you that extra several hundred dollars' room for negotiating.

Mrs. Smith:	*Well, if we take the house Ed was telling us about that sold for $125,000 and add on our kitchen remodeling and the carpet and draperies, it comes to $137,400.*
Mr. Smith:	*Beth, are you crazy? Anyone will tell you that you don't just put a house on the market for what it's worth. You have to add some room for negotiating.*
Cousin Ed:	*He's right, Beth. Alice says everyone negotiates. You should put in at least a few thousand dollars.*
Mr. Smith:	*About $5,000, I'd say. The way things are today, everyone wants to think he's getting a bargain. I think $142,400 sounds pretty good.*
Cousin Ed:	*You ought to make that a nine, John. Everyone has a nine. I think $142,900 sounds just about right for this house.*
Mr. Smith:	*Sold to you, Ed. When would you like to close?*

Everyone laughs. But the Smiths list their house at $142,900.

Think prices are never set this way? Think again. Real-estate agents can tell you tons of stories about this common price-setting technique, which is a little like deciding where you would like to live by closing your eyes and putting a pin in a spot on a map.

But how else, you may wonder, can you set a price? There are several solid paths to house pricing. When you have finished this chapter, you will know them all.

Tax Assessments

This is a suggestion for those who do not want to ask a real-estate agent for help in pricing their house.

You cannot call your town's tax office, ask for the assessment figure on your house, and get an accurate idea of the worth of your property. Tax assessment figures standing alone are not an accurate indicator of market value. First, some towns do not base their taxes on a 100 percent evaluation. Instead, their assessments are 60 percent or 80 percent or whatever percentage they designate of the market value at the time the assessment was made. Second, even in towns where the evaluation is 100 percent, the assessment is sometimes inaccurate. In fact, it was inaccurate the day it was announced.

Why is that? General tax assessment or real-estate assessment throughout a town takes a year or more to complete. In today's market, a year can mean considerable change.

Still, by all means, call your local tax assessor's office. What makes the difference is the information you request and how you use it.

Tax records are in the public domain, which means that you can request assessment information on any piece of property in town. So when you call or stop in at that office—some may require an in-person visit—ask for the assessments on your house and on several others in your neighborhood. Choose houses both larger and smaller than yours and compare the figures. Where do you stand in your neighborhood?

Now, zero in on market value more closely by getting the assessment figure on a house that recently sold somewhere near you. Then get the actual selling price. You can get that from a realty agent, or you can find it in the property transfer records of the town or county. That information is available to the public too.

Compare the actual selling price to the assessment. How many thousand dollars of difference is there? Or, better still, what percentage of the actual selling price is the assessment? The larger the number of recently sold houses in your neighborhood that you calculate this way, the more accurate a picture you'll get of the real relationship of tax assessment to market value in your area. Using this information, you can figure a ballpark selling price for your house.

INFORMATION

You might also be able to check the Sunday real-estate section of your local paper to learn the recent selling price of houses near you. Many papers offer the service, in long columns of listings of recent sales, giving the name of the buyer, the address, and the sales price.

All this talk of "replacement cost" might bring to mind your home owners' insurance policy and your coverage in the event of a catastrophe. However, you can't really use that figure for replacement cost in the selling context. Some owners insure their houses for just 80 percent of the replacement value, while others insure for 100 percent. And most owners just guesstimate their house's value before signing for the insurance.

If houses have not been reassessed for years in your town, and if you are sure that your house, assessed twenty years ago at $60,000, is now worth $120,000, and if recent sales of comparable houses show that to be true, then consider that your market value is probably twice the assessed value.

For a more precise estimate (which sounds like an oxymoron) of your house's worth, you need to consider a number of other variables such as lot size, location, condition, improvements, decorating, extras included in the sale, need to sell, and market conditions.

Replacement Cost

What would the replacement cost be today for a hundred-year-old Victorian mansion, crafted with materials imported from Europe and handmade by artisans? Right, you could not duplicate that today. Who is going to want to spend that kind of money importing stone and other materials, unless they are building a present-day Hearst Castle? And we certainly do not have those kind of craftspeople today, at least not in any great numbers. Houses are just not handmade like that these days.

Because so much of the value of a piece of property depends on its location, too, the cost of physically duplicating it or replacing it is not an accurate indication of its potential selling price. Replacement cost is valuable only as a negotiating tool. It is a number you can throw out when arguing for your price.

If you want to use that tool, and do not mind going to some extra trouble, you can calculate the replacement cost of your property by calling a local or regional home builders association and asking for the average cost per square foot on new-house construction in your town. It varies tremendously from one part of the country to another, and from one part of the state to the next. (For example, housing costs are quite high in northern New Jersey, where many towns serve as bedroom communities for New York City commuters. In the southern part of the state, costs are considerably lower for similar-size properties.)

Then measure the foundation of your house and calculate the square footage. Don't forget both floors in a two-story house. Multiply this by the cost per square foot. Next, add the value of the

land—check the price of lots being sold near you—and the value of the extras (wall-to-wall carpeting, special lighting fixtures, appliances, draperies) as closely as you can estimate them. Now you have a number. You might compare it with the number you got from your work with tax evaluations, but you still have more zeroing in to do.

Personal Comparison Shopping

This technique is not mathematical (that's a relief), but it's more immediate and vivid than figuring replacement costs or comparing tax evaluations.

Take the ballpark figure you got from your calculations with tax assessments, add $5,000 for negotiating room, and go out and look at houses in that price range. Really. Realty agents often place 8½-by-11-inch fliers, which give pertinent information about the property, in plastic, weather-resistant tubes that are attached to the signs on the front lawns. So you don't even have to call a real-estate agency to ask your questions. Note the asking price of houses that are like yours, as far as you can determine.

Check, too, for extras—lot size, neighborhood—anything that can help you compare that house with yours.

If you do this little exercise properly, you should get a good idea of the asking price. Houses that are grossly overpriced should stand out.

Here's another tactic. Call for-sale-by-owner sellers listed in the classified advertisements in your local paper. If an ad does not give the address, ask for it and tell the seller you'd like to drive by the house and neighborhood first before calling to see the inside. Ask the price as well, although that is likely to be included in the advertisement. Here, too, you will have to gauge the size of the house for sale, and how your neighborhood compares with that enclave.

If you plan to move to another part of your town, you can call a realty agent and ask her to show you a house that is actually as much like yours as possible. She can take you through properties so you have an even better way of comparing your house with them.

Agents will do this and will try very hard to get your listing when you are ready to sell. By all means listen to the spiel, but do

Be realistic about your own house in comparing it with others. Don't instinctively think "mine's better." You will never get a clear picture of the value of your property if you can't be objective about it.

not sign automatically. There is a full discussion of working with a real-estate agent in chapter 10.

A Professional Appraisal

A licensed real-estate appraiser's job is to come up with the fair market value of your property. The point of that appraisal is to determine that figure *in the absence of a buyer*.

To find it, an appraiser will first make a careful inspection of the property, measuring the rooms and noting the desirability of the location, the condition of the structure, and the extras included in the sale. Then he will research the records of past sales kept at his office to find houses of like size and condition that have recently sold, and he will note their selling prices. He may also call brokers in the area and ask for recent sales prices on houses similar to or located close to yours. He may even ask about activity patterns and interest in houses near yours that are listed but haven't yet sold. Then he will judge and weigh the information and arrive at the price he thinks a buyer will pay for the property. That price is an educated opinion, usually fairly accurate, but like all opinion subject to error.

So, should you hire an appraiser?

Don't bother. An appraisal can cost $250 or more and is used mostly by lending institutions in refinancing; in divorce when there is disagreement and dissension between owners; by corporations that are transferring employees; and for purposes of estate settlement. In almost all other cases, a professional fair market value appraisal is neither necessary nor warranted.

Why spend that much money? You have already read some suggestions for setting a price on your house. Here is another solid, no-cost way of arriving at that figure.

The Comparative Market Analysis

This analysis uses comparables to determine the fair market value of a piece of property. "Comps," as they are known among realty agents, are listings of houses that have been sold during the previous year or two that are similar in location, size, features, and price range to the property in question. In this case that's the house *you* are selling. They are kept on file in every real-estate office.

Here is how it works. A new listing comes in to a realty office. A sheet is drawn up for that property listing location, size, price, and so on. Let's say that after two months there is a price reduction. That is recorded on the listing sheet. After another month an offer is accepted on the property and contracts are signed. The agent notes that on the listing sheet. Finally, there is the closing. The actual selling price is then released to all agencies belonging to the multiple listing service. The sales price is also noted on the listing sheet. Now that sheet of paper has all the pertinent information about that property. These files used to be kept in large, sturdy books, but most offices now keep them on computer.

To determine the fair market value of your property by using comparables, you would follow the procedure of the professional appraiser. First, gather data for all recently sold (within a year or two) houses in the immediate neighborhood and for all houses of similar size and structure in the whole town. Note the asking and selling prices (they should cluster within a range of about $10,000) and time spent on the market. Then compare each property to yours. You want to come up with a figure as close as possible to the mark. Try to get as many comps as you can to compare with your own house. After you've done the comps, you will feel more secure about the probable selling price of your house.

"Well, sure," you may say, "all that sounds sensible. But how do I get these comps?" Simply stop in at a nearby real-estate office. You do not need to make an appointment. Real-estate associates love walk-ins. There is always someone there who will have been assigned "floor time" for that day.

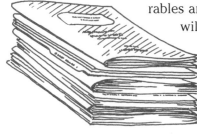

Tell the agent who greets you that you are considering selling your house and that you would like to look at comparables and discuss selling price with her. You will be welcomed warmly and she will bring out the books or computer printouts immediately. Then proceed with your selecting and comparing. You can do the market analysis yourself and

INFORMATION

The methods sellers use to set sales prices vary around the country. In some areas sellers set an asking price at or very near what they expect to receive, and don't expect to haggle. In other regions—the Northeast, for one—asking prices include a negotiating leeway of $5,000 to $10,000, maybe more with higher-priced properties. Ask your real-estate agent what is common where you are.

Many realty offices require salespersons to take a half-day or a certain number of hours of *floor time* each week. That means they must be physically present in the office to answer phones and talk with walk-ins while other agents are out. The agent you get when you walk in is not necessarily the best or the worst in that office. She's just the one "on duty" at the time. Agents usually don't mind floor time because it gives them dibs on sellers who might be calling or bringing in new listings, or on buyers interested in particular properties.

come up with a price, and you can always ask that real-estate agent for an opinion.

Using Competing Real-Estate Agencies

You can be sure that just about every real-estate office within a five-mile radius, sometimes even farther away, would be absolutely delighted to compete for your listing. Listings are the backbone of the real-estate business. Every salesperson in every real-estate office is coached first and foremost in getting listings and in using the "listing tools" available. The competitive market analysis (CMA) is one of those tools, and is freely offered by just about every agency. In fact, you may have received a letter or postcard in the mail—perhaps several of them—over the years from a local agency with the heading "How Much Is Your Home Worth?" The note offered a free CMA and then offered to sell your property. You probably tossed it away, not wanting to sell at the time.

Now you do want to sell. You are going to call for a free no-strings-attached CMA. But since you might sign with the agent who comes to your home at some point, pick one who is likely to be good.

Once you know whom you are going to talk to, call the real-estate office and ask to speak to that sales associate. Tell her you are considering selling your house and would like to have a comparative market analysis to help determine the asking price. She will come to your house with comparables in hand. She will do a careful inspection of the property with you and then discuss its pros and cons, compare your property with the comparables, and come up with her estimate of fair market value.

You should do this with at least three different agents (five is preferable, but you may wilt after three). When you've finished with the visits and the talking, you will have three (or five) professional opinions. There may be one that is particularly high or low, but generally they will cluster within a narrow range of agreement.

There is one drawback to using competing real-estate firms in this manner, but it also happens to be an advantage. Along with doing the CMA, every agent who comes to your house will want to tell you why her firm should get your listing, and how they can do

Comparables—How Your House Fits In

As you have read, studying the sales of properties much like yours can aid you in setting a solid price for your house. Here is a worksheet to help you see how houses that recently sold compare with yours. You might want to photocopy this sheet, so you can study comps from five or six or more houses.

	HOUSE #1	HOUSE #2	HOUSE #3	YOUR HOUSE
Address				

Neighborhood
  Like yours
  Not like yours				

Lot size				
Square footage				
Number of rooms				
Number of baths				

Garage
  (1-car)
  (2-car)
  (3-car)				

Fireplace				
Central A/C				
Other features				
Taxes				
Asking price				
Time on market				
Selling price				

the best job for you. This may bore you or make you nervous, but please listen, even if you are determined to try the for-sale-by-owner route. You can learn a lot from these agents and you can get some fine insights into the operations of their particular offices.

Right now you should know that setting the price is a time of listening and evaluating, *not* signing. No matter how competent an agent seems, no matter how efficient her office operation, no matter how much you like her personally (even if she is your cousin by marriage!), *do not sign a listing contract on the day of the competitive market analysis.*

Talk price for as long as each of you can bear it, listen to her stories of wonderfully quick sales—then say good night and let the matter rest. The next day see someone else. One agent will eventually surface above the others. She will not necessarily be the one who says your selling price should be the highest either (she may just be telling you that to get your listing).

Do not feel guilty about taking up realty associates' time with a CMA. It is one way they get listings. Take advantage of their expertise and question them *extensively.* When you are confident of the price you are asking, you can enter the actual selling experience with a positive, sure attitude.

Does what you stand to make when your house sells seem like a lot of money to you? It can if you have lived there for quite a few years and are likely to reap a tidy profit from the sale. But *is* it all profit? Not to burst any bubbles, but please read on to consider some points that might not have occurred to you.

CHAPTER FIVE

How Much Will You *Really* Make from This Sale?

S o you are rubbing your hands with glee at the thought of your profit. Some home owners back themselves into a bad financial corner by using the market value of their present house as the down payment on their next, more expensive one. They have completely forgotten that selling a piece of property costs money. These costs must be deducted from the profit to arrive at a realistic working cash figure. (This does not apply, of course, if your move is supported by a transferring company, which is likely to absorb the extra costs.)

The worksheet on page 51 will help you see how much you can expect to net from the sale of your house. Write your expected selling price in the upper right-hand corner. Then, as you read this chapter, list the expenses to be subtracted along the left-hand side of the page. Total those expenses and deduct that amount from the expected selling price. That's your net gain.

How much of your selling price is that profit likely to be? Alas, there is no one figure that will help everyone across the country. Requirements, practices, and rates vary nationally. But here are the most common expenses, plus suggestions on where to go for better estimates or definitive figures. (There is a more complete discussion of closing expenses in chapter 17.)

1. The legal costs involved in selling your home fall into two categories: *fees and taxes imposed by the municipality, county, or state*, and *fees paid to an attorney*. You might dig out the closing statement from the day you bought your house and check through the seller's expenses. That may not give you current dollar amounts, but it will tell you in what broad categories those expenses will fall. Your agent or lawyer should also have a government booklet handed out to buyers and sellers to help them understand their rights at the closing.

To give you some examples: Most states impose some kind of *real-estate transfer tax*. Often it is a small percentage of the sale price, say 0.05 percent or not too far from that. Or it can be written as $1 for each $500 or fraction thereof of the sale price. Or it might be a flat fee up to a particular amount and then a percentage after that. (Check in your area. Sometimes that tax is paid by the buyer.) A local *recording fee* is also common. These are usually flat figures, but percentages are sometimes used.

Calculating Your Profit

These are the most common expenses you will have to deduct from the price you get for your house. Some additions might be the custom where you are. You are legally entitled to a list of closing costs, from your lawyer or your realty agent. However, there are other expenses you will have to deduct from your gross profit that are not related to settlement costs.

EXPECTED SELLING PRICE $_____

EXPENSES

Municipal fees and taxes	$_____
Real-estate transfer tax	$_____
Attorney's fee*	$_____
Special assessments, liens, or judgments	$_____
Pro-rated real-estate taxes, association fees, utility bills	$_____
Points	$_____
Balance on the existing mortgage	$_____
Prepayment penalty	
Expenses related to getting your house ready for market	$_____
Real-estate broker's commission	$_____
Moving	$_____
Other _____	$_____
_____	$_____
_____	$_____

      TOTAL $_____

      MINUS TOTAL EXPENSES   – $_____

      EQUALS   = $_____

              NET PROFIT

* *Your attorney's fee is likely to include any charge for work he or she contracted for you such as title search, survey, and the like.*

INFORMATION

The buyer pays a good deal more in closing costs than the seller, so you won't be hit with that 3 to 5 percent of the purchase price you paid when you bought your present house. Sellers pay closer to 1 percent.

The cost of some services required by the state, the lending institution, or a contractual agreement between buyers and sellers will appear as part of the attorney's fees, since he or she must do the work to satisfy the requirements. Most common among these are a *title search and title insurance*, which is a guarantee that you have clear title to the property, and an *abstract of title.*

Both the cost of title insurance and the fee charged for an abstract vary from one title company to another, and from one attorney to another. According to local custom in the area, these charges can be required of the seller or the buyer.

There is no "standard" closing fee among attorneys. Each law firm has its own price and those prices are becoming more and more competitive. You may be very surprised at the differences in cost among several law firms for exactly the same services. So unless you already have a lawyer, you might want to do some shopping. Simply call among the lawyers listed in the Yellow Pages and inquire as to their fee for representing a seller at closing. Fees can range from around $100 to $500 or more for very complicated transfers of title. Be sure you know exactly what services are included in each lawyer's fee so you can make accurate comparisons.

If you have any qualms about reputation and competence, ask the real-estate agents with whom you will be working about the lawyer, or call your local or regional bar society and inquire about firms that handle closings in your area.

2. In some parts of the country lending institutions will not give a mortgage without a *survey* of the property. Usually the buyer pays for this, but sometimes the seller gets the nod. Who pays should be specified in the sales contract. If it is you, you might be able to save this cost if you had a survey done when you bought the property, and if you have made no changes in the house (the outside of the structure or on the grounds). If this applies to you, have your attorney contact the buyer's attorney or the lender's attorney to see if the old survey, with a notarized affirmation of no change, would be acceptable. It often is.

3. Then there are *points*. They are another lender-imposed charge that could cost you a considerable bit of money at the

closing. If you are like most nonprofessionals in this field, you have probably heard the word *points* and understand that it has to do with mortgages, but do not know very much more. Points are fees that some lending institutions charge to make giving a mortgage more profitable for them. One point is usually 1 percent of the mortgage amount, and points are paid at the closing table. However, not every lender charges points with every transfer of title.

You can get current information on points in your area by calling several banks and asking how many points, if any, they are charging on traditional loans, and on those insured by the Federal Housing Administration (FHA) and the Department of Veterans Affairs (VA). Many home owners negotiate very hard on FHA or VA mortgage sales in order to keep the selling price high enough to cover any points they will have to pay at the closing. Some sellers simply will not accept an offer contingent upon a mortgage involving points.

In some markets, buyers will ask sellers to absorb points that they (the buyers) expect to be charged.

4. If you have a *mortgage* on your house, call the lender and ask the current balance. Deduct that amount, too, in your "expenses" column.

5. If you have owned the house you are selling for, say, fewer than five years, you may also have to pay a *mortgage cancellation fee*, or *prepayment penalty*, to the bank that holds your loan. This is usually 1, 2, or 3 percent of the outstanding balance. A mortgage-cancellation fee is not written into all mortgages, however, and it is sometimes waived in the event of a company transfer or if you are financing the new house you are buying through the same lender that holds the mortgage on your current house. You can find out what your obligation is by getting out that mortgage and skimming through it. Cancellation fees will be specified in a separate paragraph or item number.

6. Among other charges that must be paid at the closing table are outstanding *special assessments* such as for sewers or sidewalks, any *liens or judgments* against the property, and a fair *apportionment of property taxes and annual fees*, such as those for a

An ***abstract of title*** is a synopsis of the history of a title, indicating all the changes in ownership and including liens, mortgages, charges, or any other matter that might affect the title.

Do You Need a Lawyer?

- If you have a real-estate agent and have sold a house before, you might decide you can get by without legal counsel for this sale.

- If you are selling a house by yourself, you will definitely want a lawyer to draw up a sales contract and help you through the sale in many respects the way a realty agent would.

- If you do not have a lawyer and any trouble arises—buyers threaten to cancel a sales contract, buyers cry "foul" at one element or another of the sale—run, do not walk, to a law office! A lawyer's fee is not that much when you compare it to the money you stand to gain from the successful sale of your property.

- Finally, if you do not want a lawyer for the entire transfer of property, or cannot afford one, hire him or her just for negotiating and for drawing up and supervising the sales contract, not the closing. The closing is simpler and its procedures and costs are pretty much watched over by federal law. You need help in the "open-season" atmosphere of bargaining over price and other details.

homeowners association, and sometimes *final utility and disconnect fees*. Some charges you won't be able to calculate until you know *when* the house is to be sold; others, such as liens, are flat figures that will simply have to be paid off.

7. Don't forget the *expenses related to getting your house ready to put on the market*. (Save all of the receipts!)

8. Although it is almost at the end of the list, this is likely to be the largest single expense attached to selling your house: the *real-estate broker's commission*. If you are selling your house yourself, you can, of course, forget about writing this check. But it wouldn't hurt to add it to the list just in case you are unable to sell on your own and must at some point engage an agent. Figure 6 percent of your fair market value, which is usual.

9. Finally, there is *moving*. This can cost you from a few hundred to several thousand dollars. For a detailed look at the costs attached to relocating, turn to chapter 20.

Now deduct all of your expenses from the fair-market-value estimate you wrote down at the outset of this exercise. What you get is the dollar amount the sale will net you.

Your Plans?

Think about that sum of money carefully. Do you plan to spend it? Use it as a retirement fund? Put it into another house? Is the real equity enough for a down payment on the house you want? Is it enough for the investments you want to make to secure your future?

In the ideal situation your answer is yes, but even then there is still one more somewhat painful point to explore. What if, for some unknown reason, you cannot get someone to pay the fair market value for your house? Then what? What is the least amount of spendable cash you need from your house to enable you to fulfill your motivation for selling?

When you arrive at that figure, you can also get a rock-bottom selling price on your house. You should calculate this figure and

INFORMATION

Some 80 percent of FHA-insured home loans are made to first-time buyers, according to the U.S. Department of Housing and Urban Development.

TIP

Try to avoid a prepayment penalty clause with your next home mortgage, saving you that charge if you sell early.

discuss it with whoever is selling the house with you. Write it down, and put it away. (But don't forget where you put it!) *Do not discuss this bottom figure with any real-estate agent you see.* You do not want agents or buyers to know how low you will go.

All of this paperwork should be done before potential buyers begin to troop through your house. And especially before the stress of reaching the negotiating table. If you learn and follow what you have read in this chapter and the preceding one on setting a sales price, your time and efforts will be rewarded in dollars at the closing.

CHAPTER SIX

Major Buyer Turn-ons—and Turnoffs

DEFINITION
PLEASE

Curb appeal is a term you will often hear from real-estate agents. It means that the exterior of a house for sale (its facade, front lawn, and driveway) is so neat and attractive that would-be buyers who drive past want to make an appointment to see the inside.

Now we leave paper and pencil and get down to the practical work involved in selling your house: getting it ready to be shown. This chapter will concentrate on heavy-duty repairs; the next chapter involves smaller jobs.

Actually, getting your house ready for sale is interrelated with setting a price, but since one chapter has to go first, you initially read about finding the right price. In practice, though, you should be juggling both topics. Try to have your property more or less "ready to go" before you open it to realty agents for a comparative market analysis. As those salespeople go through your house, note their comments. Again, since you are considering this property in a businesslike manner, be objective about any criticism. Remember, it is a house, not a home.

Not that you will hear much outright negative talk. You will need to be able to listen to how specific points are made and pick up the implications and hints in the agents' words. Be sure to notice what they notice most, and pay attention to what attracts their attention. These are professionals looking at your special property. They and you both will be looking at it with a view to its worth.

It is impossible to give suggestions that will apply to each specific home seller in the nation. So it is truly up to you to develop a critical eye when looking at your place. This can be difficult. We all—or at least the overwhelming majority of us—love our "home." But we often do not notice it either. Really. Are you oblivious to the jackets perennially draped on each of the dining room chairs? Do you see that your collections take up too much space in the living room? Do you notice the cat odor in the house? If you are like most of us, you do not see (or smell) these things because they are part of your everyday living pattern.

Buyers, however, *will* notice and mentally deduct points from the attractiveness rating of your house. These folks do not know you personally. Everything in the house that is of a personal nature is, frankly, annoying to them and gets in the way of imagining themselves in your house. And that's exactly what you want house hunters to do—picture themselves living in those rooms so perfectly that they want to buy your house!

First, you will want to see to your house's "curb appeal."

If you are unsure how your house is going to appear to potential buyers, go to a few open houses, as suggested earlier. See what you notice first, what appeals to you and what is jarring. What did you spot when you first drove up the driveway? What caught your eye in the living room? bedrooms? kitchen? bathrooms? Now drive up to your own house as if you were a buyer and ask yourself those same questions.

You may find plenty that is amiss. The front windows are a little dirty, there are kids' handprints along the stairway to the second floor, the garage definitely needs work, particularly sweeping. And the backyard hasn't been touched in quite a while, since you've been spending your spare time working on the front lawn.

All of this will be an eye-opening experience. Let's look at the major areas that might present problems, and could turn off house hunters.

Exterior Painting—Take a walk around your property, and look objectively at your house's exterior condition. Could it really use a coat of paint? Maybe on closer look you see that it's not so much the house that needs painting as it is the trim. Sure, that's only a temporary face-lift, but sometimes scraping and repainting the trim can save you a couple of thousand dollars you would have had to give up at the negotiating table.

While considering painting the trim, think about giving it a different, spiffy color. Paint stores can help you with interesting combinations of colors for both the house and the trim. Try something new!

*The front door—*Maybe you don't pay much attention to yours. You might use the back door 99 percent of the time, or the door leading from the garage into the kitchen.

Now is the time to look at the front door the way a buyer will. If necessary, give the door a fresh coat of paint, and make that an interesting color too.

Fix the hinges if they squeak. Take down an out-of-season wreath, make sure any glass in the door sparkles and any lights are clean and work.

WATCH YOUR STEP

If you have bought several gallons of paint for sprucing up your house, be careful where you store them. Keep them away from the area around the water heater. Fumes from the opened paint and heat from the heater's pilot light can meet and start a fire.

TIP

For free guidance about grass, plants, and bushes, inside and out, call or visit your local cooperative extension service, a county government agency located just about everywhere in the nation. You can bring problem plants, or just leaves, with you to help the agent understand your problem. He or she can give you printed material, also at no charge. Look in the county government section of your telephone book. The service is listed under "Department of Agriculture."

• • •

Suggestion from a weary home owner: If you're selling in the fall and your grass doesn't look great, don't rake up the leaves as they fall. Let them lie there. It's a nice autumn look!

Prospective buyers will be standing there for several seconds, maybe longer, waiting for you to answer the bell. They have plenty of time to notice chipped paint, scuff marks, dead flowers or plants in a tub on the stoop, dirty porch lights, and anything else you would rather they didn't see.

Be sure the doorknob works perfectly too. A rattling knob does not make a good first impression.

In fact, here is a good spot to remind you that all doorknobs in the house should be in good working order. If an agent goes to turn one and it comes off in her hand, a buyer cannot help but wonder what else is wrong with the house. It's unfair, but it's a quick mental leap for buyers: a problem (of any size) equals a poor-quality house.

Also, check to see that the doorknobs are not surrounded by your children's fingerprints.

And . . . While you have the paint supplies out, don't forget the fence if you have one, and give a fresh coat of paint to the mailbox. Or maybe it's time to buy a new mailbox.

Landscaping—Take an objective look at the grass. How is it *really* doing? You might need some plugs for bare spots, or sod for larger areas. You might also treat yourself to a lawn-treatment service. Have them come every month or two to fertilize and spray for lawn pests while the house is on the market. You can expect to pay $40 or so per visit.

Look also at plantings around the foundation of the house. Very often shrubs become shaggy and overgrown while their owners pass by day after day, oblivious to the gradual change. This happened to one family about eight years into owning their present house. Trees that had been there when they moved in had now grown even taller and fuller. The plantings that had previously received full sun were now in the shade. Many of their leaves had turned brown and dropped off, leaving bare branches. Neither busy home owner particularly noticed until they began getting the house ready for sale. They ripped out the dying bushes and replaced them with ones that do well in shade.

If it is feasible, do some pruning and trimming all around your house. Be especially careful of walkways. Shrubs growing over a walkway become an obstacle, making the entrance to the house less attractive. And if you have a good sampling of weeds in your lawn, and you do not go with a lawn-care service, then keep the grass cut short, or as short as is healthy for it. Weeds are less recognizable that way.

Your goal for the outside of your property is the same feeling of "clean decorating" that you will want indoors. Keep the yard and driveway free of clutter and debris—no children's toys, no empty clay pots, no cars on blocks in the driveway. Neatness can be worth several thousand dollars and weeks (sometimes even months) of on-the-market time to you.

If you have two cars in the garage and two more in the driveway, see if you can park one or more at a neighbor's or a nearby friend's while your house is on the market. It will make your place look more spacious, and allow plenty of room for agents to park.

The Garage—Does yours look as bad as the basement? *Worse?* This is another area that is often neglected, with stuff crammed into the space often willy-nilly. Now you will really have to organize it all. Arrange cartons neatly against a wall. Shelving is attractive and can create an organized look that appeals to buyers.

The Basement—Wet basements are the biggest worry home owners have about a property. That is understandable this problem belongs to a mysterious plumbing system few of us know much about—especially someone else's—and can portend even more serious troubles. If you have such a basement, be honest. There is more on this subject of what you must, or should, disclose to a buyer in chapter 11.

Don't try to hide a sump pump under piles of things or under a bench. An honest explanation and evaluation of a water problem will hurt you far less than the nagging suspicions in the buyer's mind, and your own worries about a possible lawsuit.

Should you paint the basement walls and maybe the floor if you've had water problems? By all means. You will likely have to tell a buyer about "the problem" anyway on a disclosure form. Also, buyers are savvy these days and look with suspicion at a freshly painted basement. It practically screams "I was painted to hide water stains" or, worse, "a high water mark."

TIP

Are oil or rust stains in your garage or driveway bothering you? You can buy commercial driveway cleaners in automotive and home-improvement stores. You might also consider renting a pressure washer. Or it might be easier to have an individual or company who provides that service do the job for you. It isn't that expensive.

• • •

A good reminder for changing the furnace filter: Do it each month when you pay your utility bill.

• • •

If you have a termite bond, have a copy handy for your agent to show would-be buyers.

DEFINITION PLEASE

If you have a sump pump, you certainly know what it is. For everyone else, a *sump pump* is an automatic water pump set into the basement floor to prevent groundwater from seeping into the basement.

Also in the basement, on a lighter note—pardon the pun—be sure the light switches work and that all the bulbs on individual pull cords work as well. It is somewhat disconcerting when an agent pulls a light cord in a particularly dark part of the cellar, and no light goes on. She feels foolish; the buyers feel a little suspicious and begin to look at that area a little harder. Are these people trying to hide something? they wonder.

Cobwebs and piles of sawdust from a workshop should also be cleaned out of the basement. No one expects the area to blind the buyer's eyes with its shine, but no one wants to cough his or her way through years of dust either. Don't worry about boxes, old toys, gardening tools, and other collectibles; that's what people expect to see in a basement. Do arrange things neatly, so people can walk about safely.

Don't forget to change the furnace filter if you have been lax about that chore. Sooty heating units can perform sluggishly, and you do not want to give a buyer—or the buyer's house inspector—the sense of a problem there.

If the laundry is in the basement, check to see that the area around the washer and dryer is clean and well lit. If you have "stuff" around those appliances, you may want to nail up a single shelf for the detergents, bleach, and fabric softener. An inexpensive area rug can give the area definition, and make the minus factor of a basement laundry (buyers aren't crazy about climbing stairs with a laundry basket) almost a plus.

Termites—This is another major worry for potential buyers. These days the majority of real-estate contracts have a termite-inspection clause written in as a contingency to the sale. It provides that a professional exterminator will inspect the property, and if termites are discovered, the seller will have them eliminated at the seller's expense and repair any damage they may have caused. This must be completed before closing. If a seller refuses to cooperate, the

buyer may void the contract and have his or her deposit money refunded.

A good many home owners have termite contracts, since they live in condominium or patio-home communities where houses share joint walls, and the by-laws require that protection from each owner. The contract calls for a yearly checkup by the exterminator. Maybe *you* already have such a contract.

Although this clause and the termite check are standard almost everywhere now, waiting for the termite inspector always causes some uneasiness among sellers who think they have their house sold. You can avoid that twitching, and/or the embarrassment of having an inspector actually find termites, by doing a little "inspecting" yourself. Take an ice pick or a pocketknife and poke at the support beams near the foundation walls all around the perimeter of your basement. The knife should not sink easily into the wood. Also, walk around the outside of your house and look for mud tunnels (lines about a quarter inch wide) on the foundation, running up from the ground maybe six inches or so. Termites use these tunnels to enter and exit the house.

If you suspect termites, call for an inspection by a professional exterminator before you list your house for sale. If he doesn't find anything, his report will usually satisfy the termite contingency in the sales contract. If he does find an infestation, have it eliminated. Chances are you would have to pay for the elimination anyway; and if it is discovered as a contingency, it could rock the deal. Most exterminators also give a warranty of a year or more after treating a house, and this can be turned into a plus when you are negotiating.

Why Buyers Are So *Nervous*

The common thread running throughout this chapter is "neatness counts." One reason for this warning is that buyers want a house in move-in condition; they don't want to cope with someone else's problems. Neatness also counts because so many buyers are insecure about their purchase. If a house is clean, they like to tell themselves, the owners must be just as conscientious about maintenance and repair.

Be sure there is a handrail along the stairs to the basement. That's required by law in most states. If it has become dirty or stained from years of use, give it a coat of enamel.

Biggest Buyer Turnoffs

- *Poor physical appearance of the house and property.* Dirty, peeling paint, loose railings at the front door, broken doorbell, unkempt lawn and landscaping, cracked or loose bricks, driveway, or steps. Also dirty dishes in the sink and dingy, dirty windows

- *Obvious plumbing problems.* Dark brown stain on the ceiling in the den sounds off alarms, even if the original problem in the bathroom above was repaired. So do neglected bathrooms with cracked, stained, or loose tiles; mildew; crunchy floors (sign of water damage or warped or de-laminated plywood); low water pressure; old, cracked, or chipped fixtures; loose toilets; bathtub rot; and dripping faucets

- *Water in the basement.* Signs of a wet, damp basement, such as water marks on the walls, dank, musty odors, and mildew

- *Dingy kitchens.* Dirty appliances, loose handles, missing components of appliances, worn countertops, old stained sinks, poor flooring (even old linoleum), and bad lighting

- *A chilly house.* A very cold house in early spring will leave most buyers unfriendly and disinterested. If they can see their breath, or if they rub their hands together often to get the blood circulating, either your thermostat is set too low or the heating system has a problem. Same goes for a very hot house in summer, particularly in warm climates where cooling systems are a key element in any house

Source: HouseMaster
(home inspection company)

Every buyer wants to get a "good" house, but very few know much about the standards of home construction, or how the working systems function within the house. In their confusion buyers get neatness confused with good maintenance. Of course, this is not always true, but it does bring up a problem sellers must face: how to convince a twitchy buyer that their house really is solid and is not going to fall apart ten days after the new owner moves in.

As a seller, you can help nervous buyers by being as open and honest as possible about defects. You might consider having an inspector over, too.

A House Inspection for Sellers

To help reassure buyers, some sellers have a house inspector or an engineer look at their property, and then they offer that report to house hunters. These days almost all buyers stipulate in the sales contract that one contingency for the deal going through is a house inspection with results that are satisfactory to the buyer.

Your getting a house inspection and offering that report to interested buyers can work to your advantage and move a sale along to a successful conclusion. The relieved buyer will know exactly what's going on in your place.

The report should be detailed. A buyer will want every question answered, not just the superficial ones.

House inspections can cost anywhere from $150 to over $500, with the average running around $250. The inspection usually takes one to two hours to complete. The price you pay depends on the area of the country, the size of the dwelling, and the individual inspector's, or inspection company's, rates.

The Inspector's Job

The inspector should bring to light any important problems in the house—disasters already there or those about to happen. A buyer might still purchase your house after seeing the report, but he or she will have more room to negotiate if serious problems are found. For example, he might say to you "Well, the house inspector says the roof's in very bad shape. He estimates it's about twelve years old, so it's about due for replacement." Those comments can open

INFORMATION

So far California, Oregon, Minnesota, and Texas are the only states that even minimally regulate professional house inspectors. Inspectors are often retired contractors or appraisers or others connected with the home-building industry.

bargaining for a lower price and/or repairs or replacements. No house is perfect. So rest assured (or somewhat assured), no buyer is expecting perfection.

By all means go along with the inspector as he or she looks through your house. You can learn something, and have time to digest any problems and think about what you intend to do about them. You can make the repairs and increase the asking price for the house accordingly, or not make the repairs and wait for the buyer's inspector to find the faults and then do your negotiating.

Finding a House Inspector

You can ask friends, neighbors, and work associates for the name of an individual or company. You might also call your mortgage lender or your lawyer for recommendations.

Finally, in a pinch, check the Yellow Pages. You will find large, nationwide concerns and small local firms there. One is not necessarily better than the other. You might look for companies that belong to the American Society of Home Inspectors (ASHI), which sets standards for its members. On the other hand, some of the nonmembers—usually small, independent local services—may still be fine. For the names of ASHI members in your area, call (800) 743-2744 or visit *www.ashi.com.*

Other Inspection Concerns

Are you curious, and worried, about radon, asbestos, and lead paint? You can read about those problems in chapter 11.

Your house inspector might not check those special concerns for you. Inspectors do not always look at *everything.* For example, some will not go up on the roof; they only look at it from the ground and try to determine its condition from there. Each company has its own style and laundry list of what it *will* investigate. Ask what's covered by the firm you engage and make sure the situation that concerns you is on the list of what *is* explored.

Incidentally, there is no one "house inspection report form." Each company has its own reporting format. You might ask the one you are thinking of hiring to show you a typical report, so you can see what is covered (and what is not).

If you are already registered with a real-estate agent as you read this, do not ask her to suggest a house inspector. Agencies can make recommendations, but those individuals or companies might not submit a report that shows too many flaws (that is, a house that might be hard to sell). That kind of report might convince the real-estate agency not to refer that agency the next time. Steer clear of this conflict of interest.

The Ten Most Frequent House Problems

1. Improper surface grading/drainage*

2. Improper electrical wiring

3. Roof damage

4. Heating systems

5. Poor overall maintenance

6. Structurally related problems

7. Plumbing

8. Exteriors

9. Poor ventilation

10. Miscellaneous (sticky windows, dripping faucets, and the like, as well as environmental concerns, such as lead-based paint and asbestos)

Source: American Society of Home Inspectors

* This was the number-one problem in homes, reported by 35.8 percent of the home inspectors surveyed. It is responsible for the most common of household maladies: water penetration of the basement or crawlspace.

How about a Warranty?

Growing in popularity is the Home Owners Warranty, another effort to allay buyers' fears. Yes, buyers may have had the termite inspection and the radon and asbestos check and the lead-paint inspection and, for that matter, the *house* inspection. But still they worry, particularly with older houses.

A Home Owners Warranty is a prepaid service agreement with a customer (the seller, to pass on to the buyer), in which the warranty company promises to repair or replace certain covered systems and appliances in that household in exchange for an annual premium paid by the home owner. A seller would purchase a one-year policy.

There are several companies around the country offering these policies. Your real-estate agent can tell you about the company her office works with. Policies range in price from $300 to $400 a year, with a low deductible of maybe $50 or so.

These are not insurance policies. Indeed most home-warranty companies exclude coverage for items covered by the standard home-owners insurance policy.

The policies are growing in popularity and the renewal rate is high. Many new buyers renew the policy after the one-year purchase by the seller expires.

You might want to look into this purchase. In addition to reassuring your buyer, the policy covers *you* from the signing of a contract through the settlement. If anything goes wrong with the house, you will not have to worry about paying to have it fixed before the buyer's walk-through just before the closing.

That's the big stuff. The next chapter concerns itself with smaller, but no less important, details in getting your house ready for sale.

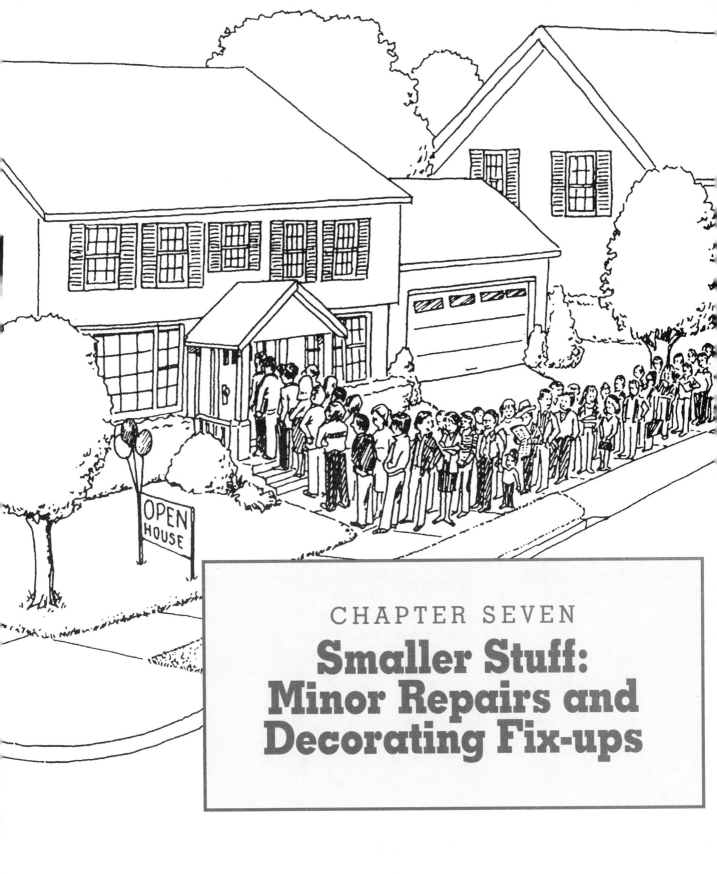

CHAPTER SEVEN

Smaller Stuff: Minor Repairs and Decorating Fix-ups

OPEN HOUSE

TIP

A real-estate agent can suggest what you might want to do around your place, but politeness is likely to keep her from telling you the absolute truth. Your friends probably won't be totally honest either. It's up to you to assess your house's good points—and the flaws that can fairly easily be remedied.

• • •

If you are a working person or a working couple, with little free time, you might consider hiring a cleaning service to clean your house initially. Then you can maintain it relatively easily while it is on the market.

Okay, you've read about painting the exterior and cleaning the basement and the other important checks that need to be done around your house before you plunk that For Sale sign on the front lawn.

But there is more. Before you sell your car, for example, you clean it inside and out, empty the ashtrays, perhaps replace the floor mats and try to scrape off the decals. You must also do all the little things to your house that are necessary to make *it* salable as well, and at the best price.

Funny thing is, many of us live with, and ignore, the small stuff. Buyers, however, will notice everything.

Remember, if there is something wrong, even a teeny bit wrong, with your house, a buyer is going to think:

1. the whole place is poorly constructed and ready to tumble down, and/or
2. you haven't maintained it well, and/or
3. it's too small.

Let's get to some of these areas now, those nitpicky things others will notice that you might not. Or you might, but you just shrug and say, "It won't make a difference." Ah, but it probably will.

One of these "small things" could be pretty big around your house, although it has nothing to do with mechanical systems, crowded garages, or troublesome termites.

Eeeeuw—Dirt!

Real-estate agents say a house hunter's biggest turnoff is dirt inside a house (and around it, too, for that matter), and we aren't talking about soil either, but *dirt*. So the place must be shining and, unfortunately for you, you must keep it that way while it is on the market. Yes, that can certainly become a drag after the first week or so, but you never know who is going to ring that doorbell and you want your "product" to look good.

We can somehow stand dirt in our own house, up to a point, without being repulsed, but dirt in someone else's place—*ugh*. Funny, though, it's the same kind of dust, grime, and scuff marks.

Get Rid of Clutter

"Clean" also means devoid of clutter. Buyers want that, too. They are attracted by rooms with just enough furniture—and no more—and just enough nice touches to look finished. The personal items that you see as "homey" simply crowd a room and detract from the viewer's overall impression of the property. So pack away the fifteen framed photographs of your grandchildren in the living room! Hide the five bowling trophies in the den! You may be trying to show that "nice folks live here, and folks with a life, too," but no one is interested. In fact, they are distracted, which is what you don't want. Do you ever see anything personal in a model home at a new development? No, except for the occasional framed photograph on a night table. That is the look you are trying for.

You want people to imagine themselves living in your house, and they cannot do that if *your* life intrudes on their thoughts.

Experiment with taking things out of your rooms—a few pieces of furniture, an extra chair, magazine bins, plant stands—and then see how the room looks. Airier, right? More spacious? Space sells! Once you begin looking at each room with that eye, you will automatically be able to decide what stays in that space and what goes.

Try putting all that you have taken away from various rooms in one space for now. Perhaps that will be the garage or the basement or a somewhat empty spare room. Do you have a neighbor or friend who can keep those extras while your house is on the market? Chapter 20 will give you some tips for storing things—renting a self-storage unit for the duration, for example—or getting rid of unwanted items permanently. After all, as you read in chapter 6, the garage is supposed to look neat and well organized too.

In the you-can't-win department: Be careful not to go overboard clearing out the clutter. The "too bare" look is not good either!

Sprucing Up the House

Windows and Coverings

Windows need to be clean, all of them—and what a chore that might be! But almost every house hunter will walk over to a window

Fix-up Checklist

Here is a worksheet to help you with jobs that need to be done around your place. Under each area of the house (and the lot) are two or three blank lines. Fill them in with what exactly needs to be done there. As you complete specific jobs, cross out those lines. When all of the lines under a heading are crossed out, put a check mark on the line in front of that part of the house. Under "Mailbox," for example you might jot down "Paint" on one line and "Straighten it" on the other.

This should help you chart your progress.

OUTSIDE

❏ Mailbox

_____

_____

❏ Front lawn

_____

_____

❏ Front shrubbery

_____

_____

❏ Exterior paint

_____

_____

❏ Exterior trim

_____

_____

❏ Front door

_____

_____

❏ Sidewalk/driveway

_____

_____

❏ Garage

_____

_____

_____

_____

❏ Backyard

_____

_____

_____

_____

INSIDE

❏ Basement

_____

_____

_____

_____

First Floor

❏ Entry hall

_____

_____

❏ Living room

_____

_____

❏ Hall closet

_____

_____

Fix-up Checklist (continued)

INSIDE (CONTINUED)

- ❑ Dining room/area
  ____
  ____
- ❑ Downstairs powder room
  ____
  ____
- ❑ Den
  ____
  ____
- ❑ Kitchen
  ____
  ____
- ❑ Kitchenette
  ____
  ____
- ❑ Pantry
  ____
  ____
- ❑ Stairway to upstairs
  ____
  ____

Second Floor

- ❑ Hallway
  ____
  ____
- ❑ Master bedroom
  ____
  ____
- ❑ Dressing room
  ____
  ____
- ❑ 2nd bedroom
  ____
  ____
- ❑ 3rd bedroom
  ____
  ____
- ❑ 4th bedroom
  ____
  ____
- ❑ Bath
  ____
  ____
- ❑ Bath
  ____
  ____
- ❑ Hall closet
  ____
  ____

Third Floor

- ❑ Attic
  ____
  ____
  ____
  ____
  ____
  ____

to check the view. Similarly, what is on and around the window will need your attention. Replace torn or discolored paper window shades with something new, clean, and maybe spiffier. Blinds should be washed, and any curtains or draperies cleaned and ironed.

Hall Closet

We've all seen the cartoons about a person opening a hall closet and everything in the world falling out. What a riot! And what a job you're going to have to do to put that closet in shape if that is what yours looks like. However, it is probably the first door house hunters will open in your place (since you or the agent will have opened the front door for them). You must make the closet look as if there is room for more things to be stored there. If it looks crowded, and there are just three of you living in the house, a would-be buyer is likely to think, "Gee, they don't even have room for the three of them, and there are four of us." Enough said?

Living Room

If folks step right into your living room from the front door, their first impression is particularly important. Watch out for worn spots on the carpet. If you elect to cover a bad patch in a wall-to-wall carpet with an area rug, you are not hiding something and therefore in violation of any disclosure requirement you will read about in chapter 11. Prospects can always lift that area rug if they choose.

You might also want to consider taking up threadbare wall-to-wall carpeting entirely and having the floor refinished. Perhaps you could add an area rug or two.

This next part is difficult if you *live* in that room. Try to keep newspapers and magazines neatly stacked, not lying about on table-tops and on the floor. Drinking glasses, soda cans, chip bags should also be cleared away, certainly at the end of each day.

Do you have a ceiling fan in the living room? Clean it!

Dining Room

Do you have jackets and shirts on the dining chairs? Sweep them off to the closets. Clean the lighting fixtures and make sure they're in working order. Remember earlier advice about too much furniture? That can apply particularly to the dining room. Don't try to cram a table, six chairs, a china cabinet and buffet, and maybe a ficus tree into a space just not made for that much furniture. Get rid of some of the chairs at least. Remember—think airy!

Kitchen

This is one of the two most important rooms in a prospective buyer's eyes, the other being the bathroom.

You will be relieved to hear that realty professionals say there is no need to have an outdated kitchen remodeled. You do not know what plans your buyer has for that area anyway, so don't bother. Just keep its old-fashioned state in mind when setting your price.

But whether your kitchen is vintage 1960, or designed so cutting edge you can slice a finger on it, there are some things you will want to keep in mind about that space while the For Sale sign is out front.

- Dreary doesn't sell. Make sure the room is bright, both with sunlight and light fixtures.
- Paint or paper the room, or at least the splash area or any problem spots.
- If you need a new appliance (or two), replace it now. Buyers don't want to be faced with the thought of purchasing a new dishwasher or refrigerator after just moving in. New appliances can add to the "plus" column of what your house has to offer.
- Paint the fronts of outdated dark cabinets.
- Replace knobs on cabinets with something trendier or more expensive.
- Replace worn linoleum, perhaps with tile.
- Remove magnets from the refrigerator door, and whatever notes, cartoons, and children's art they are holding up.
- If you have a display of copper pots, they should be gleaming.
- Clear countertops of *almost everything*. Put the juicer, the blender, and just about every other gizmo away, either in cabinets or, if they are used rarely, in the garage or basement. Leave out the microwave, the electric can opener, and anything else you use almost every day. Your countertops will not look too empty. Think again of that model home in

TIP

If your house is old, or is a work in progress, do not expect buyers to "use their imagination" and consider all the possibilities. They can't. You must *show* them everything.

TIP

There are now decorators who will help you "stage" your home for sale, for a fee of maybe $50 to $75 an hour. They work with what you have, although they are also likely to make suggestions for some purchases. Ask a real-estate agent if there are decorators in your area who do "staging."

a new development. What is on the counters in that kitchen? Developers and their decorators know there is no need to show would-be buyers what goes on in a kitchen. We all *know*. Usually a model-home kitchen will sport a plant or two on a countertop, or perhaps a few cookbooks between attractive bookends. And that's all! Why not try for that same clean, serene look? It doesn't have to be perfect if real life gets in the way of maintaining an uncluttered look day after day, but doing even a little bit better, if you need to, will create a room more inviting to buyers.

Pantry

For those who are not familiar with this area, it is a small room usually located between the back door and the kitchen. The pantry is used to store canned goods and dried foods, and is also a drop-off point for the family's coats, umbrellas, and boots.

If you have a pantry, make sure things are arranged neatly on shelves and on the floor. If coats are just being left on a table or a countertop, you might hang them on a row of large hooks or pegs you can buy at a home center.

Stairway and Hallway

Are the stairs safe, with no sliding mats or slippery edges? Does the handrail wobble? Is the "artwork" along the wall your kids' fingerprints? Maybe that stairway area could use a fresh coat of paint. An arrangement of pictures would be an attractive addition to catch a visitor's eye while he or she is walking up the stairs.

Check the hallway between upstairs rooms to be sure it is in satisfactory condition. How about the carpeting there? Is that in good shape?

Master Bedroom

Perhaps you have one of the very popular master bedroom suites, with a bath and dressing room adjoining the bedroom. Play it up! Decorate attractively, stashing rows of shoes and tons of cosmetics away so that nothing looks like *too much.*

You might want to tie all three areas together, decorating-wise, if they are not already. Without spending too much money, you can give the dressing room a coat of paint that complements a color in the wallpaper pattern in the bedroom. Or mix and match in some other fashion—towels in the bathroom coordinated with the comforter in the bedroom. Or how about the same ceiling wallpaper border around each of the rooms?

Bedroom Closets

With all you have to do these days, it is asking a lot for you to clean out the bedroom closets. But you really will have to dig into this job. When your house is on the market, there is no such thing as putting a Keep Out ribbon across a door. You may have seen that on house tours, but certainly not with houses for sale. Would-be buyers want to see *everything.* Remember, if clothing, boxes, and so on, are crowded into a closet, it will look too small—a negative perception buyers will carry away with them.

Children's Rooms

"Good grief, must we look?" Yes, even if you've tried to avoid going into your child's room for the past two years. When your house is on the market, you must bite the bullet, step inside, and assess what you see. If a child is creative and has painted the room fire-engine red, by all means give it a coat (probably two coats) of white paint. Don't forget the woodwork.

Stuffed animals, schoolbooks, posters of rock singers, toss pillows, and toys are all expected ingredients of a child's or a teenager's room. Still, those spaces *can* be clean and well organized. And the closets can look roomy.

Bathrooms

They must sparkle! Remove grime around the shower and tub, and recaulk if necessary. Bleach any stains in the tub or sink. Clean glass shower doors. Get rid of mildew. Make sure no faucets drip. If the porcelain on your tub or sink is chipped, have it repaired.

TIP

If your hallway is dark—or if you have a dark bathroom or any other space—consider having a skylight installed. It's a marvelous look that buyers love, and costs only about $1,000. If you can afford it, and your house can use the light, you might want to spring for more than one.

TIP

If you must repaint, stick to a neutral color, preferably in the wide range of whites and ivories. In a like vein, pick a quiet wallpaper pattern, also in a neutral color. You are trying to please the greatest number of people (buyers), and neutrals do that.

• • •

Do you have relatives—or a very good friend—who might store your family's out-of-season clothes while your house is on the market? That would free up a lot of space in everyone's closets.

(Check the Yellow Pages under "Porcelain Repairing and Refinishing.")

If you have perfume bottles on display, or china gizmos or any other countertop decorations, be sure they are all washed and sparkling. (Try to keep the counters relatively clear, too; put away medicine bottles, vitamins, and other personal or beauty products.) A nice touch on a bathroom counter is a bowl of potpourri.

Replace the shower curtain, if necessary, and don't forget a new liner. Actually, you may only need the liner.

Don't forget to straighten up the linen closet.

Remember, these rooms and the kitchen could sell your house. If they need it, spend money in both these areas!

A final note about bathrooms: Most buyers these days want more than one bath, or at least one full bath and a powder room. If you want to spend the money for another bathroom, you can recoup that expense when you sell. Equally important, a two-bath or one-and-one-half-bath house can sell more quickly than a one-bath one.

All Around the House

Repair molding and woodwork nicked by the family over the years. Check woodwork to see if it needs a fresh paint job, too. Sometimes painting the woodwork brings enough brightness to an area to make painting the walls unnecessary.

You also might want to check electrical outlets, especially if you're used to running extension cords around a room, jamming several wires into one extension cord and then into one outlet. That can give house hunters the impression the electrical system is inadequate (and it's not too safe for you either).

Try to have any "dud" outlets fixed.

Odors

Can you smell your house? You shouldn't, except maybe for potpourri or burning wood in the fireplace, or something marvelous in the oven. Watch out for pet odors, unpleasant cooking odors (fish or cabbage versus a cake or cookies), cigarette smoke and its smell, as well as damp and musty odors in the basement.

Can you actually live in this perfect house, this movie set, for a few months? That's one of the hardest parts of having a house for sale. You will probably never truly relax in your own— let's say it—*home* until it is sold. You will always be telling someone to pick up something, or fluffing pillows or looking around to put a gadget you have just used into some drawer, any drawer, just to get it out of sight.

What Will All This Cost?

Not all that much, really. The average seller spends around $500 to fix up a house for sale. You might spend more, or less, depending on the state of your house right now.

Buyers need that important impression of your house as neat, clean, and *in working order*. If they want to turn the den into an office, or take down the wall separating the kitchen and dining room, or totally repaint, that's their business. You cannot be expected to have a place that will suit everyone. You *will* be expected to meet their most basic needs and wishes in a house, though. Accomplishing what was discussed in this chapter and in chapter 6 will help you attain that admittedly tough goal.

Besides curb appeal, real-estate agents have a term for a house that is virtually perfect inside and out, and therefore easier to sell. They call that house a "cream puff." Wouldn't you like that label attached to your house, with word of its good condition making its way through the real-estate agent grapevine?

What's "In" These Days

Here is what's considered trendy in houses nowadays. Do you have any of these features to offer a buyer? Good for you if you do!

- Gated community
- Water garden
- Jacuzzi
- Center island in the kitchen
- Pop-out windows (new, bay-type windows that might be found, say, over a kitchen sink)
- "Open" plan for first-floor living area—no arrangement of rooms with walls
- Deck or patio, open or enclosed
- Master bedroom suite
- Feng shui, the Chinese art of designing and decorating a house to invite peace, happiness, and good fortune. A seller might boast of this design and expense, pointing out to would-be buyers how *they* can retain that "good fortune" after *they* live there.

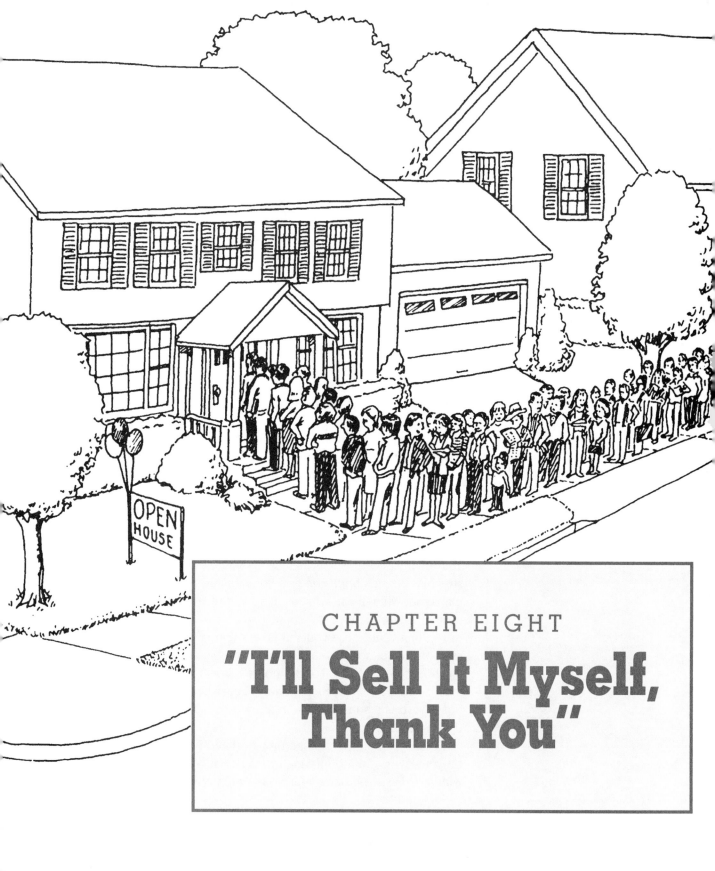

CHAPTER EIGHT

"I'll Sell It Myself, Thank You"

TIP

When you picked up this book, you might have turned immediately to this chapter. Please do read the other chapters as well. There is information in Part I that will help you in one area or another of selling a house on your own.

• • •

These are the primary reasons that FSBO sales fail.

- Overpricing
- Poor marketing
- Lack of financial savvy
- Poor negotiating techniques
- Legal snarls
- Bad luck

Okay, okay, okay, you may be saying about now. Let me at it, I want to sell my house by myself.

Who could blame you? What seller wouldn't like to save a 6 percent commission he or she would otherwise have to hand over to a real-estate agent? Think of all the furniture that piece of change would buy for the new place. Think of the moving expense tab it would pick up. If you sell your own $95,000 house, you save $5,700. Sell a $250,000 house and the commission you don't have to pay comes to a tidy $15,000. Or look at it this way: How long would you have to work to *save* that amount of cash?

You might say selling your house all by yourself is the ultimate do-it-yourself project!

But wait. Think for a moment of two roads to the same destination: the successful sale of your house. One road is a major interstate highway, smooth and direct. The other is a meandering country lane, with many curves and turns and sometimes no signs or directional signals. Do you get the picture? Guess which represents doing it yourself?

Still, while using a real-estate agent may be more direct (the faster path to a sale), the meandering way can also sell your house. Sometimes you can drive on *it* quite fast, but you need good control and an excellent sense of direction.

Are you hesitating? You have definitely decided to sell. But after reflection, you are unsure which road is better for your particular piece of real estate? Alas, no one can help you with this decision. Your own situation is specific, just as your neighbor's down the street is. But this book *can* give you detailed maps of the two roads, maps that will tell you what's ahead before you get there. This chapter is the map for the country road.

Selling your house yourself is an exciting way to go, and everyone who is even remotely interested in and capable of doing so should give it a try. For the home owners who take the time to learn some basic procedures and safeguards, the risks are slight and the reward is a substantial sum of money that stays in *your* kitty and doesn't go into someone else's.

One very important point, though: Keep in mind that by doing it on your own, you are missing the most valuable ingredient of a sale with a real-estate broker. Your house will not be on the multiple listing service circuit and will not immediately be seen by house hunters all around your area. (Sellers who sign with discount brokers do have some access to the MLS. More about that in chapter 10.) *You* will have to do all the publicity and advertising. Take a look at the questions in the box on page 84, to see if you really could—or should—take on this job.

Taking the Plunge

So are you ready to give it a try? Before you act, read what follows in this chapter and the next one. They will offer a good many suggestions and some pretty firm guidelines to help you make a successful sale.

Tactic #1: Don't feel that you've made a permanent commitment. Choosing to sell without a realty agent is not an irrevocable decision. If you find the going too difficult, you can list your property as quickly as snapping your fingers.

In fact, while you are on the for-sale-by-owner road, you should monitor the traffic on the real-estate highway. You do that by watching the real-estate pages of your newspaper and listening to the agents who call you. Newspaper advertising and reported sales will tell you a lot about your competition and about the climate of the market in general. The phone calls from agents who are scouting for a new listing (yours!) can give you excellent

insights into the activity and working procedures of their companies. When they ask questions, answer them and ask some of your own; and if they ask permission to visit your property, invite them in.

Often an agent who is "too busy" to go on a preinspection visit to a new listing will rush off to examine a property she thinks she might list herself. And even if she doesn't get the listing (which she definitely won't on her first visit to you), she will remember the house if it does come out on the multiple listing service. That's all to your advantage as a seller. By all means keep in touch with the real estate pros.

DEFINITION PLEASE

FSBO (pronounced "fizz-bo") is a term you will encounter during the selling process. It stands for for-sale-by-owner properties.

Should You Sell It Yourself?

- Is everyone in the household agreed on the do-it-yourself path?
- Do you all know that for several weeks or months selling your house will become almost a part-time job?
- Do you have the time, not just for showing prospects through, but for all of the setting-up details too?
- Are you knowledgeable about your community and particularly your neighborhood—the location of schools and parks, zoning restrictions, and so on?
- Are you thick-skinned enough to stand quietly while a prospective buyer makes negative, even nasty comments, about a feature of your house?
- Are you knowledgeable enough about people to separate the lookers from the serious buyers, and to keep the former from taking up too much of your time?
- Are you aware of financing options in your community? (You will be after you follow suggestions in this book.)

- Do you have the money to spend up-front for advertising costs? Working with an agent allows you to pay when the sale is closed, being a FSBO means paying as you go.
- Are you available seven days a week to show your house? Buyers will want to come over when *they* want, not when you'd rather see them during your leisure time.
- Do you have good negotiating skills? You will not have an agent to act as a buffer. You'll have to do all the "money" talk yourself.
- Do you know what you are required by law to reveal about your house? (You will after reading chapter 11.)
- Do you have a lawyer to work with you on this transaction?

If you can answer yes to all of these questions (or most of them, with the intention of learning how to do the rest), then you should be able to sell your home on your own. You can certainly try!

Tactic #2: Don't allow agents to show your property to prospective buyers while you are selling it yourself. This is so important, it's almost a rule. If you break it, you will be working against yourself.

Here's what could happen. At any given time, there are X number of home buyers in the realty marketplace. When your for-sale-by-owner house comes on the market, it will draw its prospective customers from this pool of active house hunters. Most of them are already working with at least one agent. That agent will see your ad and think, "Aha, this is perfect for the Baxters!" So Agent Reddy will call you and say she has a customer just right for your house. She'd like to show it to them. If they buy, the commission will be 6 percent of the sale price. If they do not, there is no obligation to you.

It sounds tempting. "After all," you reason, "there is no obligation." Ah, but that phrase is deceptive. Whether the Baxters buy your house the day Agent Reddy shows it to them or six weeks later when you accidentally meet them at a cocktail party and get to talking about price, you owe Agent Reddy a commission.

She claims that commission because she first introduced the Baxters to your property under your oral open-listing agreement. (There is an explanation of various realty agreements in chapter 10.) That was when you said, "Yes, you can show it." It was also why you got the letter the next day thanking you for allowing her to show your house to the Baxters under the one-day agreement to pay a 6 percent commission. Agent Reddy would claim that she was instrumental in effecting the sale of your property to the Baxters, even though you came to a meeting of the minds on price at a party. She would claim (and she would be right) that you cannot sell to the Baxters without paying her commission. If you were to try to do so on the sly, she would have legal grounds to file suit.

There is a good deal involved in legal descriptions of agency relationships and "standard negotiation clauses," but that would simply obscure the point being made here. Every time you allow an agent to bring a buyer to your property while you are selling it yourself, you are taking one "fish" out of the pool in which you are fishing. You are working against yourself, since the purpose of your advertising is to bring those very same people to you *directly*.

Be sure to make several copies of your community's by-laws to hand out to serious prospective buyers. They must know if they can have several pets, a basketball hoop, a fountain on the front lawn, and even paint the place magenta if they like. Many buyers will not know to ask for these documents.

INFORMATION

You will need to acquaint yourself with local zoning regulations in the event a buyer wants to set up a home office in your house, or even turn it into a retail store. If you have no community by-laws to guide you, call your zoning department to see if your block is zoned residential or mixed-use. Usually home offices that do not change the exterior of the structure, or cause too many cars to take up residents' parking spaces, are all right. Retail establishments are another, more serious matter.

If there is one exception to this rule, it is the corporate-transfer buyer. These people usually have only a week or so to find a house and they very rarely run down home-owner ads. If an agent calls you with this kind of a prospect for a one-day/one-customer, it is usually a good idea to agree. Transferees are real estate's typical "hot buyers," and you might just as well have your property among the others to be considered.

Tactic #3: Don't show your house to anyone who will not give his or her name, address, and phone number, or who will not make an appointment to see the property at your convenience. This precaution is really little more than common sense, but sometimes it's overlooked in the excitement and novelty of the selling experience. You can give out your address to those potential buyers who want to "drive by" first, but make it clear that you will show the property only by appointment. (You might also add "Shown by Appointment Only" to the sign you have on your front lawn.) There will still be some stubborn die-hards who will surely ring your doorbell saying, "We were driving by and just fell in love with your house." Tell them you will be happy to set a date and time for a showing, but not now. If they won't return at another time, they weren't buyers, they were lookers.

Tactic #4: Don't hold out for the sell-it-yourself route too long. This last tactic grows out of the principle that there are only X number of potential customers in your buying pool.

A for-sale-by-owner house is likely to sell to a resident of the town in which it is located or the immediately surrounding area. Corporate transferees and out-of-state buyers cannot afford the time, effort, and aggravation involved in finding an individual house in an unfamiliar area. The buyer population in your pool, therefore, does not change very rapidly. Advertisements in all the local papers for two or three weeks in a row will probably reach most of your potential customers.

Your greatest number of phone calls and inspections will occur the first week after your advertise; the second and third weeks will pick up stragglers and perhaps vacationers. Beyond that, you will have a trickle of customers—the new people who come into the marketplace. Four to five weeks, then, is the outside limit you should give yourself with a FSBO house. If your house is not sold in that period, you need the larger pool of buyers from more distant areas that a professional real-estate agency and the multiple listing service can bring you.

There you are: the four don'ts. They are all potential trouble spots along your country road that leads to a sale. Still, that isn't the sum total of advice.

Companies That Help FSBOs

Over the last decade or so, companies that help for-sale-by-owner sellers have sprouted up in various parts of the country. Some firms are regional in scope; others are national.

How much help do they offer? Essentially, they give advertising assistance. These companies will place your ad—for a fee—in their magazine, which is circulated free around town. For a fee, your house will also be shown on a local Sunday morning television show they sponsor. They may also have an Internet home page.

How much you can expect to pay depends on the part of the country you live in and the individual company. An ad in a monthly color magazine might cost around $200 to $300, although there are sometimes cheaper package deals. There is another fee for showing your house on the Internet. The companies also offer signs, directional arrows, plastic tubes to contain your flier, and the like.

Look into one of these companies near you if you choose. They can help, but don't expect a good deal of assistance in other areas. And don't rely on them exclusively for advertising. Remember, no one is going to care about the sale of your house the way you will. You must get out there and beat the bushes yourself. You can find these companies in the Yellow Pages under "Real Estate."

Now let's get on to more specific FSBO suggestions.

Try to set appointments for showings when two or more people will be at home, for your personal safety and also to protect your property against theft.

If you are by yourself, arrange with a relative, friend, or neighbor to call you maybe fifteen minutes after the would-be buyers arrive. Tell that person over the phone, loud enough for your visitors to hear, that you'll get back to him or her as soon as the showing is over. A small safety ploy.

CHAPTER NINE

Ten "Must-Do's" for FSBOs

Most sellers on their own start by putting an ad in the local paper. As you may have guessed, that is the first mistake. It is a mistake because most people are totally unprepared for what will happen when that paper comes off the presses. They pick up their ringing phone and find themselves on the defensive end of every conversation, answering whatever questions the anonymous callers choose to throw their way. Often they can't distinguish between potential buyers and real-estate agents looking for a listing. Sometimes they are unprepared for the most commonly asked questions about taxes, heating costs, or square footage. And worst of all, sometimes they can't even give clear and specific directions to their own property! In other words, they botch up the deal on the phone before it has a chance to get started.

Remember, you are the salesperson here, and your house is the product. You will have to earn your sales commission (in this case, it's saving a realty agent's commission) like everyone else with a product to sell. Do for your potential buyers all the things a good agent would do for you. Here are ten "must-do's."

1. Describe the Property

There is a classic cartoon in the real-estate world that shows a brand-new agent dressed to the nines in a plaid suit, a gaudy tie, and shiny shoes, standing with a couple dressed in jeans in a room with a fireplace, two wing chairs, a coffee table, and a couch. In one hand the agent clutches a piece of paper that he is scrutinizing intently as he extends the other arm and says "*This* is the living room."

The sheet of paper from which this astute fellow derives this information is, of course, the listing. Sometimes a seasoned agent will show a house without carrying the listing with her, but you can be certain it's in the car under the front seat.

Real-estate listing sheets describe the property and answer the questions most commonly asked by interested buyers. You, too, as a house seller, must have a good description of your property, and you must have those answers. To do this effectively, you will want to make up a "listing" of your own for your property.

You may follow the format of the listing sheets the MLS uses in your area or you may use the sample that follows as a guideline. In either case, you should type it neatly so everything fits on one side of one page. Don't get carried away and poetic in your descriptions; think of this as a business form.

A typical MLS listing might look like this:

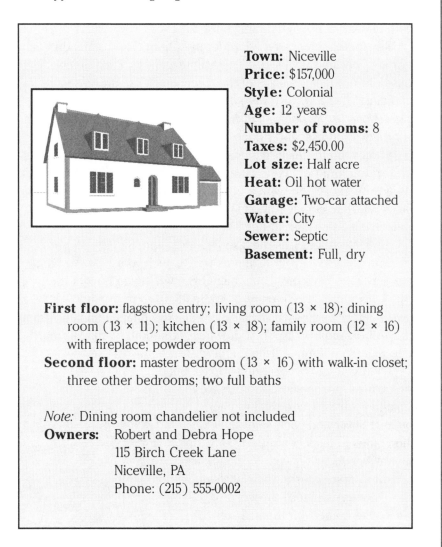

Town: Niceville
Price: $157,000
Style: Colonial
Age: 12 years
Number of rooms: 8
Taxes: $2,450.00
Lot size: Half acre
Heat: Oil hot water
Garage: Two-car attached
Water: City
Sewer: Septic
Basement: Full, dry

First floor: flagstone entry; living room (13 × 18); dining room (13 × 11); kitchen (13 × 18); family room (12 × 16) with fireplace; powder room
Second floor: master bedroom (13 × 16) with walk-in closet; three other bedrooms; two full baths

Note: Dining room chandelier not included
Owners: Robert and Debra Hope
115 Birch Creek Lane
Niceville, PA
Phone: (215) 555-0002

TIP

You can find lot and room sizes by digging up the papers you had drawn up when you purchased your house.

Your listing can follow this same format.

Note the items listed on the upper right-hand side of the sample listing. This is specific information that you should have before you begin selling. (It's also a good idea to include the amount of the heating bill for the previous winter and, if applicable, a season's worth of central air-conditioning bills.)

Now look at what's typed under the photo. The rooms on each floor are specified with sizes. The listing agent for this particular house did not feel the sizes of the three smaller bedrooms were important. They are. Give the sizes of all the rooms on your listing. Under *Note*, list any items not included in the price. Finish up with your name, address, and phone number.

When you are finished typing, and are happy with what you have written, print out your listing. If you don't have a computer, take it to a print shop. You want a clean, sharp page. Have a hundred black-and-white copies run off (that could be the minimum order required). It could cost under $10.

The realty agency listing also includes a photograph. A photo will certainly add to your listing as well. Check your files. You may have kept a copy of the listing page from when you bought the property, or find any other picture of it already used in a magazine or newspaper. Glue it down (don't use cellophane tape) on your listing page. A pen-and-ink or pencil drawing of the house will also reproduce well, so put any artistic talent in your family to use too.

When you have your listing copies, put one near each extension phone. Give the remainder out one at a time to each potential buyer and each sales agent who comes to inspect your property. In this way agents will have information to pass on to associates in their offices, and customers will take a record of your house home with them. Thus your property will compete on equal ground with the houses that are being shown by agents, and will get a little special notice in area real-estate offices even before it is listed.

2. Locate the Property

For real-estate agents, the first step in locating the property means showing prospective buyers where the street is on a large wall map of the town. That gives buyers a sense of where the house stands in relation to municipal services, recreation areas, houses of worship, shopping, highways, and schools. In step two, the agent gets the buyers into her car and drives them to the house *by the most scenic route possible.*

For you, the FSBO seller, the process is reversed and slightly more difficult. Your primary goal is to get the buyers from their home to yours *by the least complicated route.* You must make prospective buyers feel absolutely secure in your directions or they simply won't come. Therefore you must guide them by phone.

Here's how to do this: Get a good street map of your town. Mark the major roads—the streets everyone knows by name—in red. Now plot the most direct route to your house from each of these major roads with a different color pencil. Then take a separate sheet of paper or an index card, color-code it for each route, and write out those directions.

Be specific. Here is an example: "From Main Street at the post office going east, take your third left. This is Oak Street. Go through two traffic lights, and at the third light turn right. This is Cos Cob Lane. We are on your left, number twenty-nine, a white split-level with blue shutters."

If you really want to be exact and specific, go out and drive each route, noting the distances in tenths of a mile between major turns. Again, for another example: "From Ridgemont Avenue going south, turn left at Green's Drug Store. Go one and seven-tenths miles and turn left on High Street. Go four-tenths of a mile and turn right on Maple Street. We are the fourth house on the right, number one thirty-six."

When you give these directions to a prospective buyer, be sure he or she reads them back to you. You want to be absolutely certain the person doesn't get lost. Getting people to your house is half the game here!

After your written direction cards are completed, take the street map of the town, mark a star where your house is with a felt pen,

TIP

You might want to engage a real-estate agent on a "consulting" basis, paying her a flat fee for an hour or so of her time, so you can ask her any questions you might have about showing, negotiating, the contract, and the closing.

and then circle it. When you have an interested party, get out this map and point out your house in relationship to the facilities of the town, just as the real-estate agent would do in her office.

3. Know the Town

The ability to point out schools, churches, shopping centers, playgrounds, good restaurants, and entertainment facilities in town, along with a thorough knowledge of proposed highway construction, zoning changes, and probable tax increases is much appreciated by out-of-town buyers. This information is less important to local buyers, since it is already a part of their lives; but you should not entirely overlook it. Just moving from one part of a large city to another means getting used to new services, shops, and schools. It's almost like moving to another town.

At a bare minimum, you should know about the schools in the neighborhood. Also, make a point of knowing if there are exceptionally good recreational facilities nearby (a good playground, a pool). Do the same for especially good shopping or community social activities, such as drama, art, garden or bridge clubs, or senior citizen centers. Know about proposed zoning changes or construction in your area, and take heed of any predictions that corporate offices, research plants, or industrial parks being built in the town will lower taxes.

You don't have to write all this up in a formal presentation, but you should have it tucked away in your mind and be able to include it in your conversations with customers whenever appropriate. The information won't sell your house to people who dislike it the moment they walk in the front door—you shouldn't waste any effort trying to sell to them anyway—but it may tip the scales with someone who is wavering. And most assuredly, it will put your property on an equal footing with those being presented by the knowledgeable real-estate agent who can chat endlessly about the town.

You even have one advantage over that salesperson. You know your neighbors. A little conversation with an interested buyer about the nice people next door or across the street, about the families nearby who have children about the same age as the buyers' children, about neighborhood people who work where your buyers work (car pool potentials), or about the prize-winning gardener or painter around the corner never hurts a sale. This kind of intimate detail makes people feel more at home and gives them a sense of being in the neighborhood before they actually buy. It breaks down buying resistance by breaking down fear of the unknown.

4. Qualify the Buyers

"Qualify" in the real-estate world means money. Every green sales agent is told by her office manager or supervising broker that she *must* qualify all buyers before taking them out to see houses. This rule saves time and prevents disappointments, but in practice it's sometimes broken.

To qualify a buying couple, an agent needs to know the amount of their combined gross annual income, the amount of money they intend to use as a down payment, and the amounts of any large outstanding loans on which they make monthly payments. That could be car payments or credit card debt or school loans. Or it might be alimony or child support. The agent then computes these figures and compares them with the guidelines of each of the lending institutions in the area. She comes up with the monthly payment amount that the family can afford in order to qualify for a mortgage at each lender's. This, of course, also sets the top limit on the purchase price they can afford.

Many real-estate agents, especially inexperienced ones, find it difficult to ask people how much they make, how much they've managed to save, and how much they owe. Home owners selling on their own find the task nearly impossible. The result is that many private sales fall through because neither party realizes, while shaking hands and signing contracts, that the buyers simply cannot afford the house. Everyone is frustrated, hurt, flustered, and angry when the mortgage application is refused. Usually it means that the house, tied up in the pending deal, has been off the market for almost a month. Sometimes it means that the sellers have signed a purchase contract on another house, thinking theirs was sold, only to find that they are stuck with two houses. Nightmare City!

These days, more and more real-estate agents avoid prying questions by sending would-be buyers to a mortgage lender to be

INFORMATION

As a FSBO seller you can expect many buyers who will be looking to you for help with financing. If you choose to do this, there is more about seller financial aids in chapter 14.

DEFINITION PLEASE

Being **prequalified** for a loan means a mortgage lender has told you, based on the information you give him or her about your finances, how much house you can afford to buy. Being **preapproved** is more detailed and is a far better credential for a buyer from the seller's perspective. This means the house hunter has gone through the mortgage application process, and the lender guarantees to lend that buyer X amount of dollars for a home loan within a certain time frame. All that is needed to complete the granting of the mortgage is the address of the house and an appraisal by the lender.

prequalified or preapproved. The house hunter then comes back with that documentation and the agent knows how to proceed. That is, she knows how much house the buyer can afford.

The do-it-yourself seller has to do some homework here. First, call several local lending institutions and ask, "What are your current minimal requirements for a down payment on a house?" Also, ask the lenders for their guidelines in qualifying applicants for a mortgage. They will gladly give you this information, since lending money is their business and they want to make loans. Jot down the information you get from each lender, just in case you need it for negotiating later.

Now calculate some minimums of your own. What is 20 percent of your asking price? 10 percent? 5 percent? You will need to adjust this figure when you finally agree on an exact selling price, but now you are looking for approximations and working with your asking price will come in close enough. For example, if your asking price is $125,000, 20 percent down is $25,000, 10 percent is $12,500 and 5 percent is $6,250.

Next, calculate how much annual income a buyer must have to qualify for a mortgage on your house. To do this, call a mortgage lender and ask the amount of the monthly payment for principal and interest on X dollars (your house price minus 20 percent down, 10 percent down, etc.) for a term of thirty years or whatever is currently being given.

Or you can buy a little paperback that all real-estate agents have and that is sold in most bookstores for $6 or so. The book can be called *Mortgage Payments* or some similar name. It contains charts showing how much a monthly mortgage payment would be for, say, a $90,000 loan at 8 percent for thirty years, at 8¼ percent for thirty years, at 8½ percent for thirty years, and on and on for a hundred or so pages of varying amounts.

When you get these amounts, add one-twelfth of your annual taxes. This is the real monthly payment a buyer must make. Compare it to the qualification guidelines of the lending institutions in your area and calculate the gross annual income required to "carry" your property. With a smaller down payment than your working figure, the income must be higher; with a larger down payment, it can be lower.

Who Does What Here?

Do you know who will be handling different areas of this realty transaction for you? You should have that information before you actually accept a buyer's offer.

- *Who writes the contract of sale?* Try to have your lawyer draw up the contract, although the buyer's lawyer could. If the buyer's attorney writes up the contract, be *sure* that your lawyer gets to read it.

- *Who holds escrow moneys?* Your "fiduciary" agent, probably your lawyer, or a closing agent if that is common where you are, will hold the money.

- *Who will handle the closing?* Someone has to be in charge at the closing. This must be a third party; that is, someone who may be paid for his or her services but cannot profit from the transaction. That could be either side's lawyer, or perhaps a closing agent who handles a property transfer without buyer or seller present.

- *Where will the closing be held?* There are many choices— your lawyer's office or the buyer's lawyer's office. It could also be held at the closing agent's office if that is the custom where you are, and your presence might not be required. That agent could be the title company, or the mortgage lender. If you had a real-estate agent, the closing might be held at her office.

TIP

Don't refer buyers to *your* attorney. You shouldn't both share the same legal counsel.

Do these calculations before you put your ad in the newspaper. Then, when a seriously interested party appears and you begin to talk about money, you can simply say something like, "According to our information and calculations, you need at least $9,000 down, and a combined gross income of at least $37,000 a year in order to buy this house. How close are you to those figures?"

Your buyers may try to be evasive about money, but get as much information as you can. Ask about employment, debts, savings, and extra sources of income. Then if the deal seems to be going through, require that the buyers' lawyer present your lawyer with a financial statement before signing a binding contract. A copy of their last year's federal income tax return is also a good source of financial information. You should examine the financial statement and/or the tax return carefully with your lawyer, and you should both agree that your buyers can afford your house before taking it off the market.

Your lawyer should also look into the buyers' credit report, with their permission.

5. Be Prepared for an Offer

Yes, it's early in the game to bring up someone talking price with you. But you need to know how you will handle yourselves when that happens. When the buyer and the seller agree on a price and other terms, a real-estate agent takes it from there. With a FSBO, you do it.

When you and your buyers come to a meeting of the minds, shake hands. *That's all for now.* Take no money from them. For their own protection, buyers are advised never to make out a check to the seller.

Call your lawyer that day or the next and have the buyers call theirs. Your lawyer will draw up a contract, and can take escrow money from them—usually 10 percent of the selling price—to be held by that attorney until contract contingencies are met. From now on the contract and its clauses are handled by the two lawyers, you, and your buyer.

6. Advertise

A few days before you are about to begin your for-sale-by-owner campaign, you open the real-estate section of your newspaper and there you see a house just down the street from you. It is an ad with a picture and a border around it or, as is known in the publishing business, a "display ad." It has a large picture of the property and **Open House** printed boldly above it. It's being sold by a local realty office. Hmmmmm, boy, you think, doesn't that ad look terrific. Look at the size of it! That house'll sell in a day. You're . . . Yes, you're *jealous*. That's okay. It's to be expected. Everybody would like their property handled with photos and splash ads, but it's very, very expensive and has no place in a for-sale-by-owner budget.

Contrary to popular belief, real-estate agents do not advertise a particular house in order to sell it! Only a very small percentage of people who respond to newspaper ads actually buy the house they call in about. Agencies therefore advertise their most attractive houses most heavily. Those ads are come-ons, hooks to catch customers. All agency advertising is advertising for customers. Of course, salespeople will show the advertised house, but then they will shift customers who are not buyers for that house to other listings that may not photograph or read as well. (Often enough what reads well turns out to be a disaster on the outside, and what photographs well turns out to be not great on the inside!)

You, on the other hand, are advertising the property you want to sell and your approach should be honest above all else. You are not trying to "catch" customers, you only want to attract buyers who are sincerely interested in your kind of property. You do not need a large ad, and it should not include purple prose. Active house hunters carefully scan real-estate classified sections to pick out the new home-owner ads. Yours doesn't have to be more than four or five lines long.

It should begin with the general location. If your newspaper covers a large number of towns, lead your ad with the name of the town; otherwise you'll be dumped into the miscellaneous column, a weak place to begin. If your city is very large, lead with a borough name or a neighborhood or area name that is generally recognized.

Next, mention the number of rooms, style of the house (colonial, ranch, etc.), the number of bedrooms and baths, something about the kitchen (large, modern, sunny, eat-in), and some special features (family room with fireplace, garage, treed lot, full basement with workshop, privacy, view). Don't try to tell everything about the

TIP

If you like, you can send for a copy of the Model Home Sales Contract offered by the American Homeowners Foundation, an independent nonprofit consumer organization. Your lawyer might want to use that. It costs $7.95, or $4.95 each for two or more. Call (800) 489-7776 to order by credit card, or send a check or money order to the foundation at 6776 Little Falls Rd., Arlington, VA 22213. There is a $3 postage and handling charge for telephone and mail orders. You can also request a free brochure about the foundation's other publications.

house in the ad; usually a question in the minds of potential buyers will bring a phone call faster than a gorgeous description.

Then state the price. Just one number: $150,000. Don't write "asking $150,000" or "$150,000 firm," just $150,000. Follow this with "owner" and your phone number.

Don't pay extra for the words *principals only*; real-estate agents are going to call anyway, and you can use their calls to your advantage.

Here is how a sample advertisement might read (Don't worry, the newspaper's classified office will put your "copy" into the abbreviated style.):

> **NORTHBROOK HTS,** 8-rm all brk ranch, 4BR, 2-1/2 BA, 2 car gar., x-lg kit., $160,000. Owner 555-6934.

You can also save advertising money by not running your ad continuously. Usually Friday, Saturday, and Sunday are the best days to capture the readers you want (and they may be the days offered at a "package" rate by the newspaper). Friday and Saturday catch people about to look over the weekend, and Sunday is the big real-estate section day for many papers. Some readers won't get around to your ad until Monday or Tuesday, but that's all right. You'll have just about the entire week covered then.

Don't just advertise in newspapers. Take that listing flier and post it wherever you can around town—on the bulletin boards in supermarkets or at social halls, public buildings, and offices where you have access. You might also want to advertise on the Internet (see chapter 12).

7. Answer the Phone

In some offices new real-estate agents listen to the pros in their office and their telephone technique before answering calls themselves. The initial blind contact with a prospective buyer can be pivotal. If the person who answers the phone call comes across well, there is at least a fair chance of getting that buyer out to see the property.

As a seller, you must be warm and enthusiastic without being pushy or desperate. You should be well prepared and organized and answer questions without giving too much information, so the buyer does not get the feel of a "hard sell."

And above all, try to control the conversation! One of the oldest, most effective techniques for controlling a conversation is to answer a question and then ask one in return. For example:

> Seller: *Hello.*
> Caller: *Hello, is this the person selling the house?*
> Seller: *Yes, my name is Sam Seller. May I have your name?*

Or later in the conversation:

> Caller: *What are the sizes of the three bedrooms you advertised?*
> Seller: *Well, the master bedroom is sixteen by eighteen, each of the other two is twelve by fourteen, and they'll each hold twin beds. So the house will accommodate a family of six. Do you need that many?*

When the caller replies to a question, he will most likely give you some information about his family that you can then use to point up some other advantage of your property—close to schools, or privacy, or large family room, fenced yard for children.

Still later, the conversation might go like this:

> Caller: *Can you tell me where your property is?*
> Seller: *Yes, I can give you specific directions. Would you like to make an appointment to see it?*

Try always to make the appointment before you give directions. If the callers insist on a drive-by, give them the directions but state clearly that they must call back for an appointment before you will show the inside of the house. When you make the appointment, also

TIP

Practice talking to would-be buyers. If there are two of you, one can call the other from outside the house and go through a likely conversation. Then, maybe at another time, the other person can play the part of the buyer. You *both* want to be prepared for buyer phone calls. If you are selling alone, ask a family member of friend to play the role of buyer so you can sharpen your phone skills.

get the caller's phone number, "Just in case we have to change the appointment time or in case we have to cancel because of a deposit."

This usually makes real buyers jittery that you might sell the house before they can see it. It brings them out faster and more reliably.

If you suspect that your caller is a real-estate agent, try to identify her as soon as possible. The easiest way is to ask. If the caller is an agent, she is required by law to identify herself as such. You can then be very businesslike, take the name, make an appointment for a visit if the agent wants to see the property, and keep the conversation as short as possible, thus leaving your phone lines and your time free for potential buyers.

If you have guessed wrong and your caller says "No, I'm not an agent," you can turn your question into a positive stroke for the caller and a bit of competitive pressure as well by saying something like "Oh, excuse me. You sounded so professional in your questions that I thought you were an agent. We've been getting so many calls, you know, from agents who want to list this property."

8. Show the Property

If you think a real-estate agent wandering through the rooms saying, "This is the living room, and this is the kitchen and this is the bathroom" is rather foolish, think of yourself doing the same thing. "No way," you should say. Showing a property gracefully and sensibly to complete strangers to whom you hope to sell it is much more difficult than you might imagine. You can't just let them walk about alone, and you can't walk alongside them silently either. So you try to make conversation and/or give a tour. Neither is completely successful.

It's a good idea to ask questions to get people to talk about themselves. For example, after greeting your customers and getting through the introductions, walk into the center of the living room and ask, "Have you lived in this area very long?" (Don't worry, they'll *know* it's the living room.) They will look about while answering your question, and if they are talkative you might find out that they are living in an apartment or that they too have a house to sell or that they have already sold and *need* to move. Store away any information you get for that negotiating table later.

Words Sellers Wish They Had Never Said—and Why

"Look, if the Joneses could get $107,000 for that place down the street, we can get at least $125,000 for our house."

    It takes nine months to sell their house. The selling price is $114,000.

"We don't want anything to do with real-estate agents. My cousin's husband told us exactly how to sell."

    Their house sells in four days. Five weeks later they discover that the same model three streets over in the development sold two months ago for $8,000 more.

"Are you kidding? $81,000! I don't care if that's your best offer. We're asking $86,500 and we know this condo is worth between $82,000 and $84,000."

    Four months later the apartment is sold through a broker for $82,500. But the commission costs the sellers $4,950.

"We'll buy it. We can probably get $100,000 for ours, so we'll only have to carry an extra $15,000 on the new mortgage."

    Their old house sells after eight months for $89,500. A real-estate broker's commission lowers their net cash to $84,130. They then carry a new first mortgage that has a $15,000 higher principal and a 3-point higher interest rate than their old mortgage, and a $17,000 short-term second mortgage from the seller. They eat spaghetti *a lot*.

Another tactic is to point out specific features in a room. You might say, "My wife's really into cooking, she has quite a windowsill herb garden going," as you take them into a warm kitchen that seems to be the province of a serious cook. Or take them into a rather small bedroom and say, "This room has a huge double closet with storage shelves to the ceiling."

In showing your property, try to be sensitive to your customers. If they like the house, they will go through it slowly; if not, they'll be through quite quickly. Don't try to rush them or slow them down.

9. Negotiate the Sale

This step is where you will miss the help of a real-estate professional. It is difficult to negotiate effectively when all interested parties are face-to-face. One tried-and-true success tool in negotiating is, "Well, I don't know. That offer sounds pretty good to me, but I'll have to talk with ___ before I can give you an answer." An appeal to talk with an outside person of authority buys the negotiating party time to consider the offer and time to come back with a counterproposal. It also makes the negotiator look less like a bad guy because the demands come from somewhere else.

The absence of an involved party, however, is sometimes hard to stage. Perhaps the seller's wife or husband could be absent for some reason when a buying couple comes to make a first offer. Or you might have a rich aunt or a parent who is helping with the financing on the new home and therefore must be consulted about the adequacy of the price on the old house before you can sign an agreement. Or you might need to talk with your accountant. Or you can simply say, "We'll have to discuss this overnight and call you tomorrow."

Of course, you might just be presented with an offer very close to what you figured as the market value of your property. If this happens, don't quibble over pennies; *take it*. Remember, you are saving the entire commission.

Or you might come upon a buyer who is also very aware of market value and wants to get a bargain by avoiding the real-estate commission. In this case, if you can agree on the fair market value of the property, perhaps you can split the amount of the commission.

Don't try to demonstrate the good condition of any appliances or household systems, and don't try to get out on the roof or up in the attic unless the buyers specifically ask to do so. Usually potential buyers' first visit is a tour. If they like the house, they will come back for a second look. That is the time for a more careful inspection of condition and a demonstration of the working systems.

For example, on a house whose market value is $100,000, the commission would be $6,000. To split it is to sell at $97,000. The seller gets $3,000 more than if he sold through an agency, the buyer pays $3,000 less than if she had bought through an agency.

The negotiating game you play is actually much the same as that played when your house is handled by a broker. The only real difference is that you are missing an important player with considerable skill and with her own financial stake in making the deal: the real-estate agent.

Chapter 15 gets much further into the various aspects of negotiating. The succeeding chapters on various other aspects of the sale will help you as well.

10. Know When to Turn to the Pros

Remember what you read in the previous chapter: Being a FSBO need not be a permanent commitment. If your four or six weeks of for-sale-by-owner time passes without a buyer, don't be despondent. It does not mean that your house is undesirable and won't sell. It does mean that it is time to get on the more traveled road—the highway. You have learned a great deal, now dig out the business cards of the agents you thought competent and read the next chapter.

TIP

Try not to negotiate over the phone. Ask the buyers to come over to the house where you can talk face-to-face.

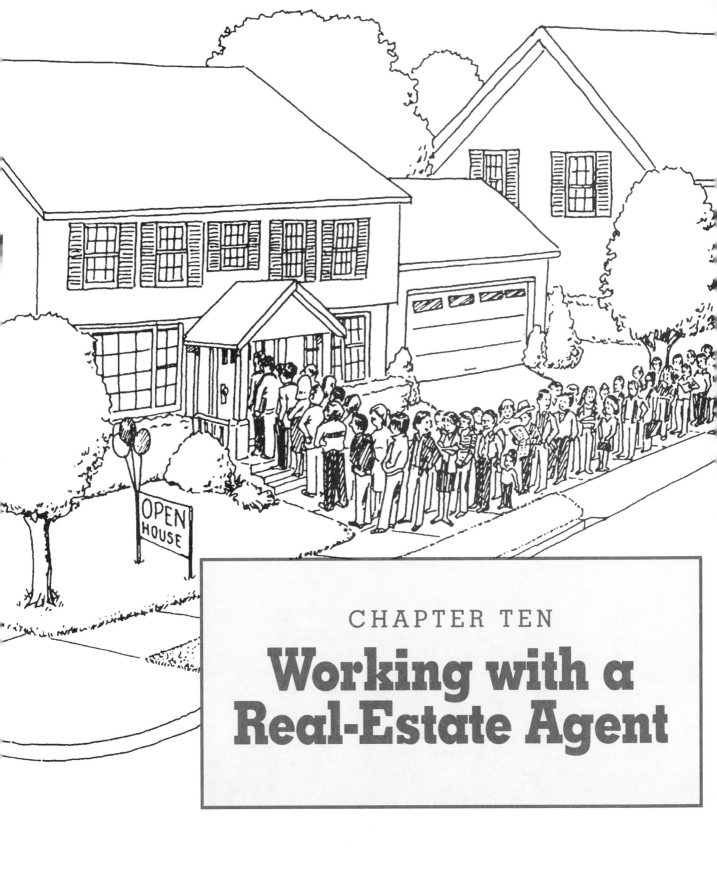

CHAPTER TEN

Working with a Real-Estate Agent

You may have read the two preceding chapters and thought, "Whew, not for me. Lead me to a real-estate agent." Or perhaps you know yourself so well you went directly to this chapter. Or you might have tried selling your house yourself, but now concede your need for the professionals to take over.

Most sellers do use a real-estate agent. And the overwhelming majority of buyers also use them in their home search, as the chart on page 109 shows.

Here is a story, a true story, that will help bring home—excuse the expression—to you the importance of distancing yourself from an emotional attachment to where you live during this process.

The house was a twenty-five-year-old ranch that had had just one owner, and it was on a busy state road. It was one of those properties that usually is nicknamed a "dog." It was also overpriced by $10,000. Yet a young, ambitious, aggressive sales agent convinced a prospective buyer that it was worth a bid. That bid was $13,000 under the asking price, but, as the agent believed, only $3,000 under market value, and therefore well worth considering. She gathered together her equipment—an impressive array of comparables, the earnest money check from her client, a signed offer form, and some extra pens—and set out to present the offer in the seller's living room.

First, she showed them the comparables, carefully pointing out the actual selling price of each house and how each was similar to or better than the property they were selling. Everything seemed to be going well; the husband and wife were listening intently. Then the agent brought out the offer form and named the offering price. There was silence for a fraction of a second before a verbal explosion began rebounding off every surface in the room. The wife was doing all the talking.

"What?!!! That's an insult, an absolute insult! We built this house and we've taken good care of it. Anyone would be proud to own a house like this. Your buyers must be blind! You just go back and tell them no! Absolutely not! And we never want to hear from them again!"

Asked of Buyers:
What Sources of Information Did You
Use in Your Home Search?

	PERCENTAGE (%)
Real-estate agents	82
Knew the seller	6
Yellow Pages	1
Home book/magazine	34
Real-estate phone hotline	4
Newspaper advertisement	51
Friends/neighbors/relatives	24
Open house	39
Television	6
Yard signs	38
Relocation company	3
Builders	9
Online/Internet, etc.	18
Other	2

Source: National Association of Realtors 1998 Report
Note: In their search for a home, buyers consult a variety
of information sources.

The realty agent made the mistake of trying to explain some basic principles of fair market value. She directed her talk to the man who was sitting quietly. The woman left the room and returned holding a broom over her head as one might hold a sledge hammer.

"You get out of here," she screamed. "You and your offer and your buyers!" She swung the broom down, hitting the sofa cushion next to the agent and then swung it up over her head again. "Get out of here! Get out!"

The agent got out. That house sold five months later for $1,500 less than the offer she had taken to those sellers that day.

Remember, this is a true story. You won't allow yourself to become that attached to *your* house, will you? Or take a broom to a real-estate agent!

Who's Who Here?

There is widespread confusion among sellers and buyers about the differences between a real-estate broker and a real-estate agent. Aren't they the same? you may ask. No, there really are differences, although the terms are commonly used interchangeably.

Every state requires that anyone who acts as an agent in the sale of real property be licensed. There are two types of licenses: a broker's license and a salesperson's (agent's) license. Only a broker can enter into a contract to handle the sale of property for its owner. A sales agent can act only for and under the supervision of his or her employing broker.

But no one seems to be able to tell one from the other. The major source of this confusion lies in the fact that hardly anyone sees a broker anymore. The vast majority of the men and women who show houses and seek listings are sales agents, also known as sales associates. Most brokers are out of public view, busy managing their offices.

Real-estate law states that under a listing contract a broker establishes a fiduciary relationship with the seller, that is a relationship of trust. The sales agent might sign at the bottom of the listing agreement, yet that contract is not valid until a broker of record in the firm also signs.

The agent you interview may promise you advertising, but the broker decides which houses are advertised. The agent may also offer to take $750 less commission during a negotiating session in order to put your deal together, but the offer won't hold up unless her broker approves it. A sales agent might show you a check for $1,000 when making an offer for a buyer, but that check must be made out to the real-estate agency or the broker. Only a broker is allowed to hold earnest money in escrow. And only a broker can collect a commission. (Usually, after a commission is paid, it is split, according to a prearranged agreement between brokers and sales agents.) And perhaps most important, a broker is entirely responsible for the marketing of your property. If one of her sales agents is guilty of wrongdoing, the broker is also guilty!

Keep in mind, therefore, that although you may be quite impressed by the personality and efficiency of the realty agent who is seeking your listing, you are in fact hiring the broker or the real-estate brokerage company that she represents. Get to know that firm before you sign anything.

Determining the Right Broker for You

Office Location

When you get ready to choose the real-estate agency that will market your property, think local. Real estate is a local business, and the marketing of your house is best handled by local people who know your area well. Choose an agency, therefore, that has an office in your town, or if it's a city, on your side of town. Agents will be much more likely to show your property if it is close to their office than if they have to go out of their way to include it in a tour.

The Nature of the Business

The agency's specialty is only slightly less important than its address. If you are selling a house, you want an agency that deals primarily in houses, not an appraisal firm that carries a few listings on the side. If you are selling a cooperative or condominium (more about them in chapter 21), you want a concern that deals with apartments on a home-owner basis, not a commercial firm that usually

A **listing agent** is the person who signs up your house to be marketed by her agency. A **selling agent** actually brings a buyer for your house. (They can be the same person.)

TIP

Sometimes a small, new agency, in an effort to build clientele (and revenue), will do a smashing job. After all, if your house goes out on the multiple listing service, the size of the real-estate agency does not matter.

sells apartment buildings. If you are selling a multifamily house in the center of a midsize city, you want a firm that works with city buyers, not one that gears itself to $300,000 houses on two-acre lots.

Choose an agency that routinely handles your kind of property. You will then be assured of the best possible exposure because the advertising for the majority of that agency's listings will appeal to your kind of buyer. In other words, many ads for a particular kind of property mean many prospective buyers for that kind of property.

Privately Owned or Franchise?

Should you go with the Joe Smith Real Estate Agency, or one of the franchises, such as Century 21, Better Homes and Gardens, or Coldwell Banker? Well, that depends.

In some communities, the privately held agency is number one in that town, while the franchises run a trailing second or third. Remember, too, that the franchised operation can be called Coldwell Banker Joe Smith Realty. So Joe Smith retains autonomy and yet is hooked up with a national concern.

Whether you go with one or the other depends on your interviewing agents (which we'll go into later) and finding the best one for you working for the agency that seems best suited for your sale.

Cooperation

You should choose a real-estate agency that will cooperate with other realty offices to get your property sold. The most common form of cooperation today is the multiple listing service (MLS) subscribed to by Realtors. You've read about the MLS in earlier chapters. The member agencies of a local Board of Realtors agree to share their listings, with the commissions to be split between the selling firm and the listing firm.

A very few cities and some rural areas, however, do not have these boards. In these areas certain groups of brokers will usually agree to cooperate with one another. Listings are not always distributed among offices, but word gets out and few sales agents hesitate to call another office to say, "I have a customer in the $200,000 price range. May I show your house on Laurel Terrace?"

Training and Competence

The competence of a real-estate sales force can vary from one firm to another and even within the same firm. Since you want the most competent group possible to market your property, choose a firm where the majority of the agents work full time, earning their living as real-estate agents (not math teachers selling real estate on weekends and during vacations). How do you know the ratio of full- to part-timers in the office you are considering? Ask.

Financial Savvy

Some real-estate firms have separate mortgage assistance departments, while others simply train each and every sales agent thoroughly in all aspects of home financing. Ask the agent from a firm that you are considering how many buyers are helped with their mortgages and how agents are trained to do this. Most agencies now require serious house hunters to be prequalified or preapproved for a mortgage loan, and will refer them to a lender for that documentation. That is good for sellers; only buyers who can afford your house will be brought to see it. Ask the agent you might engage about those "pre-" practices in her office, too.

Goodwill

Sales force turnover is as much a problem in realty offices as in other industries. Even among experienced agents who intend to remain in the career, agent hopping is common, as a sales associate takes off for what she hopes are greener pastures with another agency. Sometimes she leaves to start her own firm.

How would that affect you? Again, reputation is important here. Because sales agents work with a certain amount of anonymity (under the name of their broker) and because they tend to be more mobile than the broker who must maintain an office, their reputations are harder to pin down and to rely on. Rely, therefore, on the reputation of the broker. He or she is ultimately responsible for everything that will occur in the marketing of your property. Well-established brokers in the community take great pains to maintain the goodwill that they have forged over the years. Again, choose locally and choose a firm headed by a man or woman known in your town.

Commissions

There is no legal requirement that makes 6 percent the commission for selling a house. It is just the most common figure. Six percent has been traditional over several decades, but the law states that each listing contract is unique and that any commission can be agreed on. Some agencies ask for 7 or 8 percent and may or may not offer more services; some agencies will handle a listing for 4 or 5 percent and do as good a job as the 6 percent agency. Commission is a point you must negotiate and evaluate.

Discount Brokers

Be careful that you don't sign yourself out of the best possible marketing for your property in an effort to get a bargain commission. From time to time discount brokers seem to be everywhere, and many sellers sign contracts only to be sorry long before the contract terms run out.

A discount broker will advertise that sellers will be charged a 2 or 3 percent commission or a flat fee. Here are your problems with these brokers.

- Is the commission to be paid only on closing, not, say $300 up front and the rest, maybe $500, at closing? You should not have to pay anything up front, because the broker might not sell your house and you'd be out that advanced cash.
- An even more serious concern is a seldom mentioned one. Discount brokers may say they will put your property on the multiple listing service, maybe at a flat separate fee or maybe included in the overall charge. But how will that work in selling your place? What agent who sees that listing will want to show your house if there is not going to be a commission? And how can there be? Will the discount broker split his or her $800 fee from you? What agent would want to work to sell a house for *$400*? See the problem? Being on the MLS is good in itself, but not if realty salespersons won't pay any attention to your listing.

Discount, or limited service, brokers are licensed, and can be found in the Yellow Pages under "Real Estate."

How to Find a Good Agent

- *Personal referral.* This is the best method. Ask friends who have recently purchased a house, "Who was your agent?" and (a question whose answer can help you enormously) "Would you sign with her again?"

- *Local newspaper articles and ads.* Not everyone knows someone who just bought a house in a given area. If you don't, watch the local papers. From time to time you will see pictures of sales agents who have made the multimillion-dollar sales club in their office or who are being given recognition for other achievements. They are probably competent agents (it's hard to argue with success). Call the agent's office and ask for him or her personally. One teeny concern here: the super-duper five-star agent might be very, very busy and a house with a *lower-end* price tag might be lost in the dust with him or her.

- *Open houses.* This takes time, but by attending open houses you will meet and get to talk with the agents who are running the open house without being obligated to work with them, even for a short time. Ask questions! You will leave the open house with a sense of their personality and at least a gut feeling about their competence.

- *Your cousin Vinnie.* Working with relatives is tough in all situations, but extra tough during the already stress-filled time of selling your house. If you possibly can, avoid relatives and "old family friends."

Interviewing Agents

You will want to interview three agents before you make your choice. You may want to reread chapter 4 about now, which covered setting a price. One of the best ways to interview sales agents is to have them come to your house with their list of comparables. Remember, you were not to sign with any agent at that time. But now you can call back the one(s) who interested you, or any new ones you think could help you, or any you have heard about since that time.

Here are questions to ask of the three sales associates you will be interviewing. Their answers will help you decide who can best sell your house.

- *How long have you been selling real estate?* You want someone with at least three years' experience *in residential sales.*
- *Do you work at real estate full time?* You need to eliminate part-timers.
- *What town (or neighborhoods) do you concentrate on?* It should be yours, or your side of town. You want someone familiar with each block in your area.
- *How many houses (or condominiums) did you list or sell last year? May I have the addresses of two of them? How long were they on the market?* You'll want to drive by to be sure the houses are in your part of town, and that they are structures at least roughly resembling yours. If you are selling a center-hall colonial, and the addresses the agent gives you are for two condominium communities twelve miles away, continue looking for an agent. Naturally the less time those properties were on the market, the better. The answer to this question will differ from one locale to another, based on the population of that community and how quickly houses turn over there. Also, some agents may count houses they got listings for, but did not sell, so it's hard to interpret answers. Still, you want someone who says she sold more than one or two!

PLEASANTVILLE REALTORS
ASSOCIATION

ANNIE FINLEY
REALTOR

PHONE 651·774·9712   FAX 651·774·7791

- *What do you think is a good asking price for this house? Why do you say that?* You read in chapter 4 how to set a price for your house. One way is to get suggestions from three agents.
- *What is your minimum listing term?* You want to sign for ninety days, not six months. If she says she must have a six-month listing, tell her that's too long. When the chips are down, she will very likely allow ninety days. If she doesn't, keep looking. Here is the reasoning: If you are satisfied with this agent at the end of ninety days, you can renew with her. If you are not, you are free to look for a new agent. Six months ties you down to an agent who might not be working all that hard for you.
- *How would you market this house?* You want an agent who will advertise your house at least weekly, personally contact successful local agents about the listing, and send a brochure, or at least a postcard, to a hundred or so of your closest neighbors announcing your house for sale. What about putting on an open house for your place? There are comments about that marketing strategy in chapter 13.

    You will have to interpret in all of this the difference between an agent who sounds as if she is going to go to the ends of the earth for you and one who sounds cheap. Get the marketing plans in writing.
- *May I have the names and phone numbers of two of your recent sellers?* Do call and ask them if they were satisfied with the agent's service. Ask them, "Would you list your house with her again?" That should bring out how they *really* feel.
- *How often will you report to me about sales activity on my house?* You want an agent who will call or e-mail you at least once a week. Actually, telephoning is better, because it gives you an opportunity to ask her any questions you might have. If it turns out she does not contact you weekly, then you can call her, preferably on a Tuesday or Wednesday, to ask about the previous weekend's traffic.

WATCH YOUR STEP

Beware of agents who promise to sell your house. No one can *guarantee* a sale.

Keep in mind the agent with the top suggested price for your house may only be saying that to get your listing. Use your judgment and go with the one who has had the best answers to your questions and who "feels" right to you.

Fair Housing

By law when you list your house with a real-estate broker, you make a commitment to fair housing. That prohibits discrimination in residential housing on the basis of race, sex, religion, or national origin. You cannot legally ask a real-estate agency or the members of a Board of Realtors to bring only fair-haired Russian women or not to bring any dark-haired Presbyterian athletes to your property as prospective buyers.

What a Listing Contract Should Contain

No matter what type of listing you choose, remember that you are signing a legally enforceable document. That's why it's called a contract! Be sure that it contains the following:

1. *The date.* This should be the day on which you sign it.
2. *Identification of the property for sale.* A street address will do, but block and lot number on the tax map is better; the apartment number and name of the condo or co-op is essential for shared-space housing.
3. *Identification of the sellers.* This includes the first and last names of everyone who owns an interest in the property. This is especially important when parents and children own a house together or when a divorce is imminent or has been concluded.
4. *Identification of the real-estate broker.* This can be expressed as the name of the firm, but the listing contract must be signed by a broker who is authorized to represent that firm.
5. *The price at which the property is offered for sale.* The price may be changed through negotiation, but if a buyer offers you the full amount specified and meets all the other conditions of sale, the property is considered sold. That is,

Choosing the Type of Contract

These are the most common contract choices when signing with a real-estate broker.

- *Exclusive right to sell.* This contract is most often used and most preferred by real-estate brokers. It gives the broker the *exclusive* right to sell the property during the term of the listing. If any sale occurs, the broker is due her commission. The exclusive-right-to-sell contract does not, however, prohibit the broker from sharing the listing with other brokers. In fact, most MLS groups require exclusive-right-to-sell contracts before they will accept a property for general distribution. An owner can request that his or her property not be listed on a multiple basis. In this case only the broker named in the contract and his or her sales agents can advertise and show the house.
- *Exclusive agency.* Few house sellers are familiar with the exclusive-agency listing and few real-estate people are likely to volunteer the information. The exclusive-agency listing gives one broker the exclusive right to act as the seller's agent, but reserves to the seller the right to get a buyer through his or her own efforts and in that case not to pay a commission to the broker. Some Boards of Realtors accept exclusive-agency listings for distribution on MLS.
- *Open listing.* An open-listing contract gives a broker the right to act as the seller's agent, but reserves to the seller the right to employ other brokers or to sell the property himself without the payment of a commission. A seller may sign any number of open-listing contracts with different brokers all to run concurrently. There is never any commission splitting among competing brokers in an open-listing situation. Open listings, therefore, are never distributed by MLS. Their term should be short (usually weeks) and the contract should contain a clause stating that the open listing is automatically terminated if and when the seller signs an exclusive-right-to-sell or an exclusive-agency listing with any real-estate broker.

Your best choice is to sign the exclusive-right-to-sell contract for ninety days.

Earnest money is an amount paid by the buyer at the signing of the sales contract. It is usually held by a third party until all contract contingencies have been met. There is more on this subject in chapter 16.

the broker will maintain that he has done his or her job and that you owe the commission agreed on.

6. *Any special conditions regarding possession or financing.* These items may be as important as the price in determining when a property is sold. Special conditions include availability of mortgage money, for example, or a particular closing date.

7. *A list of items included in the sale.* Many contracts contain preprinted lists. Read through them carefully and cross out any items that your property does not have: a water softener, for example, or room air-conditioners.

8. *A list of items not included in the sale.* Be specific and thorough. Do you plan to keep your dining room chandelier? Your patio furniture?

9. *The amount of the commission.* This is usually stated as a percentage of the sale price of the house. Less frequently, a flat fee is named or a combination of fee and percentage.

10. *A statement that the commission is to be paid at closing.* This clause protects the seller from being required to pay the commission if a buyer tries to back out of a contract.

11. *An expiration date.* Every listing *must* have one. It should be a named, specific date—October 9, 2000, for example. Do not accept "three months from the date of contract." Like the price, the closing date can change throughout negotiations.

12. *Signatures.* The signatures of everyone who owns an interest in the property must appear on the listing along with that of the broker who owns the reality office.

Some contracts also include a carryover or protection clause that states that if the property is sold to anyone who viewed it with a licensed real-estate agent during the period of the listing, a commission is still due to the listing broker. This clause should have a time limitation; three to six months is generally acceptable. The clause protects the broker against the collusion of a buyer and a seller who agree on a lower price after the expiration date by eliminating the commission.

Some listing contracts also state who will hold the earnest money. Try to have it held by your lawyer or an escrow agent, not

the real-estate broker. (The lawyer won't be owed a commission in the event something goes amiss.) If the broker is to hold earnest money, be sure that you write "fiduciary agent" after the firm name or broker's name on your check, which shows that that firm or broker is holding that money in trust for you.

After you and the broker have signed a listing contract, be certain that you are given a copy. You may want to refer to it while the contract is in force.

Can You Ever Get Out of a Contract?

Yes, you can. A listing contract's primary purpose is to assure the broker that she will be paid her commission when she brings you a willing and able buyer for your house. Nothing in the agreement requires you to go through with the deal. Of course, in theory she could hold you to the letter of the contract and ask for her commission when she brings you that suitable buyer, but in practice things are different.

Let's say that your expected company transfer has been canceled and you won't be moving to Brussels after all. Or maybe you don't *like* your agent. She tracked mud on your good rugs, dropped cigarette ashes, and worst of all, let the cat out! You want to cancel.

Or let's say you just decided you don't want to sell–you can't bear leaving your house.

Generally a listing contract contains withdrawal clauses that allow sellers to be released from their agreement if there is a bona fide change in circumstances. (Yes, the mud, ashes, cat situation is considered a reason for a change.) There are two types of withdrawals:

1. A conditional withdrawal, where sellers agree that they will not sell the house during the rest of the original ninety-day or six-month listing period (If they do, they will pay the listing agency its full commission.)
2. An unconditional withdrawal, where sellers are free to pursue other options

The listing broker (the owner of the agency) must agree to either withdrawal clause for it to be valid. The broker might also ask

You could be in trouble if you cancel a listing contract after you've seen potential buyers who are members of a "protected class" under fair housing rights laws.

INFORMATION

If you have a complaint about your agent, first, discuss it with the agent. If that doesn't work, take it to the broker. If you're still not satisfied, take it up with your area Board of Realtors, and finally, with the state Real Estate Commission.

the seller to pay a withdrawal fee for time and money spent on the house up to that date. That fee could run $500 to $1,000, and could be especially applicable if the sellers just changed their mind about selling without any serious mitigating circumstances, like the cancellation of a job transfer.

And one final point, Please don't confuse getting out of a real-estate agency listing contract with getting out of a sales contract that you and a buyer have signed. When you sign a contract to sell your house, and the buyer signs, and all of the buyer's contingencies have been met, then you *must* sell that house to that buyer. Changing your mind then can become a messy legal and financial problem for you.

Preparing Your Listing Sheet

The information your listing agent writes on her listing worksheet is what virtually every prospective buyer will see before coming to your property. This information will be used to write the advertising for your property, and it will be used by other agents to decide whether to show your property. Make it as accurate and appealing as possible. You read about this in chapter 8, but in this chapter you will be turning that information over to a realty agent, who will give it broader exposure.

On your listing, be sure to state room sizes (measure them or have the agent do it). Check marks in the blanks after dining room, kitchen, and so on, don't tell a thing. Know your real-estate tax bill; the agent will ask for it. And be sure that any special features are mentioned on the listing sheet. Here's an example: "Beautiful hilltop view; new sixty-gallon hot-water heater; exterior painted last year; 22 × 14 foot deck off kitchen." These items attract the attention of buyers and other agents and bring about more showings.

Go over the directions to the property with the agent. Be certain they are clear and accurate and that they don't take prospective buyers past any not-so-desirable places, such as the municipal sewage-treatment plant that happens to be a mile from your property.

Be absolutely positive that your names are spelled correctly and that your phone number is correct.

Once your listing is typed up and distributed (within a few days to a week), ask the agent for a copy. Check it for errors, typographical

Documents You Will Need to Gather

House hunters will want to see the following documents and records. Try to make a few photocopies. Serious buyers will want to have their own copy of some of these papers. You may want to give your agent a copy of the by-laws, but keep the rest of them, and copies of the other forms, perhaps in a "house" file at home.

- *Disclosure form(s)* (See chapter 11.)
- *Survey of your property*
- *Association by-laws* (from condo and co-op owners, plus those who live in single-family house communities operating under by-laws)
- *Condo or co-op financial statements, record of maintenance fees, and any special assessments over the past three years*
- *Property tax records*
- *Utility bill documentation for the previous year* (electricity, water, water conditioning if you have a well, home alarm system charge; septic tank cleaning or sewer fees; trash collection fees)
- *Location of underground tanks or facilities* (drawings of location of septic tank and drainage systems, available at the buildings department at city hall; location of a buried oil tank)
- *Warranties* (for appliances, new mechanical systems, carpeting. Most of these items stay with the house, and can be a good bargaining tool.)
- *Inspection reports* (copies of a house inspection; radon, asbestos, and lead-paint tests)
- *Home Owners Warranty* (another plus that can be used in negotiating)

PAM'S
MIGHTY MOVERS

TIP

It can't be stressed enough: You need to make sure your real-estate agent has a copy of your community's by-laws or CC&Rs (covenants, conditions, and restrictions), or whatever they are called where you live. Buyers need to know what they can and cannot do in your community. If you don't tell them, they will still be held to the letter of those laws.

and factual; no one will do this as thoroughly as you. If you find any, have your agent send corrections through the MLS or whatever interoffice system is used. If there is a major error, such as a wrong address, a picture of your next-door neighbor's house instead of yours, transposed room sizes so your living room reads "12 × 12," while your child's bedroom is "22 × 14," or "slab" is listed instead of "full basement," insist that a new, corrected listing sheet be printed.

Photograph

It's true in real estate, too—a picture *is* worth a thousand words, or a few thousand dollars, or a few weeks' shorter or longer marketing time. You cannot sell your property unless prospective buyers come to see it, and nothing brings more buyers out than a good picture.

If the MLS or office photographer took your house picture on a gray day, or from a bad angle, or when the garage doors were open, the garbage can was out front, and two tricycles and a wagon were on the lawn, ask your agent to have it retaken and to distribute a new listing sheet.

Also—and this is very important—if your house was listed in February, and the photo showed it snow-covered, have a new photo taken if it is still on the market in May. Do the same if your house has a year-end holiday wreath on the door and it's now February. People are not terribly interested in houses they think have been around forever.

The Lockbox

This device looks like a large padlock. The loop is designed to go over the doorknob and then securely inside the cast-iron body of the box so it cannot be removed from the door except with a master key. The master key opens and lifts off the front panel of the box where the key to the house is kept. Every working sales agent and broker member of a Realtors board has a master key. This system allows agents to show a property when the owner is not at home. There is a more detailed explanation of life with a lockbox in chapter 13.

Next, what you must, and should, tell a prospective buyer about your house.

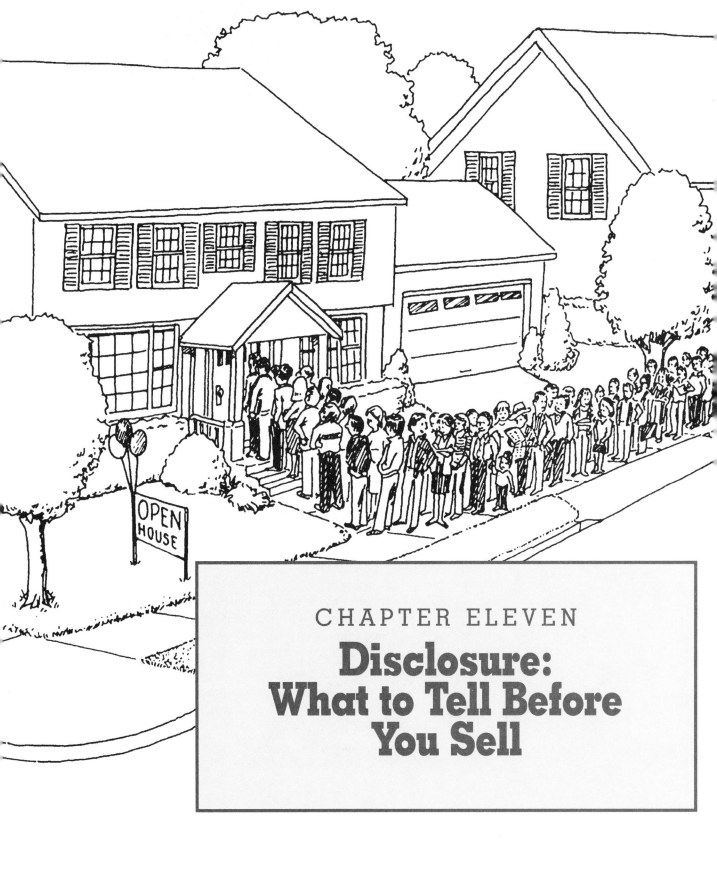

CHAPTER ELEVEN

Disclosure: What to Tell Before You Sell

Disclosure is required whether owners use real-estate agents or sell on their own.

There was a time, maybe twenty years ago, when the rule in purchasing a house was strictly *caveat emptor*: Let the buyer beware. Here is our house, the sellers said, and they did not have to open their mouths about what worked and what didn't or what other nasty secrets the house was hiding.

Does the basement flood regularly? Are there plans to build a thruway that will run practically next door? Is radon gas seeping into the lungs of its inhabitants? Is this where that murder took place ten years ago? You had to poke around to find the answers in those days, if it even occurred to you to ask the questions.

Then . . .

In 1984 the first states passed laws requiring that home sellers tell buyers about any known defects or serious problems in the property to be sold. Most states now require sellers to sign some sort of disclosure form about the condition of their property. Those requirements vary around the country, but the mood of the courts on the subject favors the buyer.

In theory, you must disclose any known factors that could negatively affect a buyer's assessment of your property's worth. In practice, however, the operative word is "known." You are not giving a guarantee here; you are just required to be honest about the reality of things at your place.

What Most States Say You Must Tell

You may be presented with two forms: a Disclosure of Property Condition form and a Lead-Based Paint Disclosure form. Your real-estate agent can provide you with these documents, or your lawyer, or the Real Estate Commission office in your state capital can give them to you.

Although a disclosure form certainly protects the buyer, it looks out for the seller too. By signing that document the buyer acknowledges the condition of the house. That means he or she can't come back to sue you for the cost of making repairs to anything on the list of defects on that form.

Here is what the forms are all about.

Disclosure of Property Condition Form

Most of these documents—and, again, they vary among states—ask your knowledge of the roof, basement, septic tank, sewer system, central heating and cooling, electrical system, and pest infestation (termites and carpenter ants). They also include questions on radon, asbestos, and lead-based paint (see pages 127–128). You might also be asked if your house is in a floodplain and if there are any flooding or grading problems; if you know how the property is zoned; and if there are any structural defects.

The forms usually try to make things simpler for you by providing boxes where you can just check off your answer. The most common boxes are "yes/no" and "defective/not defective."

Can you say you don't know about a certain condition? If you have had a house inspection, as discussed in chapter 6, you probably will know exactly what is wrong in your house. But perhaps you have not had an inspection. Let's say, for example, you are asked about the condition of the roof. You haven't had an inspection, have never been up on the roof, and have never had a roofer look at it either. It doesn't leak, but it *is* seventeen years old. You would answer that question "unknown." That notation will help a buyer make certain the house inspector they engage checks that part of the house.

Lead-Based Paint Disclosure Form

Exposure to lead-based paint can place children at risk of lead poisoning. Very young children have been known to break off paint chips and chew on them. The Atlanta-based Centers for Disease Control estimates nearly a million children have unacceptably high levels of lead in their blood, which can result in behavioral and growth problems, learning disabilities, and low attention span.

If your house was built before 1978, you must fill out a lead-based paint disclosure form. You will state to the best of your knowledge whether you know of the existence of lead-based paint in your house and whether you have any written materials, such as reports, that buyers can look through. Buyers then acknowledge on the form that they have received copies of any information you have. Buyers can then investigate that potential problem on their own if they choose.

You must be honest in filling out disclosure forms or you run the risk of a lawsuit.

Radon and Asbestos

Consumer protection extends even further these days, and includes radon and asbestos hazards.

Radon

This is a colorless, odorless gas that seeps up through the ground and enters buildings through cracks and gaps in the walls and floors. Once inside, it can build to dangerous levels. Continuing studies show that radon can be a carcinogen. The longer the exposure to high radon levels, the greater the cancer risk.

In 1999 a study in the Proceedings of the National Academy of Sciences found that cells could be more sensitive to genetic damage caused by radiation from radon gas than was previously believed. It is thought that radon causes more than twenty thousand lung cancer deaths each year, second only to smoking.

Not every house has radon gas, however. Some ten years ago we thought we were all dying from radon fumes in our houses, but in the years since that panic has subsided. A 1998 National Academy of Sciences study estimated that only about 6 percent of American homes have radon concentrations that require attention. So don't start hyperventilating as you're reading this; you may have no problem at all where you live. However, because radon has no odor, color, or feel, it can only be detected through special testing devices. You can ask your real-estate agent or check with your state Department of Environmental Protection to see if your state has a radon problem and how you should proceed. If you learn your house has levels that are above what is considered safe, you will be told how you can get treatment for that problem.

Asbestos

Asbestos is a hazardous material found in most houses that were built before 1980. Sources include old roofs, deteriorating or damaged pipe insulation, fireproofing or acoustical material, and floor tiles. Interestingly, remodeling or attempting to remove the material can actually increase the risk of exposure. Asbestos is harmless unless it is disturbed and becomes airborne. Often, it can be better to let it remain the way it has been, but covered or somehow sealed to reduce exposure. You will want to ask your realty agent or lawyer what to do about any asbestos problem in your house, and where and how you can have it checked.

Other Disclosures: Necessary or Voluntary?

Here are a few other somewhat common concerns.

- *What about city plans to build a highway near my house?* Tell about this, with or without a disclosure form. This information can certainly affect a buyer's assessment of your property's worth.
- *What if they're going to widen the street in front of my house, taking about two feet of my land?* This is a gray area that might call for individual interpretation. How much frontage do you have now? Taking two feet if you have forty feet of frontage is not the same as taking two feet from a condo community where the units have maybe twelve feet of front lawn. In the first case, two feet taken from forty feet may not affect how a buyer feels about the value of a house and how his offer to buy it might take into account that encroachment. In the condo community, the buyer might feel differently. This is one for your real-estate agent or lawyer to answer.

  In both examples interested buyers can check with city hall to see exactly what is planned for that block, but that does not affect the need for disclosure, if there is one.
- *We had our house treated for termites four years ago. Do I have to tell that?* If they have been totally eradicated, no need to tell. You probably have a termite bond now, which calls for annual check up visits from the exterminator to see that the problem does not return. In showing a buyer that bond, you might mention that everything's been fine since 1995 when you first called the exterminator.

TIP

For up-to-date information about asbestos, you can call the federal Environmental Protection Agency at (888) 372-7341 (this is the EPA–New England number, but it is used nationwide).

- *When we moved in ten years ago the seller disclosed that the basement flooded in a hurricane. In our time here there's been no flooding. Do we have to tell what that seller said?* Many disclosure forms say "Has your basement flooded within the last five years?" You would be truthful in just writing "no."

"Traumatized" Properties

Then there are less common concerns some sellers may be faced with when preparing their property for sale.

Airport Noise

You have no responsibility to disclose that concern to would-be buyers. They are expected to know that that property is close to an airport, even if they do not hear planes when going through your house. This can be a problem when it comes to selling, though, and there is no way around it but to wait for a buyer. It may take a while, but someone will buy that house. *You* did.

Problem Neighbor

It's a free country, and an unpleasant neighbor is entitled to live where he or she wants and can afford to buy. There is no need to call the buyer's attention to Mr. Mean.

Threatening Dog Next Door

Better ask your real-estate agent or lawyer on this one. "Threatened" is not the same as "attacked," but . . . ask.

Crime Scene

If there has been a murder in your house, you can expect it to take a while, sometimes a year or two, before that property will sell. And then it is likely to be at a reduced price. If the murder happened before *you* bought the house, there is usually no need to mention it to a buyer unless your state says you must.

Death from Natural Causes

Check with your real-estate agent about whether this should be included in a disclosure statement according to the rules in your state. Sometimes it must. However, it certainly should not affect your ability to sell and at a price you want, all things being equal. Incidentally, AIDS cannot be disclosed in selling a house, for privacy reasons.

Near a Cemetery, Jail, or Sewage-Treatment Plant

Buyers can certainly see those properties for themselves. It could take you a bit longer to sell such a house. Although if it blends in with the rest of the community, it should not be a problem. For example, park-like cemeteries with greenery and low markers set into the ground are usually not too objectionable to many buyers.

If you have owned your property for many years, you may have seen it drop in value after the cemetery/sewage-treatment plant/jail went up. But if those facilities have been there for a while and are not offensively ugly for the neighborhood, the value of your house might have made its way back up again.

If you hear that a cemetery or other development that residents are not likely to want in their backyard is about to be erected near you, you *must* disclose that to potential buyers. This information could affect a buyer's perception of the value of your property. (And no telling yourself, "Oh, those plans'll never come to anything, it's just talk.")

Handicapped Access

There is no "disclosure" involved here, of course. Any modifications made to your house for handicapped access will be plain for prospective buyers to see. You might be fortunate enough to have a buyer who is looking for a house with access for a disabled relative or friend. Usually these properties sell fine if the changes in the property (outside ramp, widened doorways to accommodate a wheelchair, etc.) have been done well. If the place is a jumble of do-it-yourself projects that someone didn't do very well, then the house may sit for quite a while and then not sell at a satisfactory price, unless you spend some money to undo the mistakes.

Haunted House

Is the fact that a "spirit" resides in your house going to dissuade buyers? Some states do have laws requiring you to tell about ghosts,

TIP

One solution to selling the problem property might be the lease/purchase option, allowing renters or buyers to gradually become accustomed to the house and its history or current "problem." Read about this buying strategy in chapter 14.

but most say real-estate agents and sellers do not have to explain any perceived spectral inhabitants.

Actually, some buyers are likely to be entranced by the idea of a haunting, while others don't believe in the spirit world and pooh-pooh the notion. The ones who would be truly frightened will stay away, but there are enough of the others to form a reasonably sizable buyer pool if you must tell.

What about "Fixer-Uppers"?

So can't you sell a house, problems and all, "as is"? Certainly. But you must still fill out the disclosure form. A house that needs a great deal of work can be tumbledown in areas that have nothing to do with termites or radon gas or a new exit ramp to the interstate going up next door. Selling a "needs work" house that has nothing to do with mandated disclosure regulations is perfectly fine. In fact, the "handyman's special" is a real-estate tradition.

If It Bothers You Not to Tell . . .

Overall, in an iffy area, where there are no state laws requiring you to tell what is not on a disclosure form, you may feel it ethical to inform a would-be buyer of some particular problem with your house. If there is doubt in your mind, it is best to tell. You will feel better, and you won't worry for the next year or two whether the buyer is going to come after you about that little "problem."

This is important, and probably the bottom line: In all areas of disclosure, rely on the professionals—your real-estate agent and your attorney—for guidance. They should know the answers far better than you. By all means, lean on them.

CHAPTER TWELVE

For Sale by Internet

Realtor.com Is Number 1

Realtor.com, home page of the National Association of Realtors (NAR), is far and away the online leader in real-estate listings. The site has some 1.2 million listings, 3.5 times more than its closest competitor.

Home views increased from 33 million in January 1998 to 174 million in January 1999. On average, each home listed on realtor.com is viewed 129 times a month, up from 33 times a month in January 1998.

NAR listings are of properties for sale by member Realtors around the country. Buyers can click and see what is for sale nationwide, statewide, citywide, and in specific parts of town.

So, you don't have a computer. Or, you have a computer, but you're not online.

Relax. Every other home owner is not selling his or her house with wild success from a computer image of it. The ship has not sailed without you on this one.

But if you *can* visit Web sites, then there are some addresses you might check out. Although more and more buyers *are* using real-estate Web addresses to shop around, it's still mostly a tool for real-estate agencies to get their message out to the buying and selling public.

Interest is certainly growing, though. The National Association of Realtors reports Web shoppers for houses was 18 percent in 1997, up from single digits just a year or two earlier. That is still not a large number, even allowing for some growth between 1997 and now, but the increase is enough to make everyone in the field confident of eventual resounding success on the screen.

Often throughout these pages, you have seen Web addresses of companies or associations that can help you with specific areas of your house sale. You can see how clicking on to house-inspection pages, government programs, and so on, can help you in practically every step of your house sale. What about actually *selling* your house on the Internet?

If You're Selling Your House Yourself

Look into some of the national or regional companies that aid FSBO sellers by helping them with advertising, including Internet listings (check the Yellow Pages under "Real Estate"). Some will design your advertisement and run it for $35 or so with others under the umbrella of that FSBO company.

Ask the company you are thinking of hiring how many daily or monthly hits they get, or how many people click on to read that company's message. Go with the outfit with the largest number; you want as much exposure as you can get.

Here are some sources. Abele Owners' Network at www.owners.com offers a free listing. The network has about 35,000 properties around the country, a small number when compared with NAR. Yahoo! (www.yahoo.com) also features listings of houses.

Sometimes you can list your house for free, but if you want anything a bit special, you must usually pay extra. There are two larger kits from owner.com containing such aids as photos of your property, lawn signs, directional signals, and other items. They cost $89 and $140.

By all means include a photo, or more than one, with your ad. Not every seller does.

Keep in mind that real-estate sites are constantly changing: growing, increasing or slashing rates to advertisers, expanding into new areas. There are new ones setting up shop all the time, too. Do some playing around at the screen to see what's new since this writing. Probably there are a number of new home pages!

Working with an Agent

No doubt the real-estate broker you sign with will advertise your house on the Internet, along with others the agency has for sale. These days every national franchise and probably every small real-estate office around the country has a home page that features current properties on the market, some company advertising, and perhaps a few consumer tips. Most regional Boards of Realtors have such a page, too.

Most shoppers want the addresses of houses they see on the screen, but professionals hesitate, citing the privacy and security of their clients. Still, some regional real-estate boards and agencies do provide an address if an agent

okays it. Then it is shown along with a photo of the house, directions, the price, a listing of features, and sometimes even floor plans.

If for some reason you do not want your house shown on the screen by your own real-estate agency or by a regional Board of Realtors, say so. You might even want to insert that restriction in your listing contract with that agency.

WATCH YOUR STEP

If you do get your house listed on the Internet, don't relax and wait for a buyer. The listing is not going to do your work for you. Keep in mind, it is just a *lead* for browsers. Shoppers still have to see your place in the flesh, as it were, not just a grainy photo of it on a screen.

• • •

When selling a house yourself, it's safer not to give your address in an Internet ad. Just list your telephone number.

A Long Journey

A study a couple of years ago by a Palo Alto, California, technology company found house shoppers roaming all over the Internet. The technologist who conducted the survey said at the time that real-estate searchers "are getting to where they want to be much more slowly than other users. Some may not even be getting there at all."

The problem was, he went on, many users tend to try out real-estate terms to find what they want, entering words like "MLS" or "listing" or "agent" or certain states or metropolitan areas as key words in their search engines. Well, you may say, that makes sense, doesn't it? In reality, though, the survey found that most Web sites are not keyed into that terminology, so a lot of people were getting lost.

The study, the first of Internet real-estate key words, concluded that until a common language emerges for finding properties, entering something like "chicago-illinois-real estate" will work best.

These days, for example, besides the sites mentioned earlier, you can also check out the International Real Estate Directory (IRED) at www.ired.com. This is essentially a search engine for real estate. IRED Web masters went through the Internet for real-estate sites, saving you frustrating time spent in front of the screen. All you need to do is click on a specific region of the country, and you'll have lists of many real-estate properties for sale in that area. That's how the NAR listings work too.

You can expect to see more real-estate shopping sites cropping up all over the Internet, with some addresses more valuable than others. More houses for buyers to shop for translates into more opportunities for sellers. Who knows how far technology will have advanced by the time you sell your *next* house!

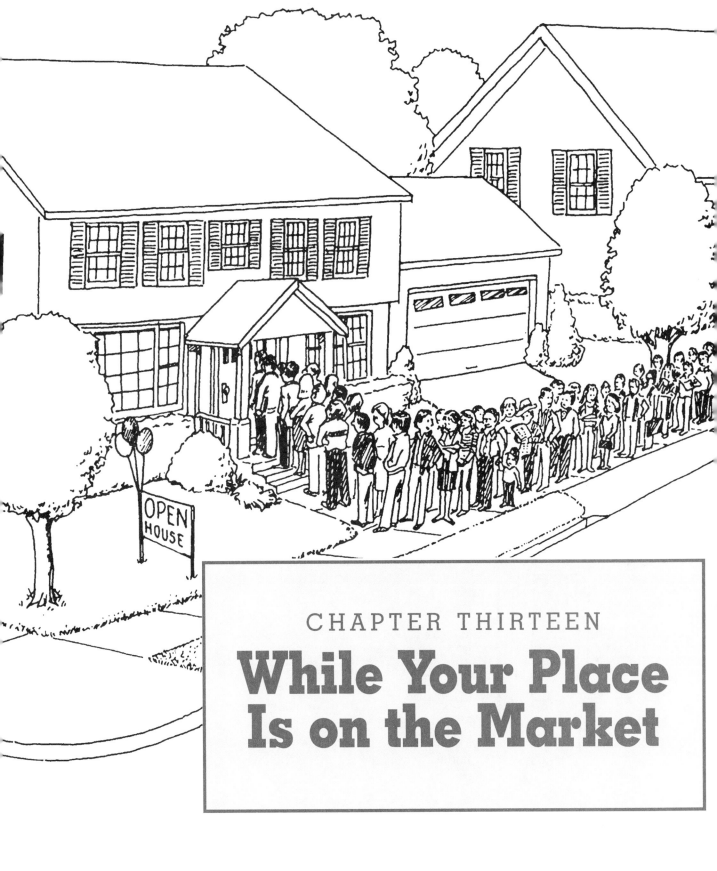

OPEN HOUSE

CHAPTER THIRTEEN

While Your Place Is on the Market

So there you are, upstairs in your bedroom, dining on Chinese takeout straight from the box, and watching the evening news when . . . you hear your front door unlock and open, and then you hear voices. Good grief, a burglary!

If your house is on the market and you have a lockbox, it is more likely to be a real-estate agent showing a prospect through. It certainly doesn't happen often, but now and then an agent will come into your "home" while you are there. She'll be as surprised as you are. "But I called you just a little while ago," she'll explain, "and no one answered." Well, maybe you just got home. In any event, she should have rung the doorbell even when she got no answer to her phone call, but some don't.

That scenario is probably not going to happen to you. But while your house is on the market, you will feel . . . Well, if you have sold a house before, you will know. Trying to explain to someone who hasn't is, as the song goes, like trying to tell a stranger about rock-and-roll.

You will have a lot of physical and emotional sensations during this time, but you won't be quite sure what they are and why you have them. On-the-market time is exhausting and sometimes confusing. And to add to the complexity, it is also an experience filled with emotion. Anger, resentment, astonishment (at the incompetence of some people), anticipation, suspense, respect (for professionalism), impatience, anxiety, frustration, and gratitude are almost unavoidable. They come at different points in each seller's game, but they come. Be ready for them and recognize each feeling for what is: a normal reaction to the stresses and demands of the situation you are in.

So let your anger, or whatever emotion you are feeling, run its course. But don't *act* in anger or emotion. Being rational is one of the strongest assets a player can have in this game. And a good part of being rational is recognizing when you are not rational and waiting until you are.

Suffice it to say, there are many stress stories from sellers. What follows in this chapter are some of the most common on-the-market experiences. You can tie your own emotions and resolutions to them (and learn from the tips that will be passed along, too).

The Lockbox

The lockbox—sometimes referred to as a keybox—symbolizes your commitment to opening your house to strangers. Lockboxes are not used everywhere in this country, but they are prevalent, especially near major cities and in densely populated suburban areas. Most of them look like a very large padlock. The loop goes over the doorknob and then snaps back into the box itself. It cannot be removed unless the face of the box is opened. This is done with a special key that is carried by all sales agents and brokers who belong to the Board of Realtors. The key to your house is placed inside the lockbox.

Once your listing agent snaps a lockbox on your front door, entry to your house is available, in theory, to any and every member of the local Board of Realtors. Most listing sheets ask that the agent call first, and most agents do. But a few will always drive up unannounced, ring the bell, and if no one is at home, use the key in the box. Most of these agents, however, are courteous enough to leave their card, usually on a kitchen counter, so you know the house has been shown.

With the lockbox in place, there is always the remote possibility that you will be caught in the shower or sleeping and won't hear the doorbell. (The example used at the beginning of this chapter, when you are home and the agent bounces in unannounced, happens rarely.) If at any particular time, however, you are especially concerned that agents and prospective buyers will drop in on you without prior notice, you can prevent use of the lockbox by locking the storm door or screen door. But remember that you have it locked and unlock it before you leave the property by the back door! If you do not have a storm or screen door, you can take a piece of masking tape, cover the keyhole on the lockbox, and print "Do Not Disturb" on it with a felt-tip pen. Again, don't forget to remove the tape before you go out.

Some sellers object to lockboxes because they don't like the idea of strangers going through their homes, especially when they are not there. In general, however, the boxes work quite well. Almost to a person, real-estate agents are honest people and there are very few incidents of damage or theft reported in the course of each year.

Lockboxes enable many agents on an active board to show your house without depending on the listing agent to open the house, and without requiring you to stay home while your house is for sale.

In some areas realty firms use the new, electronic lockboxes. They are computerized; entry is done by a code. Every agent has her own code. The lockbox records who was at the house and for how long. The listing agent gets a printout of that information. This provides more supervision for lockbox visits.

If you do object to a lockbox, however, whether the old style or the new electronic type, you can ask the listing agent to note that there is not one on the house and to type "Shown by Appointment Only" on the bottom of the listing form. Or you can leave a key at the office of your listing broker. This works fairly well only when the listing office is located close to your property. Few agents will drive miles out of their way to get a key, drive back to the property, show it, and then drive back to the listing office to return the key. They will simply recommend other houses.

Some Boards of Realtors, especially in the more rural parts of this country, do not have lockboxes. There the listing agent is totally responsible for every showing and will meet selling agents from other offices at the property in order to open it, answer any questions, and lock it again. It is a relationship based on trust and it works beautifully in quiet, geographically limited areas.

If you are fortunate enough, therefore, to live in an area where your listing agent is present for each showing, rejoice, for you could not get better service. If, on the other hand, you must be content with a lockbox, know that the system, impersonal as it is, has been working for many years and working well.

A Sign

Before your listing agent leaves your house the day you sign the listing contract, she will also have to settle the question of a sign. Some sellers object to a real-estate office's sign on their front lawn. It is, of course, their prerogative, and the property will eventually sell without one, but your best bet is to go with the sign. Here's why.

In the first place, not having a sign will not keep the fact of your selling your house a secret from the neighbors. Besides the arrival of the police, fire engines, an ambulance, or the exterminator, nothing is more obvious to the neighbors than a steady stream of visitors to your property. Especially when the visitors are almost always a couple accompanied by a single person who drives a car with an "R" decal on the back window, and a fluorescent magnetic sign reading GO GET 'EM REALTORS on both front doors!

Second, signs can really be helpful to your sale. More often than you think, a neighbor two blocks away will see that sign on the way to work, and then tell a coworker about the new house for sale near him. Also, that sign will help an agent who has not previously visited your property locate it without scanning each doorway and mailbox for numbers. (Condo owners will want to turn to chapter 21 for information on signs when *they* sell.)

The Open House

While your listing agent is bending over to snap the lockbox on your front door, she will probably mention open houses to you. There are two kinds, a Realtors' open house and a public open house, and you will have to be away from home for both of them.

The Realtors' Open House

This is always on a weekday soon after a listing comes out. It is announced in the MLS bulletin with a date and specific hours. Fifteen minutes or so before the announced time, your agent will arrive to play host to your property. While you are out, agents from the surrounding area will arrive singly and in office groups for inspections. The listing agent will point out any special features of the property and answer any questions. Often she will also arrange slips of paper and a bowl on a table near the entranceway and ask visiting agents to leave anonymous predictions of an actual selling price for the house. The agents do this as a courtesy, hoping that that listing agent will do the same for them at their open houses. Those "predictions" are helpful to agents.

If your agent does this, ask to see the estimates. Expect a range of several thousand dollars; this is a walk-through response of sales professionals, but it is not a competitive market analysis. A cluster of estimates around one figure should, however, come close to that

TIP

A Sold sticker across your For Sale sign, left there on the lawn for the two months between signing a contract and closing, is just advertising for the agent and that realty office. If you like, you can take down the sign once you *know* the sale is assured.

DEFINITION PLEASE

When one or several open houses are announced for new listings, real-estate offices often set aside a few hours, or a morning, for their salespeople to visit those properties. In some offices four or five agents will go in one car, in what is called in the trade a *caravan*. So when you call your agent the receptionist might say, "Oh, it's Tuesday morning, they're all out on a caravan."

market analysis figure. If there is no cluster, or if the cluster is several thousand dollars away from your asking price, you might want to re-evaluate that price. Don't be in a hurry to make any price changes now, however. Let the house stay on the market at your original price for at least a month, so you and your listing agent can evaluate buyer response.

Some agents' open houses are very successful, with anywhere from twenty-five to fifty agents making preinspection visits; others draw only a trickle of visitors. If you have a big draw, that's excellent. The more agents who see your house, the more potential customers you will have—a point that has been repeated a few times in these chapters. If, however, the response is small, do not be overly concerned. Sometimes it's the weather, sometimes a crowded schedule for that date, sometimes a slightly out-of-the-way location, sometimes a general laziness about open houses that prevails throughout your particular Board of Realtors.

Agents' open houses are a tool that you should use. Accept all the benefits that you can get from the day, and don't worry about so-called success or failure. If it seems advisable, your house can be scheduled for another open house later down the road, especially if you put through a price reduction at some point.

The Public Open House

These open houses are chancier, and less effective. Sunday afternoon is the most popular time for their scheduling. Usually there is an ad in that Sunday's morning paper. Your listing agent will arrive about half an hour early and set out signs—a large one on your front lawn near the street, and sometimes several directional arrows at cross streets nearby. She then waits for the people. Usually they are few, and usually they are just curious. Sometimes the "potential buyers" are actually neighbors, who want to see the inside of your house and to know what you are asking for it. Often the visitors are trying to get a feel for the market before they begin

serious house hunting. And, as you have read in chapter 4, they can also be FSBO sellers looking for some idea of how to price their own houses.

Except in new developments with model homes, few pieces of property are actually sold through open houses. Most often, real-estate agents sit through them because they hope to pick up the names of a few potential customers from among the people who do stop, and because open houses usually please the sellers, who think something special is being done for them.

If you and your family are going out on a particular Sunday afternoon and your listing agent wants to run an open house, there is probably no harm. Don't expect too much, though, and do put away all valuables. The people who walk through your house will be strangers to the agent, and she may not be able to supervise their inspection as closely as desired, especially if two or more groups come in at or near the same time.

This is a good time to talk about valuables. As you have read, most real-estate agents are honest, and so are most home buyers. But it is unwise to offer temptation. The agent assigned to your house cannot possibly accompany every person or group walking about the property. Some agents pair up on an open house to reduce this possibility, and more than one has asked a party to wait outside on the porch while she shows another group through the house.

If your children have some particularly favorite, and therefore precious, toys, put them out of sight before going out and having your property shown. Some buyers not only allow, but encourage, their children to play in a child's room while they inspect the rest of the house. The results are sometimes destructive and therefore heartbreaking to the children of the seller.

Well, Look Who's Back

If an agent schedules a repeat showing to a very interested party, it is imperative that you leave the property, even more so than on a first visit. Repeat showings usually precede an offer, but they take a long time. Would-be buyers often tour round and round the house several times, re-entering rooms and imagining

Protect Your Property During an Open House

These tips are for those selling with a realty agent. Selling it yourself? *Do not hold an open house*. There are too many potential problems when you are on your own.

- Put away anything of value, whether monetary or sentimental, as well as prescription drugs.
- Put away small electronic items, such as cameras and cellular phones.
- Don't leave receipts around that could have your credit card numbers on them.
- Make certain there are no guns in the house.
- Don't call buyers' attention to a particularly valuable collection.
- Don't leave keys, credit cards, or cash in obvious places like a sock drawer or jewelry box.
- Watch out for your garage door opener. If you leave it in plain sight, someone could take it, come back to your house at another time and break in.

the placement of their furniture. Sometimes they even measure windows, climb into attics, test plumbing, and poke into the corners of closets and basements. They can spend a half hour, an hour, or even more talking with the realty agent. All of this is discomforting to a seller. Go out, even if you watch from behind a neighbor's curtains! And don't worry about being around to answer questions. If there are any, the agent will call you later.

The Telephone

Very, very important in your selling experience is your phone. Once your listing is "out" (on the MLS), agents will call you to make appointments, ask questions, change or cancel appointments, and sometimes do some preliminary negotiating or testing for the firmness of your price. So even if it means a temporary change in lifestyle, try to keep your personal phone conversations short. Most agents are diligent in trying to reach home owners for an appointment. If busy signals are constant, however, they will sometimes put the listing aside for another day—maybe—or they will appear at your door without the advance notice they tried to give you.

Many sellers are angered by agents with customers in tow who stop without an advance appointment, and in some instances the anger is justified. If the house is a wreck, someone is ill or sleeping, or you simply do not want a showing at that moment, just say so. Tell the agent that this is not a convenient time, but you would be happy to make an appointment for later in the day or another day. Unannounced arrivals, like negotiating, are just part of the realty game, and you should be prepared to deal with them.

Sometimes drop-in customers are actually very strong potential buyers. Here is a common occurrence: Your house was not among those selected by the agent for showing that day because it was just a couple of thousand dollars over the limit the buyers had set for themselves. As the agent was driving down your street to another house, however, the buyers spied the sign on your

The **TIP** text reads:

Be careful of your computer during an open house. If you leave it quickly when you hear prospects are coming, be sure to save what's on the screen or, what might be better, close down the machine. Kids might play with what you are working on, or even grown-ups could hit a button accidentally and . . .

front lawn. "Oh, I love that one!" says the woman. The man asks, "Could you drive by it once more?" On the second time around, the agent slows and stops in front of the house. The couple agree that your house is "beautiful, exactly what we want," and they ask the agent the price. When she tells them they look at each other and one says, "Well, maybe we could go that high for something that looks perfect. Do you think we could go in and see it?"

Now you, as the seller, know nothing of this conversation when the agent comes to the door, and you must make your decision based upon the state of your world. Consider this, though: Most people drawn in by a sign on impulse have a strong, positive attitude toward the property before they begin their inspection.

Actually, with cell phones in virtually every agent's car it's not likely you will be that surprised to have her ringing your bell. Still, maybe you don't have a call-waiting service and you've been chatting with a family member for half an hour (remember about keeping those lines open!) and she has not been able to reach you.

The No Show

Every bit as annoying as the agent who arrives without an appointment is the agent who makes a firm appointment and then doesn't show up or shows up two hours late. This too is a common occurrence in the real-estate business and one that you must also try to take in stride. It happens because people are unpredictable. Here's an example.

When a selling agent (not your listing agent, but rather every other agent interested in your property) calls you at 10:00 A.M. to make an appointment for a showing at 3:00 P.M., she is most likely scheduling a series of five or six house visits along a planned route. Let's say your house is number five.

Her customers arrive at her office at 12:30 P.M. They enter house number one at 1:00 P.M. They have no interest, spend fewer than five minutes there (the agent allowed fifteen minutes on her schedule), and go out. They arrive at house number 2 at 1:20 P.M., despite the fact that their appointment was scheduled for 1:45.

They *love* it. They walk through every room at least twice. They walk around and around the outside of the house. They send the

TIP

If you do not already have a telephone-answering machine, you might want to invest in one now. A cell phone is a pricier purchase; but if you have been thinking about buying one, this is a good time to do it. Then you will never be out of touch with your agent or anyone else related to your house sale.

Fifteen Minutes to Get Ready

Good Grief! Your real-estate agent just called and wants to bring someone over. They will be at your door in fifteen minutes. Here's how to make your place look better in a hurry. (If it looks like a lot of work in fifteen minutes, keep in mind you're not likely to have to do *all* of these cleanups.)

- Pick up newspapers and magazines lying around the living room. Spray *lightly* with an air freshener if someone has been smoking.
- In the kitchen, stack dirty dishes in the sink (the dishwasher if you have time), straighten countertops, wipe up any spills on the floor with a wet paper towel. Spray with air freshener any cooking odors that aren't *great* smells.
- Hang up any stray clothing you find on the first floor in the hall closet.
- Pour some clean litter in the cat box (there's no time to change the litter).
- Get rid of anything on the stairs that is waiting for someone to take it upstairs.
- Make unmade beds (here's hoping you have comforters, which are much easier to use than a bedspread).
- Hit the bathroom(s). Straighten up, toss used towels in the laundry bag, and reach for the set of towels you're using just for showings. Run a paper towel over the sink (you're keeping a roll under the sink), check the tub/shower. Use a wet paper towel to mop up spills or dirt on the floor.
- Check pets to be sure they're out of the way.
- Take a deep breath, put a smile on your face, and answer the doorbell. You made it!

agent back inside for the survey map that the sellers had left on the dining room table, and they walk the boundaries of the property. They go back inside, linger in every room, and mentally begin to place their furniture. They flush some toilets, poke some beams in the cellar, and finally sit down in the living room and ask questions about the neighborhood and the schools. They have spent more than an hour at the house, but the agent does not rush them because she can sense an impending sale.

Finally they decide to look at the other houses on the day's schedule. They arrive at house number 3 late and go through it quickly. They walk through, but hardly look at, house number 4. As soon as they are back in the car, they tell the agent that they want to go back to house number 2.

Now *you* are house number 5 and you know (or would know if you were aware of all of this) that your house is nicer than number 2 and more fairly priced. Perhaps the agent even thought that your house and number 6 were the best things she had to show and had therefore intentionally scheduled them at the end of the day. Will that agent then try to persuade her customers to see the last two houses on her schedule? *Never*. Not if she has had even a half hour of experience or training.

When customers want to drop everything and return to a house, they are ready to buy. Few agents will complicate matters by trying to show other properties. You, as house number 5, will be left that day with a "no show." If the agent is courteous, she will call you to apologize and explain later in the day, or she will have her office call you to cancel. Try to grin and bear it. One day, you will probably be that second house.

Patience, Patience

In all likelihood, however, you will play the role of house number 1, 3, and 4 several times before you are the lucky number 2. Customers will walk through your house, uninterested. Some will be more courteous than others; they will make appreciative remarks, ask a few questions, walk around the yard. Others will be in a hurry. Sometimes they won't look at the yard or the cellar, or even the upstairs bedrooms. It will be a whirlwind, five-minute showing. Then they are gone, and you end up thinking "For *this* I washed the kitchen floor?"

Try to restrain yourself from fury at the agent. Real-estate agents are a little like matchmakers. They can bring a buyer and a house together, but they can't make them love each another.

Also, do not try to point out the special features and attractions of your property to customers who obviously are not interested. You will only end up looking foolish and overanxious. Let the realty agents do their work. They know their customers; they know what will appeal to them. Cordial silence on your part is the stronger hand.

If you are at home when an agent and customers arrive for a showing, smile through the introductions, and then gather all the family members in one room and remain there throughout the showing. The living room or family room is usually best, especially in winter when you can have a roaring fireplace and pleasant music on the stereo. Try to stay out of the kitchen; people like to feel roominess there and like to look closely at appliances. Outdoors is also a good place to pass the time of a showing in pleasant weather. You can sit on your patio or in your lawn chairs and relax with a beer or a glass of iced tea.

If you have a young child or someone who is ill or napping when customers arrive, tell them. Mention that the door to that bedroom is closed and you would appreciate it if they would not go in. If they are considering your house, they will return to see that room later.

Your Kids and Your Pets

Let's go with the pets first. Animal encounters are among the most common "war stories" told by real-estate agents, yet few home sellers have any idea of the terrifying intimidation felt by customers and agents faced with a German shepherd barking, snarling, jumping, and clawing at the door as they approach. Some people, seeing the dog, will not even get out of the car. Once they are convinced the dog is on a leash held by the owner, most will go through the house, but there is a constant sense of uneasiness that is in direct proportion to the size of the dog and the frequency and ferocity of the barking.

TIP

You might be able to borrow a crate from your veterinarian, if you know him or her well. To make that gesture worthwhile for the vet, assure him or her that you will still be visiting that clinic after your move.

The best place for a dog while a house is being shown is in a fenced enclosure at the back line of the property. Customers see him there as unthreatening and are not annoyed or pressured by the barking.

You may not want to build an outdoor pen, however, just for the on-the-market time ahead of you. In that case, consider purchasing a dog crate.

Crates suitable for every breed are available at almost all pet shops and their price is small in comparison to the security against accidents that they provide. (You will also find the crate useful for traveling with your dog, housebreaking future puppies, introducing a new pet to the household, etc.)

Cats are less of a problem, except when very young children accompany their parents house hunting. Toddlers tend to pounce on sleeping animals or chase moving ones. Almost invariably the child gets scratched. It is safer, therefore, to confine the cats in one room with a note on the door reading "Cats inside—do not let out."

It is also a good idea to indicate on your listing form exactly what animals are on the property and where they are. This is particularly applicable if you happen to have a python, iguana, or other exotic friend. And *please* be sure whatever you keep it in is securely fastened.

Any pets you have are going to be somewhat disturbed by the changes in your house and lifestyle, the comings and goings of agents and customers, and the increased emotional tension in your family. Sometimes a docile dog will snap, or a stay-at-home cat will disappear for several days. But the stress and confusion that the animals feel and demonstrate is only a small part of what your children will be working through while your house is for sale.

Teenagers and school-age children are always curious about what's happening. They want to know the asking price, what the agents said, what the customers said, and how the negotiating is progressing. Depending on your particular family style, you may have some difficulty discussing some of these points, and you certainly shouldn't go beyond what you consider the prerogatives of adult privacy. But try to talk about the selling experience with your children. They have fears and uncertainties about selling, about family finances, and about the forthcoming move. Their questions are far

TIP

A real turnoff to virtually all house hunters, even those who are cat owners themselves, is a litter box that needs changing and a smell that permeates the house. Keep the box clean and tidy for the duration.

If you can, try to keep very young children from answering the telephone while your house is on the market. Potential buyers will not think they are cute and will not be interested in chatting with them. You could lose a sale that way.

better answered by you than by their imaginations or by the ideas and deductions of their friends. And if you share your house selling with your children, you have an opportunity to teach them about an experience they will probably have to face as adults and for which there is little training and education available.

Preschoolers are different and perhaps more difficult. They respond emotionally to the tension, the need to keep their toys picked up, the strangers walking about their rooms. Often their response is fear, so it is most important that you spend some time talking with them about what is happening. Explain that you will soon have a new house and that you are going to sell the house you now have. Tell the child a little about what a real-estate agent does, explain about the sign on the front lawn, and why the child is not allowed to answer the phone during the selling time.

Most of all, try to help the child understand that you and the real-estate agents are trying to find the "right" family for your house. This is important because some children do not understand why the people who come through the house do not buy it, and sometimes they feel personally rejected.

You must walk a fine line here between overburdening a young child with facts and explanations and helping him or her feel comfortable with the changes in the family lifestyle that selling has caused. Above all, try to answer questions honestly and clearly.

This advice sounds simpler than it actually is. You may find yourself confronting your own unanswered questions and fears more often than you'd like to admit, and you may find that your responses are sometimes both emotional and irrational. This is especially true if your house does not sell within the time frame you allowed. You feel you did everything right, yet the question persists, "Why isn't it selling?"

That can be hard to answer, yet the answer is essential to the solution—getting it sold. First, try to stop worrying and then take a clear-eyed look at the points discussed in the next chapter.

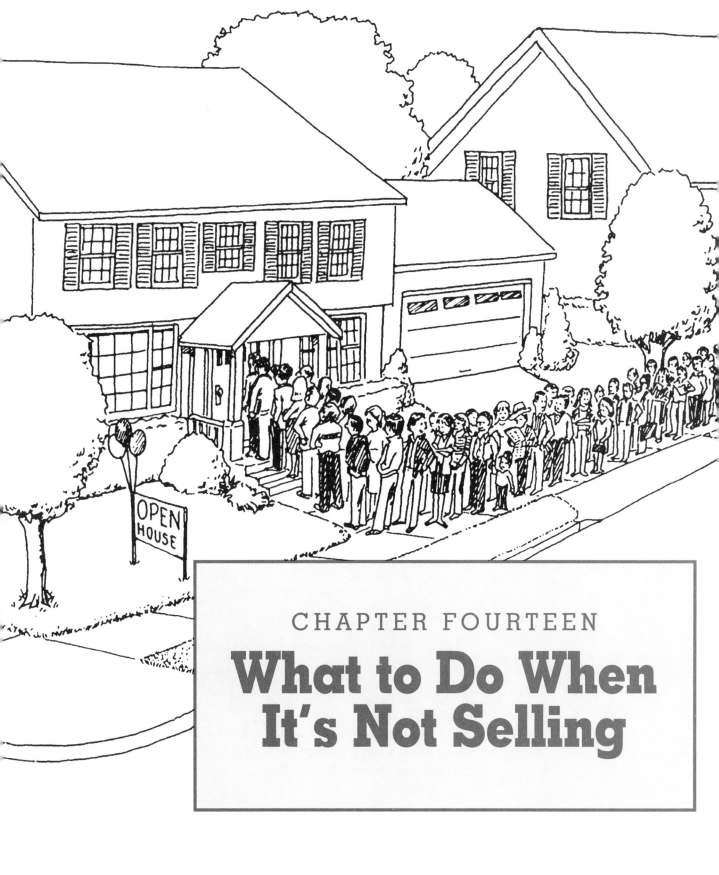

CHAPTER FOURTEEN

What to Do When It's Not Selling

I f you sell your house with no effort on your part—oh, maybe you give the buyers the patio furniture in the negotiating back and forth—then good for you. But maybe your house is not moving and you are understandably concerned. What could be wrong? Is it the house or the economy or what? Here are some circumstances that might be holding up a sale, and some proactive strategies.

Buyer Response

It's an awful thing to consider, but is there something about your place that is unappealing to buyers? Something you have not noticed? Do most of their comments touch upon condition, decorating, location, or price? And how do you find out?

Finding out is relatively simple; doing something about it is not always that easy. To monitor buyer response, save all the cards of the agents who show your house and mark each with the date of the showing. When you have a large collection, gather them together, sit down at the phone with pencil and paper, and call each agent. Introduce yourself, mention that you are the owner of the property for sale on Bliss Lane that that agent showed on (name the date). Then say something like "Do you remember how your customers responded to this property or any particular comments that they made about it?"

Most agents will be happy to take a few minutes to talk to you about their buyers' responses. (Agents always have a secret hope of picking up listings that expire, so they are always nice to sellers.) Watch for patterns of repetition in your conversations.

If customers are mentioning "condition," you may want to spend some time and money on paint and redecorating. But you must listen carefully to what those agents are saying. Few will say "too dirty"; you are more likely to hear, "Well, it needs more work than my customers wanted to do." Try to get some specifics. "Did they mention anything in particular? We were all down with the flu the week before you came through and the house really wasn't looking its best." That gives an agent the opportunity to pick up on your necessary neglect and explain further if she chooses.

Comments from Would-be Buyers

Use this sheet to write down remarks your agent or other agents pass on to you about what "lookers" have said about your house. Even allowing for politeness in sparing your feelings, some repetition in answers should surface, giving you an idea of why your place isn't selling— and how you can make some positive changes.

DATE	COMMENTS	AGENT

Comments like "too small," "too close to a major road," "don't want to live in that town," "not enough trees on the property" all indicate that the house was not quite right for those buyers and/or the price was not sweet enough. You can't do anything about a busy street, but many buyers seem to notice it less at a lower price.

If you are shy about calling all the agents who showed your property, or if you simply don't have the time, you can ask your listing agent to do it for you. Remember, however, that you will be getting the information secondhand, or filtered. On those realty boards where it is customary for the listing agent to be present at every showing, you won't be able to call selling agents since cards are left with your listing agent, but you can ask her what she saw and heard at each showing.

Price Too High

Are most customers saying that? Then you can send a price reduction through the MLS. It does not have to be large; a price reduction of $2,000 indicates that an owner is anxious to sell and willing to negotiate.

If all the answers you are getting in your investigation of buyer response sound like variations of "too much money," and you absolutely cannot reduce the price and you must sell, there is a shot in the dark you might try. You can wait for the listing to expire and then advertise the house again *for sale by owner* with a price reduction reflecting your saving the amount of the commission.

What if you try all this and there still are no buyers? What do you do then? If you do not need to sell, you might want to take the house off the market completely for a few months. Then try again with a new season and a fresh group of buyers in the pool. If, however, you must sell, then you can relist with the agency that showed your house best and most often (this may, of course, be your original listing agency!) and then try to wait . . . patiently.

Being patient is very hard when you need to sell. Remember, many people have been in your position. And remember, too, *every* house is eventually sold. Have you ever heard of a house that never sold? Keep your place as clean and well maintained as you can and

watch that patience. Your turn will eventually come and *you'll* catch the brass ring!

The Money Market

Have mortgages become difficult to secure? If so, spend some of your time hunting down banks and other lenders, like mortgage brokers, that are still offering money. Yes, agents check, too, but none of them is going to be as interested in selling your house and as highly motivated as you are.

You can do this by phone. Call within a wide radius of your house; you'll have a large phone bill that month, but if you find some sources of money it will be well worth it. Some lenders in large cities forty or fifty miles away may still be giving home mortgages when no institution in your immediate area is lending. Keep a list of the requirements and terms of each lender that you call. If you find some sources of money, have your listing agent send a memo through the MLS that says "Financing available to a qualified buyer." Then when an interested buyer appears, discuss your mortgage leads with the selling agent.

Also, if the money market is very tight and banks are requiring high down payments of one-third, or even more, re-evaluate your own financial needs to see if you can help a buyer. (There's more about that coming up later in this chapter.)

The Local Marketplace

Look back to chapter 3, the section on the national and local economy (pages 32–35), and then investigate the mood of your local real-estate marketplace. If it's depressed, you may not be able to do much to help your house sell more quickly, but at least you may feel better about the fact that you are not alone. Never fear, there are some tips for selling in a down, maybe *really* down, market.

Some Suggestions

Whether the problem is your own house or the local or national economy, here are strategies that are more serious and require more

Ask people who come to see the house on your second for-sale-by-owner try if they have seen it previously with a real-estate agent. But don't despair if they have. Although you must contact that agent, the fact that those buyers have come back indicates a strong interest. Perhaps you can work out a price acceptable to you both and/or perhaps the broker will accept a slightly lower commission because the listing has expired and the buyers contacted you directly.

TIP

With a lease/purchase plan, put a banner on your For Sale sign announcing "Rent to Own." Make sure that statement is in all your newspaper advertising.

participation from you, and for a longer time, than other tactics. However, they may help you eventually sell your place.

Lease/Purchase Option

This is often touted as a good way of finding, if not an outright buyer for your house, then at least a tenant who will, it is assumed, eventually buy. This option is very popular among buyers, particularly those who can afford a monthly mortgage payment, but who have not been able to put together the amount of a typical down payment.

If you take this route, you will have a *lot* of applicants!

It works like this: You and the buyer agree on a purchase price for your house. The buyer will rent for eight months or one year or eighteen months or however far into the future you want. (Don't make it too far, you want to be certain the economy will not change too much in that time.) In this three-part contract, the tenant agrees:

1. To pay you a specified rent each month for an agreed-on length of time
2. To have a portion of that rent (any amount you choose, $100 a month or $300 a month, or a percentage of the rent, maybe 25 or 30 percent) applied toward a down payment if he or she wants to exercise the option part of the contract (The tenant might want to have 50 percent of the rent going toward a down payment, even 100 percent, but keep a reasonable portion nonrefundable—at least half, if you can, preferably more.)
3. To pay you a small, up-front, nonrefundable payment of maybe 3 or 5 percent of the purchase price

At the end of an agreed-on time the tenant can exercise the option to buy or cancel the plan, thereby losing the rental credits.

If the sales price of houses in your area has gone up in that time, and the buyer wants to go ahead with the sale, then the buyer wins and you lose what might have been a greater profit on the sale. (Remember, though, you did receive several thousand dollars in rent during that year or so).

If the sales price of houses in your area has gone down, and the buyer says no thanks, he or she can walk away without any penalty and you have to start selling (or leasing) again. Unless, that is, you want to renegotiate a sales price with your exiting tenants, a price more in line with the current market.

Lease/purchase, also known as "rent to own," can be set up on any terms you want (and a tenant-buyer will agree to)—length of the lease, amount of rent, amount of small down payment to be paid up front, and duration of the lease.

This can work for you—or it can be a pain in the neck. Here are some points to consider.

- Naturally you will be conducting this type of "sale" on your own; there is no commission to interest a real-estate agent.
- Be sure your tenant is preapproved for a mortgage. What is the point of offering a buying option if he or she will not qualify for a home loan in a year or eighteen months? You want someone who will be able to come up with the remainder of the down payment, too, after subtracting your rent credits from the total amount needed.
- On the plus side: Tenants in a lease/purchase plan seem to take better care of the rental property, probably because they are going to buy and consider themselves home owners.
- On the minus side: Your house is off the market during this time, with the outcome—a sale for you—assumed but not 100 percent certain.
- Either plus or minus depending on how you view it: You become a landlord, and have management responsibilities that go along with that role. (More about that in chapter 22.)

A variation on this, which might work better for you, is to rent to someone who voices interest in buying, offering him or her right of first refusal when you put the house on the market again. This is not a rent-to-own plan. Naturally, that tenant does not receive any rent "credits" toward a down payment. In a year or eighteen months, or whenever the market has improved where you are, you can sell to him or her at current market value. If the tenant is not interested, there will probably be a pool of likely buyers by then.

You will definitely want to talk to your accountant to see how you can benefit tax-wise with a rent-to-own strategy, or even just renting and then trying to sell again in a year or so.

Seller Financing

With this strategy, the seller might want to offer his buyers a second mortgage to cover the amount of extra money they need to buy his house, an amount they have not been able to finance with a first mortgage. Let's say a bank will lend them 80 percent of the purchase price, they have 10 percent to put down and need another 10 percent. You will lend them that 10 percent.

What's in it for you? Well, when yields on certificates of deposit and money-market funds are as low as they have been in recent years, a seller can earn much more by offering this loan secured by property—his home. The higher rate may be worth the paperwork and risk. This strategy is also useful to the seller who does not need cash from the sale of that house to buy another one. Here again you will want a lawyer to work out the details, although you may want to consult with your financial adviser first. The types of loans offered here usually run from three to seven years, with the balance due at the end of that date.

Interest rate and length of the loan can be whatever you and the buyer agree to—everything is negotiable. You will want to talk with your financial adviser about these interest-only loans, with the balance, or principal, due at the end of the agreed-on number of years. These are known as *balloon mortgages*. Presumably the buyers will be in a better financial position at that time to secure longer-term standard financing.

Interest payments can be paid to you monthly, quarterly, or annually. Again, whatever is agreed on is fine.

Some sellers are willing to offer primary financing—or a first, long-term, maybe thirty-year, mortgage—to their buyers. These buyers might be self-employed or otherwise unable to secure regular financing from a bank. You would do this if you want a steady income at a higher interest rate than what you would earn leaving your money in a bank. If you decide on this strategy, be sure to follow the procedures any regular lender would. Do a credit and income check, making sure the buyers put at least 10 percent down and have the cash to pay closing costs.

What if something goes wrong here? Then you foreclose, which can be a time-consuming and aggravating process, but if you choose your buyer carefully you can minimize that risk.

Tactics for the Seller in a Buyer's Market

Maybe the problem is not your house; maybe all sellers are having difficulty right now. Here are some tips for when times are really grim for sellers, as in a splendid buyer's market.

1. *Be certain of the market value of your house.* If you are not satisfied with the figures you get from several competitive market analyses, go ahead and pay for an appraisal.

2. *Make your property more attractive than its competitors.* Add a new appliance, have a ho-hum front professionally landscaped or paint the exterior.

3. *Try a widely distributed open listing.* This tactic is neither well known nor often used, but it is very effective. Its success is predicated upon two factors. First, your property must have been listed and distributed throughout the member offices of a multiple listing service for several months, so that a standard listing sheet complete with photograph and property specifications has been readily available to all sales agents in member offices. Second, you must call the broker-owner or office manager of *every* agency that showed your property during its multiple listed time and arrange for an office-generated open listing that would guarantee the sales agent who actually makes the sale 50 percent of the office commission.

By effectively doubling* the potential commission (without spending an extra penny yourself), you will get many more showings. What you have done is to increase competition, with the added incentive of greater reward for the winner.

* When *exclusive* listings are entered into a multiple listing arrangement, any sales-agent member of the MLS can sell the property. When a sale is consummated, the commission is split between the listing broker and the selling broker. The usual split is 50/50 or 60/40 with 50 or 60 percent going to the selling office. The commission due to each firm is then split again between the broker and the salesperson in that office. The man or woman actually doing the leg work to sell your property, therefore, is working for approximately 25 to 30 percent of the commission.

An Auction

If you are really in a hurry, or perhaps selling an estate you inherited some miles away, you might want to consider having an auction. This is explained in chapter 22, "Selling a House You Inherit." It, too, is not a perfect solution to a house sale, but it could work in certain situations, allowing you to sell a property that you cannot (or do not want to) spend much time trying to market.

CHAPTER FIFTEEN

Negotiating:
The Art of the Deal

I f you were shopping for pottery in an outdoor bazaar, "discussing" its price would be called *haggling.* When you get up to the big-ticket items—and you can't get much bigger than a house—those discussions become a more polished *negotiating.* Now you are dealing with an art, and a bit of a game too.

There aren't likely to be screaming matches, tears, hysteria, fists pounded on a table, and the slamming down of telephones in arguing over the price of small items. But in negotiating for a house, the emotion expended by both sides could provide enough energy to launch a rocket!

So is this chapter going to be called "Ten Ways to Avoid Emotion During Negotiating"? Not at all. Negotiating is an emotional experience, and you have every right to feel those emotions, good or bad, profitable or futile. What this is leading up to, however, is some insight and suggestions that will help you make your moves and responses rationally despite the emotions you may be feeling.

It is not possible to give you specific suggestions for handling yourself in your own particular negotiating sessions. Each situation is different, as different as each buyer and seller and their particular temperaments, so choosing the "right" negotiating move is often as much a matter of art as of science. But let's explore some fictitious situations and then follow the most common moves to their usual conclusions. Your own particular "game" may not be among these, but pieces of it, certain moves, will be there. So view each of these scenes as choices you might make, experiences you might have.

To save some setting-up time, let's bring back the sellers you met in chapter 2. Their reasons for selling now become part of their negotiating profile, along with time on the market and the temper of the local marketplace.

The Browns

The Browns were our first family in chapter 2. They were being transferred with company support. The "fair market value" figure (reached by two professional appraisals) on their property came in at $133,600. They listed their property at $136,500. Within a week an agent brought them an offer for $130,000.

The Browns sit quietly in their living room listening to the agent as she explains how very well qualified the prospective buyers are.

"They sound like good buyers," Mr. Brown says, "but our company offer is considerably higher than $130,000."

"What was the offer?" asks the agent. She is hoping to make a sale by matching the offer.

Mrs. Brown counters with "I don't think that's as important as the question, 'How much will your people really pay for this house?' On paper it looks as if they can afford to go considerably higher."

"That's true," says the agent. "But they are determined to keep their mortgage payments within the limits of Mr. Buyer's income. Mrs. Buyer is expecting a baby in three months and doesn't plan to go back to work for two or three years."

The agent is telling the Browns that the buyers' negotiating will be tight, and that they probably will not pay full asking price.

"I see," says Mr. Brown. "Well, perhaps they would like to make a higher offer. Their offer is not acceptable to us."

"I think I can get them up a little," says the agent. "At what price would you be willing to sell?"

The agent is fishing for a counteroffer so she can begin to narrow the difference between the two parties.

"Tell them $136,500," says Mr. Brown. He is not going to reduce the asking price to any major degree until he sees exactly what the buyers are willing to pay.

"I don't think they'll go that high," says the agent. "But I'll try."

"Well, we know we can always take our company offer," Mrs. Brown notes. "It would be foolish for us to sell anywhere below that."

That evening the agent returns. She now has an offer of $132,500.

The Browns shake their heads. At this point they get out the written offer form from the company and show it to the agent.

"Look," Mr. Brown explains, "we can get $133,600 from the company and we can get it immediately. Your people don't want to close for two months. That will cost me money. I have to leave for the West Coast in three weeks and I'd like to bring my family out there as soon after that as possible. In order to make your deal worthwhile, we have to get at least $136,000."

Keep in mind that every single dollar Mr. Brown gets above that company offer is spendable cash for decorating his new house or vacationing in his new location. He was also correct in showing the

agent the company offer at this point. It becomes a negotiating tool for the agent, who can say, "I saw the papers on the company offer. It really is $133,600, and the Browns can have that immediately. And you know, this figure was arrived at by the averaging of two professional appraisers, so even if you go a little higher, you are not overpaying for the house." This is both pressure and reassurance to the buying couple.

The agent returns the next day with an offer of $134,800.

"This is my buyers' top offer," she says. "It is $1,200 over your company offer and they are willing to close in five weeks."

The Browns could hold out for the $136,500, but they are pleased to have the extra $1,200 and they like the five-week closing. They decide to accept the offer.

The Greens

You recall the Greens—you met Mrs. Green in the kitchen with her fourteen-month-old daughter who was splattering the walls with her spaghetti dinner. Things never got much better. The house was shown frequently, for buyers in the $70,000-plus price range were abundant. But it seems that no one could see beyond the unmade beds and cluttered floors, the ironing board always standing in the dining area, the fingerprinted hallway, the puppy-stained living room rug.

The asking price of $75,900 did not bring even one offer in two-and-a-half months. The listing agent came by and asked for a price reduction. The Greens were adamant; other houses just like theirs had sold recently for $75,000. They insisted they had to get that amount in order to buy the larger house they needed.

Finally, an offer came in at $67,000.

"Are they kidding?" Jerry Green asks, astonished. "That's almost $10,000 under our asking price."

"They're serious buyers, Mr. Green," the agent replies. "Have you had any other offers on your house?"

The agent knows perfectly well there have been no other offers on the Greens' house. Before presenting the offer, she called the Greens' listing agent for background information.

"No, we haven't," says Alice Green. "but we aren't under any pressure to sell."

What You Need to Know about a Buyer

There are people who really seem to want your house. Now you will need to know the following about these likely buyers.

- *How much of a down payment can they make?* The larger the down payment the greater the likelihood of a mortgage being approved.
- *Have they been prequalified or preapproved for a mortgage?* Ask the agent if she has done a qualification profile in her office or whether a lender has. This is a major benefit of using a realty agent, so don't hesitate—ask!
- *How large a mortgage can they carry?* Does the amount of their down payment, plus the maximum mortgage they can carry add up to anywhere near the figure you might take for your house? No? Then talk to the agent about the likelihood of this deal fizzling.
- *Do the prospective buyers have a house to sell?* Your signing a contract contingent on the sale of their house is a bad move. Talk with your agent about a *right of first refusal*.

In a right-of-first-refusal contract, the buyers and sellers work out a sales price. Agents continue to show your property while the buyers continue to try to sell their present house. If you receive another offer that matches or exceeds the agreed-on price, the buyers with a right of first refusal have a stated period of time, usually two or three days, to enter a binding contract to purchase, or to withdraw.

- *How soon do the buyers want to close on your house and move in?* Once you know that date, you can use it in your negotiating. Let's say that your second counteroffer is higher than their second offer, but to accommodate their schedule you are willing to wait four months to close. Or maybe you're willing to close in thirty days, if that's more convenient for them. What you're doing with this strategy is holding out for more money, but giving them something they want, and perhaps need, badly: a convenient closing date.

"Well, you know the old saying, Mrs. Green," the agent points out, "the first offer is usually the good one." The agent is trying to undermine the Greens' confidence in their asking price.

"We really couldn't even consider your offer," says Jerry Green.

"Well, what would you consider?" asks the agent.

There is silence for a minute, and then Jerry says, "I don't think we want to make a counteroffer to so low a price. If your buyers are really interested, tell them to make a more realistic offer and we'll discuss it."

The Greens do not want to start negotiations with so great a span between themselves and the buyers; the midpoint is just too low. After the agent leaves, they talk about the price and decide that they could take $74,000 and come out all right. Then they call their listing agent and ask her to bring over copies of all the comparables they had originally used in setting the price on their house.

When the selling agent returns with a "top offer" of $70,000, the Greens bring out the comparables and show the agent that most houses like theirs have sold recently between $74,000 and $76,000. They tell her they will accept a minimum figure of $74,000.

The agent takes the comparables with her and comes back with an offer of $72,500. "This is a final figure," she says, "and it is dependent on a professional house inspection showing that everything is in good condition. My people just can't go a penny higher. They can't qualify for any greater mortgage."

"Everything here works fine," says Alice Green, "and we would have no objection to an inspection. But we can't take less than $74,000."

"Folks," says the agent, "your house has been on the market for two and a half months with no buyers in an area where houses often sell within two or three weeks. I know others like it are selling for $74,000, but your property needs complete redecoration inside, new carpeting in all the rooms, and the outside trim needs painting. No buyer is going to pay $74,000 and do all that too. And besides, my people are willing to wait four or five months for a closing. This will give you plenty of time to find another house at a good price."

This last sentence is the agent's trump card. She knows the Greens do not yet have a place to go.

"Oh, Jerry," says Alice, "that would mean the herds would stop stomping through here, and we could go out looking for a place without worrying."

"Yeah, that would be good," says Jerry. "But we just can't go down to $72,500."

"We could manage," suggests Alice. "It's a thousand less than the going price in this development, but this house really does need some TLC."

"Okay," says Jerry, "We'll take $73,000."

"I don't know if I can get that for you," says the agent. "My buyers are at their limit. But I'll see what I can do."

The next day the agent returns and announces that her buyers cannot go up another dollar.

"I'm sorry," says Jerry. "We can't go down. If we have to, we'll buy a hundred dollars' worth of paint, fix this place up, and get $74,000. As is, we won't sell under $73,000."

The agent wants very much to make this deal. She knows that buyers will often go to another agent and another area when a deal this close falls through. She does not want to lose these buyers and she does not want to lose the commission on the Greens' house. She makes her final play.

"I have one more idea," she says. "It's a little offbeat, but we really want to make this sale. My broker is willing to deduct $350 from the commission you would pay us for selling this house. That would be the equivalent of a selling price of more than $72,850. We're talking about a difference of less than $150, folks. Certainly having a good buyer who wants your house, and plenty of time to move out, is worth $150."

"What do you think, honey?" asks Jerry.

"Let's do it," Alice replies enthusiastically.

The Whites

The White family was moving to a more luxurious home—trading up. Early in March they listed their house at $139,000, knowing that the price was high, but testing the market anyway. Their builder had just broken ground for their new house and they had plenty of time.

INFORMATION

Some real-estate agencies take strong objection to shaving a bit off the commission. They never, never reduce their commissions. But other agencies, while they do not like to admit it, concede that in a really tight deal it does happen. And it happens for a good deal more than $350, too—like a few thousand dollars! No commission is set by law, and even the 6 percent you agreed to in the listing contract can be changed if all parties who are affected agree to the change. However, you should never *count* on your agent's cutting her commission.

Their four-bedroom split-level showed beautifully. Over the course of three months the Whites refused negotiation with top offers of $135,000 with a six-week closing, $131,000 and $134,000 with two-month closings and $134,500 with a four-month closing.

Then one June day, the Whites receive notice from the builder that they could count on August 1 as a firm closing and occupancy date. That same evening, an agent presents an offer of $133,500.

"We've been offered $135,000 for this house and refused it," says Mrs. White.

The next day the agent returns and says her customers will go to $134,000, but no higher. They want to close September 1.

"Tell you what," says Mr. White, "make that closing the morning of August 1 *firm* and you've got a deal."

It was accepted.

In this case the closing date had become more important to the Whites than the extra dollars they may have gotten for the house. The couple did not want to carry and insure their old house after moving out, and by scheduling both closings the same day they could avoid the bother of taking out a loan for the equity in the house they were selling in order to make the down payment on the house they were buying. (There's more about this strategy in chapter 18, "When You Must Sell One House to Buy Another.")

The Whites would get the certified check at the closing on their old house the morning of August 1 and take it to the closing on their new house, which they would schedule for the *afternoon* of August 1. The Whites had known when they refused the $135,000 offer that it was a top-dollar price on their house, but at the time they had nowhere to go. Their new house wasn't finished and the buyers wanted a quick close. The $134,000 offer from a live buyer willing to close on their preferred date was close enough.

Susan Gray

As you recall, Susan Gray had decided to sell the large house where she had lived for seventeen years and move to a condominium. She invited four real-estate firms in, each to do a competitive market analysis. The figures from all four were extremely close—the low $124,000, the high $128,000.

Why Negotiations Fail

- *The buyers cannot really afford the house.* The sales agent was showing them properties above their price range with the hope that perhaps they could negotiate a bargain. Or the sales agent never saw that they were properly qualified.

- *The sellers are not ready to sell.* They still have emotional ties to the property as "home" and want to be paid top dollar. Or they simply do not yet want to move out even though they have put the property on the market.

- *Someone is given an ultimatum.* For example: "It's $145,000 and a sixty-day closing or nothing. Don't bother to come back here with anything else!" or "Either you leave the dining room chandelier or we don't want the house!" Statements like these leave the other party no space to make another proposal.

- *A buyer or seller takes a statement made during negotiations as a personal affront and refuses to negotiate further.*

- *There is racial, ethnic, or other social hostility toward the buyers.* Unfortunately, until people consider each other as individuals rather than by stereotypes, we will continue to have some problems in this area.

But Susan couldn't believe it. She knew of four-bedroom colonials in the town that had sold for $150,000. Her house had a view of the distant city and a magnificent panorama of the valley stretched below them. She and her late husband and the children had built stone walls and paths and planted azaleas, rhododendrons, and pachysandra. The inside was professionally decorated. It was a "dream house," although an *older* dream house.

Susan found a broker who took her listing for a six-month term at $149,500. (Many brokers will list an overpriced house on a long-term basis hoping to persuade the sellers to reduce the price after two or three months on the market.) There was a good turnout of realty agents at the open house, but only a few left their estimates of the selling price. Those ranged from $125,000 to $133,000. But Susan Gray was unimpressed. Her house was sparkling clean, very showable, and she could wait.

After a burst of ten customers the first week, showings leveled off to one or two a week for three months. The listing agent asked for a price reduction. Susan said no. Activity on the house decreased even more; the listing finally expired on October 25. It was not renewed.

Susan wintered quietly and in March gets two more market evaluations. Inflation and a red-hot seller's market are working in her favor. The two agents come in with $137,000 and $138,500. Again she lists at $149,500. But this spring the activity is almost frantic. Every day brings a visitor or two, and Mrs. Gray grows to hate the seemingly constant intrusions. She begins to go out house hunting herself and stumbles upon a condo community set in a wooded area near a lake. Suddenly she *wants* to sell her house.

Two offers come in at $130,000 plus, but neither buyer is willing to go over $140,000. Susan is still willing to wait, but now she waits in the real anticipation of selling.

Then an agent brings in an offer of $139,000. Susan refuses it but makes a counteroffer of $146,000. It is close enough to indicate to the sales agent that both sides are willing to do business.

The buyers say they will go to $141,000 on the house because of the beautiful location and perfect condition, but no higher. When the agent tells Susan this, she knows she has prospects who "love" the house. Now it's a question of how high they will really go.

Susan responds that $144,000 is her lowest price. The buyers say, "No way. The house is just not worth that much."

Three days pass. Susan feels despondent. She wants to move into the condo before summer.

Finally she calls the selling agent and asks if the buyers have bought another house. "Not yet," says the agent, "but they're considering one in Lake View." This is a common reply to a seller who initiates the reopening of negotiation. It is designed to induce him or her to be more generous in an offer, to restimulate interest.

"Well, I still want $144,000," says Susan, "but I'm willing to include all the carpeting, draperies, and drapery rods at that price."

She is trying to say, "I still want to sell and I'll negotiate a little more." But she does not want to give away too much until she knows what is happening with the buyers.

"I'll tell the buyers," says the agent. "But really, I don't think they'll go for it. They have a honey of a house in Lake View."

The next day, however, the agent makes an appointment to see Susan. She appears with a newly signed offer form for $142,500, including the carpeting, draperies, rods, and the dining room chandelier.

Susan hesitates but decides the chandelier won't fit well in the condo anyway. She tells the agent, "Okay. They can have the house and the extras they want for $143,000"

"It won't work," says the agent, "This is their highest offer. They'll buy the house in Lake View. They can get *that* for $140,000."

Susan will never know if there really is a house in Lake View for those buyers or if the agent is just applying sales pressure.

"Look," she says, "tell them I'll throw in the riding mower and all the gardening equipment—hoes, spades, rakes, the trimmer, hoses, the works. That's got be worth $500 to them."

"I'll do my best," says the agent.

The deal is made at $143,000.

This was a case of selling readiness for Susan Gray. She knew she was near top dollar at $141,000 since the house had been on the market for an extremely long time and all offers had been considerably lower. She also recognized the buyers' sincere appreciation for the property and was therefore correct in making a move to reopen negotiations. She was able to get more for her house by

INFORMATION

Generally, whatever is attached to the house is part of the sale, unless otherwise negotiated between seller and buyer. Lighting fixtures, wall-to-wall carpeting, and window shutters are some examples.

adding extras, items of personal property that did not necessarily stay with the house, and actually were not likely to have fit into her new life in the condo.

The Paynes

You remember Tom and Sarah Payne. They were the couple who lived the nightmare of owning two houses. Their original price on the two-story "older home" they were selling was $162,900. Then came the mortgage crunch and the trouble at the high school. They reduced their price to $159,500. No offers. They rented to a young couple. Still no offers. Realtors began calling them to report that the tenants were uncooperative. They were refusing appointments or locking the storm door so that the lockbox could not be used. A few agents reported that the place was so untidy that buyers had to pick their way through the debris and dirty laundry scattered all over the floors. The kitchen counters could not be seen beneath the dirty dishes, cereal boxes, and leftover food.

The tenants were asked to leave. The Paynes withdrew the house from the market, took a week off from work, and cleaned and scrubbed and painted. They even put new wallpaper up in the kitchen and hung curtains at the window.

Then they figured their bottom dollar. They had given up all hopes of a big profit and a new car purchased with the extra money from the house. What they *needed* was $153,000. That would give them enough cash to pay off the bridge note and get back to owning one house. They put another price reduction notice through the MLS when they reactivated the listing. It read "Price reduced to $155,500. Home vacant and newly cleaned and decorated. Owners have purchased another home and want a quick sale."

Even an old, semiblind bull would respond to so bright a red flag. Sure enough, an agent appeared at the Paynes' door within ten days. Fran Garish carries her briefcase in, opens it on the Paynes' coffee table and begins to arrange, stack, sort, and rustle papers in a way that was not only self-important, but also definitely condescending.

"Well, Mr. and Mrs. Payne," she begins, "I'm sure you're happy tonight! Here's a check for $1,000 from my buyers." She holds it up in front of her by the top corners like a six-year-old displaying a painting for Show and Tell. "These are wonderful buyers, folks, and they're ready to move in tomorrow. It's too bad we can't get a closing together that soon," she laughs, "but we'll get on it just as soon as we get these contracts signed, won't we?"

"Ah, what's the offer?" Tom asks.

"My buyers are offering you *$145,000* for that house, Mr. Payne."

"$145,000!" exclaims Sarah.

"The answer is no," says Tom.

"Now, Mr. Payne," says the agent, ignoring Sarah, "you know how long that house has been on the market, you know how tight mortgage money is right now, and you know that that neighborhood is not exactly the best in town. You're very lucky to have an offer at all, Mr. Payne, and with a quick closing too."

"Absolutely not interested," says Sarah.

The agent never even looks in her direction. "Mr. Payne, you should consider carefully now. This is a time to be rational, not emotional. Think of all the cash you'll save in carrying costs."

Tom Payne sits silently staring at the agent for what seems like five minutes, but must have been just thirty seconds. Then he speaks very quietly. "Your offer is totally unacceptable to my wife and me. We will not counter unless your buyer comes in with an offer much closer to the market value of this house."

"But Mr. Payne, you *need* to sell that property!" says the agent.

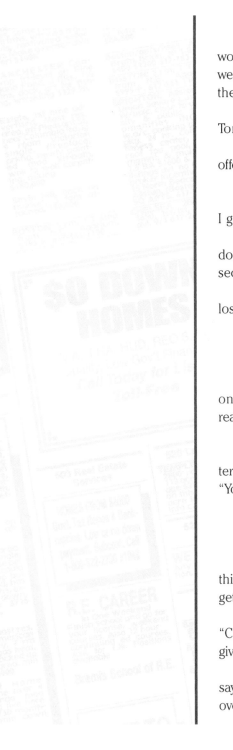

"Miss Garish," says Tom, raising his voice but speaking each word slowly and distinctly, "before we sell that house for $145,000, we'll move back into it and sell this one. Good evening. I'll flip on the porch lights so you can find the way to your car."

Does this sound final? It wasn't. The next day the agent calls Tom Payne at his office.

"Tom, this is Fran Garish. I was at your house last night with an offer, remember?"

"Yes."

"Well, I've been working, really working for you all morning and I got my people to come up with $150,000. *How about that!*"

"It's not enough," Tom replies. But he does not want to slam the door now since these buyers are obviously serious. He thinks a second and says, "Tell them we'll take $154,000."

"They'll never do it, Mr. Payne. I'm telling you, you're going to lose them. Take the $150,000 and get out."

"Tell them $154,000."

"You're the boss."

Later that afternoon, Miss Garish calls the Paynes' house.

"Hello, Mrs. Payne, this is Fran Garish. Things are really cooking on your house sale now. I can't wait to see you again. I have a really beautiful offer."

"You can come over at around seven this evening," Sarah responds.

The agent's second appearance at the Paynes' house is characterized by her virtually bubbling over at what she is about to say. "You're really going to love this one," she begins.

"We want $154,000," says Tom. "Is that what you have?"

"Almost, Tom, almost! Here it is: $152,000. Now how about that!"

"We want $154,000," Sarah stresses.

"Now look, Mrs. Payne, you can't afford to be emotional about this. You folks are losing money every day. This is your chance to get out. Take it!"

"Thank you for coming back, Miss Garish," says Sarah. "Call us tomorrow. My husband and I will discuss your advice and give you an answer tomorrow."

The agent calls Tom's office at 9:15 A.M. "We'll take $153,000," says Tom. "With a quick closing and $15,000 escrow to be turned over to us as soon as the mortgage is approved."

Tom plans to use the buyer's escrow money to make mortgage and interest payments for the month until closing, thus easing the couple's cash-flow problem.

But the deal is still not over. The buyers know the Paynes are hurting. They come back with $152,500, and refuse to go higher. The Paynes finally accept. It is better, they reason, than starting the whole negotiating process over again at some unknown later date.

Whew, are you tired just reading the Paynes' tale? This is the difficulty of owning two houses at once.

The Blacks

The Blacks' divorce would be final in three weeks; their house had been on the market for three months. Their asking price was $172,500, but they had agreed between themselves that their rock-bottom figure would be $168,000. They had agreed, that is, until a first offer came in at $168,000.

The agent appears first at Dick Black's apartment.

"Yeah, I'll take it," says Dick and signs the offer form.

Then, feeling that this may be an "easy one," the agent rushes over to see Donna Black at the house. Donna looks at the order form and at Dick's signature.

"I don't know," she says. "I need a little time to think about it. Could you come back this evening?"

As soon as the agent walks out the door, Donna calls her parents, who live just twenty-five miles away. They arrive at her house in an amazingly short time.

"Donna, you just can't take the first offer that comes along," says her father.

"Oh no, you have to negotiate," her mother adds.

Real-estate agents always reach for the aspirin when the parents of buyers or sellers get involved in a deal.

"But, Mom, we did agree that we would take $168,000 as a rock-bottom figure."

"But Donna, honey," her mom continues, "why should you take rock bottom? Get a few thousand more. You can use it to decorate your new apartment, can't you?"

To Sweeten the Pot

Here are traditional concessions sellers make when their offer of the living room draperies is not enough to light a buyer's fire.

- Make a specific needed repair or replacement—a pricey one

- Pay points

- Take back a second mortgage (see chapter 14)

- Offer a house inspection report

- Offer a Home Owners Warranty

- Pay community association dues for the first year or two

- Pay all or part of the closing costs

"Well, yes, but . . ."

"Steve," Donna's mother says, turning to her husband, "you get on the phone and call that agent. Tell her it's not enough money."

"Okay, hon, but we have to make a counteroffer."

"Well, tell her $173,000."

"Mom, we can't do that! We're only asking $172,500."

"Well, tell them $172,000."

"Mom, don't you think we ought to talk to Dick?"

"Absolutely not! This house is half yours. More than half! You earned it working and cleaning and cooking and waiting on him and taking care of his kids every day!"

"Uh, Mom, they're my kids too."

"Never mind, just call. We're going to get every red cent we can out of this place."

Donna's father calls the agent, raises his voice (for emphasis), and says that "Donna will take no less than $172,000."

The agent is dumbfounded. Dick had said the offer was acceptable. The agent told her buyers everything looked good. Now not only Donna but also her parents were into it and everything was falling apart.

An hour later Dick calls.

"What the hell is going on over there?" he shouts. "We agreed that we'd take $168,000. Let's get rid of this damn thing!"

"But Dick, I thought . . ." starts Donna.

Her mother grabs the phone.

"Listen, Dick, there's absolutely no reason for Jane to take a rock-bottom figure. If that's the price you want, you can have half of that figure and Donna should get anything over it."

"I can't believe this," Dick mutters, slamming down the phone.

Within ten minutes, it rings again in Donna's house. The agent's voice is slow, quiet, and measured. "Mrs. Black, my customers will not go over the $168,000 that Mr. Black accepted."

"Sorry, that's not acceptable to me," says Donna with a toss of her head. "And I do have some rights in this deal."

She slams the phone down.

Donna and her parents have coffee. She is buoyed up by their strokes. They tell her she's doing the right thing, being firm, independent. Then they leave, and she begins the long, lonely, nerve-wracked night.

Donna tortures herself through every hour of it, reliving the day and then reliving scenes from a hundred other days before. She is worried about the future and agonized by the past. No decision seems right. She wants to get out of the house, yet she is not looking forward to leaving its familiarity and comfort.

In the morning Donna calls the real-estate agent. Holding herself together, she explains that she has the burden of moving costs, decorating in the new apartment, and getting the children settled, which her ex-husband does not have.

She says, "We were sure the house was worth at least $170,000 when we listed it three months ago. With the way the market is going, I should think it would be worth $172,000 by now."

Donna is not making a formal counteroffer here of $170,000, but by naming the figure in this way she is effectively telling the agent she will accept it.

Three days go by. Donna is deeply depressed. She is positive she has blown the deal, but she will not give in and take the $168,000.

On the fourth day, the agent calls. "Mrs. Black, my customers are willing to go to $170,000, but only if you will wait five months for a closing so that they can put aside the extra money."

"Oh yes, that's fine," says Donna. "It will give me time to find an apartment. I'll accept the offer."

Now the agent calls Mr. Black.

"So she got the two thousand more, huh?" he says. "Well, I don't want to wait five months for a closing. Tell them no."

"Mr. Black," says the agent, "your house could sit on the market five more months. It's already been on for three and this is your first offer."

"Oh, all right! Tell my ex-wife that I'll wait the five months, but we split the $170,000 right down the middle, understand?"

The agent calls Mrs. Black and explains the situation to her. Donna has been drained by the whole procedure (and so has the agent!).

"Yes, of course, that's fine," she replies. The deal is finally made.

The Upwards

The house that Fred and Joyce were having built in Nextown was almost complete when they finally lowered the asking price on the house they were selling from $198,000 to $195,000. They had had two offers in the past five months, both in the low 190s. They refused both. Fred wanted $195,000 and was determined to get it.

One balmy spring day he gets a strange call from an agent named John Gabriel.

"I have some interested buyers for your property, Mr. Upward. They're considering several houses, but I heard them mention $185,000 as a possible bid on yours. How would you feel about that?"

This is not an offer. The agent is fishing for an acceptable price and he wants to tell Mr. Upward that something is in the wind. It is a way of saying, "In case an offer should come along on your house in the next few days, please call me so I can give my customers a chance to bid too."

"I don't negotiate without a written offer," says Mr. Upward. "We're asking $195,000 and this house is worth $192,000 if it's worth a penny!"

Mr. Upward might not negotiate without a written offer, but he told the agent exactly what he wanted to know. There was definitely some negotiating room in the asking price.

Three days later, John Gabriel from Cool 'n Calm Realty presents the Upwards a formal contract fully executed by the buyers. The offering price is $193,000.

The couple each reads through a copy of the contract silently and carefully. Then Fred says, "Ah, Mr. Gabriel, would you care for a drink or a cup of coffee? My wife and I would like to take a few minutes to discuss this privately."

So Gabriel sips coffee and flips through some magazines, while Fred and Joyce go out on the patio to talk.

"Fred, it's almost what we wanted," says Joyce.

"I know, honey, and the closing date is perfect, and they don't even want a house inspection!"

"Can they afford it?"

"Yes, they've already been preapproved for the mortgage they need."

"Wow!" Joyce is almost speechless in her delight. "So what do you think?"

"I don't know," Fred explains, "part of me says we should try to negotiate the price up a little more and part of me says, 'Take it!' It really is a good offer."

"Do you think we could get them up a thousand or two more?"

"I don't know, Joyce. But he's got a contract in there. If we sign it, it's a firm deal; we don't have to worry about it falling apart. The house is *sold*."

"The contract looked okay to me," says Joyce. "It's just a printed form with the blanks filled in. I think there was even something in there about it being subject to the approval of our lawyer."

"Yeah, there was. Honey, if we take this as is, we might be losing a couple of thousand, but we're getting all we wanted otherwise. And the thing will be tied up without any hassle. What do you think?"

"Let's go with it, Fred. I'll be glad to have the house off the market so I can start packing and leaving things lying about while I'm sorting."

The Upwards sign the contract and Mr. Gabriel calls back to his office where his buyers are waiting and says "You've got yourself a house."

So now you have read about a handful of very different real-estate deals. (There is another one in chapter 22, about selling a house you inherited.) All of these stories should give you an idea of the give-and-take that goes into negotiating. As you have seen, it is both a game and an art. You cannot move all your pieces at once; you should not play all your trumps in the first few rounds. Consider, evaluate, and try to hold some things back so that you can trade them off later for something you want.

DEFINITION PLEASE

A standard contract form with blanks to be filled in by the party(ies) signing is known as a *boilerplate* contract.

CHAPTER SIXTEEN

The Sales Contract

Whew! You've finished negotiating. You have come to a verbal agreement with your buyers on all of the important points of the sale. To get things rolling and to take your house off the market, however, you need a signed offer form, binder, tentative contract, memorandum of sale, or whatever term is used in your area to name the paper that says you and the buyers have come to a meeting of the minds and agree to have contracts drawn by your attorneys.

If you are presented with a binder, it absolutely *must* contain a sentence that says something to this effect:

This agreement is subject to contracts being drawn by a reputable attorney and executed by all parties concerned within ___ days.

Without that sentence, that sheet of paper, no matter how simple, is a legally binding contract when signed. Five working days is plenty of time to get the formal contracts drawn and signed. A check from the buyers, usually for $1,000, accompanies the binder.

Then, depending on the prevailing practice of the local area, your lawyer draws up the contract. It is passed, unsigned, to the buyer's attorney. He or she often makes a few changes or additions, and any points of difference are ironed out. Then the contracts are signed by both parties. If there are any last-minute changes made in the body of the contract, they are initialed by all parties concerned. If there is an addendum to the contract, it is initialed at the bottom of the page, again by all parties concerned.

Once the contract is signed (executed), there is usually an additional amount of earnest money deposited by the buyer. This is held in escrow.

The amount is usually sizable; the traditional figure is 10 percent of the purchase price of the house. The 10 percent figure is not mandatory, of course, and compromises are often made, especially when the buyer has a cash-flow problem because he or she is selling another house. You should try, however, to get as large an earnest money deposit as possible, certainly enough to make backing out of the deal painful, *very* painful for the buyers. Try to have this cash held in escrow by *your* attorney. This makes it easier to have the money released to you when all the contract contingencies have been met. It also increases the chances of your actually

getting that money in the event of default on the contract or other legal problems.

This has been a description of the *ideal* procedure. In actual practice, there are other ways that contracts often get drawn and signed.

First, there is usually no such thing as a standard contract of sale. There are different ways sales contracts are drawn up as well.

- In some instances the real-estate agent fills in the blanks on an agency contract form, then some changes are made through the negotiating process, and everyone pretty much agrees. But the contract is not signed. The completed form is shown to the attorneys for both parties, who check through the whole contract and usually make a few more changes to protect their respective clients. When everyone is in agreement, the contracts are executed and initialed. (This procedure usually results in a contract with lots of crossed-out clauses, written-in clauses, changed words and dates, and initials up and down the margins.)
- There is yet another way. The agent draws up the contract, the buyer signs it, and the partially executed instrument (contract) is presented to the seller. The offer is so tempting that the sellers act as their own attorneys, evaluating the contract and signing it. They are, however, somewhat protected by the inclusion of the clause:

> *This contract is further contingent upon the approval of the Purchaser's and Seller's attorneys, on content and form only, by ___[date]___.*

This allows the attorneys to rework clauses or wording, or make adjustments in negotiated points of law. However, the agreement to purchase the property at the named price is binding.

If you should be tempted by an ideal offer, written out upon a contract and signed by the buyers, if you want to tie up the deal then and there, be sure at least that this "subject to seller's lawyer's

DEFINITION PLEASE

An **addendum** is a sheet attached to a contract spelling out some agreement not mentioned in the body of the contract. This is sometimes a special provision for occupancy or tenancy, or it could be a list of personal items that are included in the sale.

DEFINITION PLEASE

Escrow is money or documents held by a third party until specific conditions of an agreement or contract are fulfilled.

approval" clause is included. If it is not, *print it in yourself and initial it.* (The buyers must initial it also before the contract is valid, but they certainly can have no objection to giving their attorney the opportunity to review the contract.)

Go through the following list of essential points that should be in the contract you are about to sign. Be sure each point is covered to your satisfaction. Remember, no one cares about, or will watch, your money and interests as closely as you yourself. And do not be afraid to question your lawyer on any point that seems unclear to you. You are paying for his or her knowledge and advice; use it!

These items are listed here rather than presented as an illustration of a contract form because it is the *items* that are important, not the form in which they are presented. They can *look* any way at all.

1. *The date of the agreement.* To be legal a contract must be dated.
2. *The full names of the sellers, their address, and the designation that they are the sellers and will be referred to as such throughout the remainder of the contract.*
3. *The full names of the buyers, their current address, and the designation that they are the buyers and will be referred to as such (or as Purchasers) throughout the remainder of the contract.*
4. *The location and legal description of the property to be sold.* The street address and the block and lot number from the local tax maps are acceptable; however, a "meets and bounds" description that includes survey points is preferable.
5. *The full amount of the purchase price.*
6. *An exact specification of how the purchase money is to be paid.* This should include the following:

   a. The amount of earnest money that accompanied the offer form (binder) and is being held in the trust account of the selling real-estate broker.
   b. The amount of additional cash to be deposited (preferably with the seller's attorney) upon execution of the contract.

c. The amount of the mortgage for which the buyers will apply. This entry should also specify the type of mortgage (conventional, FHA, VA) for which the buyers will apply and the maximum interest rate they will accept. That is usually the prevailing rate in the area, and most agents prefer to write in "prevailing rate" rather than any specific number to protect against any sudden hikes. The entry should also include the term of the mortgage acceptable to the buyers. Thirty years is most common.

d. The amount of additional cash to be paid by certified check at the closing.

Take a moment to add figures a, b, c, and d to be sure that they total the exact agreed-on selling price of the house.

7. *The kind of deed that is to convey title.*

8. *A mortgage contingency clause and cutoff date.* Every buyer's attorney will insist that if his or her clients cannot get a mortgage as stated in the contract, the contract is void and the deposit moneys are to be refunded to the buyers. You, the sellers, however, want to specify a reasonable date by which a mortgage commitment must be received. This varies depending on mortgage application conditions at local lending institutions, and the type of mortgage applied for. FHA-insured, VA-insured loans, and those with private mortgage insurance (PMI) take longer. Discuss what is a reasonable time with your real-estate agent and your lawyer. It is also a good idea to include a sentence in the contract such as:

> *The Purchaser agrees to make immediate application for such financing and to cooperate actively with the broker and the seller to obtain such mortgage financing.*

This prevents a buyer from dragging his feet over the mortgage if he should want out of the contract. It also can allow the realty agents involved to begin mortgage application proceedings for him if he has only been "prequalified"

DEFINITION PLEASE

Private mortgage insurance, also known as PMI, is a premium charged some home buyers who make a down payment of less than 10 percent. It is offered by a number of insurance companies around the country and costs a few hundred dollars a year.

DEFINITION PLEASE

Broom-clean condition means that everything must be removed from the premises and the dirt swept out; it does not mean washing windows and walls.

by a lender. If he has been "preapproved," and the guarantee of a mortgage of X dollars at X percent has not run beyond the time limit imposed by the lender, then you have no problem here.

9. *The date of the closing and the date of possession.* This can be altered by mutual consent, unless the phrase "time is of the essence" is included in the original contract, or notice to that effect is served to either party.

10. *The place where the closing will occur.* This can be and often is changed, but some location must appear on the original contract. In some parts of the country, a title company handles the transfer of ownership with no need for any of the major players to be there.

11. *A statement regarding who is holding the escrow money and when it will be released.* Buyers, of course, will want the money held until closing. You, the sellers, want it to be released to you just as soon as all the contingencies (mortgage commitment, inspections, etc.) are met satisfactorily. This money, once it is released to you, is yours to spend as you see fit. Most people use it as part of the down payment on their next house.

12. *A list of personal property included in the sale and a list of specific items not included.* This list should be as complete as you can possibly make it.

13. *A statement that liability for fire and/or storm damage remains with the seller until closing.* Most buyers' attorneys will also include a statement such as:

> *Seller agrees to cut grass and provide for snow removal until closing of title, and deliver the premises in question in broom-clean condition.*

14. *A statement that the contract is binding upon the parties who have signed it and their respective heirs, executors, administrators, and so on.* Most contracts also state that the contract cannot be assigned to another party by the buyers without written consent of the sellers.

15. *A statement that taxes, rents, interest on mortgages, municipal assessments being assumed, sewer service charges, municipal utilities, fuel oil, related club or recreation dues, and the like, if any, shall be apportioned and adjusted as of the date of the closing.* This statement assures that you, the sellers, will be reimbursed for the unused portion of the taxes and sewer use fee that you paid in advance, and for the fuel oil remaining in your tank.
16. *A statement saying how much commission is to be paid on the property and to which real-estate firm.*
17. *The buyers' signatures, identified as the buyers.*
18. *The sellers' signatures, again identified as such.*
19. *The signature of the selling agent.* This isn't really necessary, but it is an assurance that she will receive her commission.

Besides these items, there are several entries that occur quite frequently in a contract, although they are not necessary to its validity or effectiveness. You should be aware of them and recognize them.

Common Additions to a Contract

Termite Inspection Clause

One of the most usual is a provision for a termite inspection. The buyers usually pay for this, since it is to their benefit. You should check, however, that the clause providing for the inspection includes a cutoff date. If the inspection has not been made by that date, the contract should state that the buyers waive their right to the inspection. The clause should also state that the if termites are present, the seller will have them eliminated at the seller's expense and also make any necessary repairs of damages caused by the infestation. The presence of termites should not be cause for

TIP

If your buyers agree to a reduction in the purchase price to cover the cost of repairs, try also to get the real-estate agency to base their commission on the adjusted price rather than the originally agreed-on price. This will save you 6 percent of whatever the cost of repairs is.

cancellation of the contract, however, unless the damage is irreparable—a very rare case.

Professional House-Inspection Clause

More and more often these days, buyers are also including a favorable report by a professional house inspection firm as a contingency to their contract. You can often avoid this contingency by having the inspection done at your expense when the house first goes on the market (see chapter 6, pages 65–66) or by offering a warranty to the buyer (also explained in chapter 6, page 68). If the buyers insist, they have the right to request an inspection and to make their purchase contingent upon it. In this case, insist on a cutoff date and try to make it as soon as possible; a week to ten days is plenty of time to get the inspection done. If the inspection reveals some flaw in the house, the buyers can walk away from the contract and get their deposit moneys refunded. Or they can negotiate with the sellers to have repairs done or for a price reduction to cover their cost of making those repairs.

Let's say the inspection shows that the house will need a new roof within a year, even though there are no leaks in evidence anywhere at the present time. You will then have to decide between (1) repairing and/or replacing the roof yourself, using your own labor and materials, (2) having a professional roofer do the work at your expense, or (3) making an allowance in the sales price of the house.

Doing any required repair work yourself leaves you open to criticism and recall after closing if the buyers find the work faulty. Having the work done professionally can mean a time delay since closing is often contingent upon completion and approval of the work. It also means you must deal with the workers around the house while you are packing and getting ready to move. What's best here, if your buyers are agreeable, is that you get two or three estimates of the cost of that new roof (or whatever repairs are required) and then negotiate a price allowance to the buyers. Sometimes the buyers are inflexible and the sellers must deduct the entire cost of the repairs from the agreed-on sales price if they want the sale. In other cases, the buyers and sellers negotiate an agreement for an allowance that essentially splits the cost of the repairs between the two parties.

Disclosure Clause

If your state requires you to fill out a disclosure form you will not need *a disclosure clause*. However, if you do not have such a requirement, an attorney for the buyers will also include a statement such as:

The seller represents that the roof is free of leaks and that the heating, cooling, plumbing, electrical, septic waste disposal, hot water and water supply systems, and all appliances included in the sale will be in reasonable working order at the time of the closing of title.

If this clause is included in your contract, you don't have much choice but to agree to it, since a denial is bound to give rise to suspicions that you are "hiding something." Have your attorney add the following phrase: *but these representations shall not survive the closing of title.* This protects you from any kind of guarantee. In other words, if the buyers inspect everything on the day of closing, and it works, *that's it*. If the dishwasher breaks down and leaks all over the floor the next day, it is not your responsibility.

Walk-Through Clause

Most contracts will also allow a walk-through before closing by including the sentence:

The seller shall permit the purchaser or his representative to make an inspection of the subject premises on the day of closing or at a reasonably and mutually agreeable time before the closing.

This inspection is of course necessary to protect the buyer's rights in the property they are purchasing. A lot could have changed with that property since the day the buyers signed the contract and the closing. That inspection does not give them license, however, to appear at your door once a week to measure windows, check the color of your living room carpet, or test the showers. Once the agreed-on inspections are completed, you should be allowed to live in the house in peace and privacy until closing. If you wish to give

INFORMATION

In some FHA and VA deals, you may not be able to offer a repairs allowance. Those federal agencies most often insist that any required repairs be completed before mortgage approval is granted. The agency inspects and approves the repairs before closing.

permission for occasional visits, you may, of course, but this should be a matter of choice, not necessity.

Take Your Time

If you began your negotiation and sale proceedings with a binder, and an attorney has since drawn your contract, you will probably have the opportunity to take it home overnight and check it thoroughly. If, however, you have been presented with a tempting contract by a realty agent, give the agent some refreshments and something to read and take the contract into another room and check through it there. Don't worry if it takes a half hour or so, the agent is accustomed to waiting and wants to make the deal. Sign only if you are genuinely satisfied with the contract. If not, tell the agent you are satisfied with the price but you would like your attorney to look over the contract in the morning.

Next comes a step so many of us are so bad at—waiting.

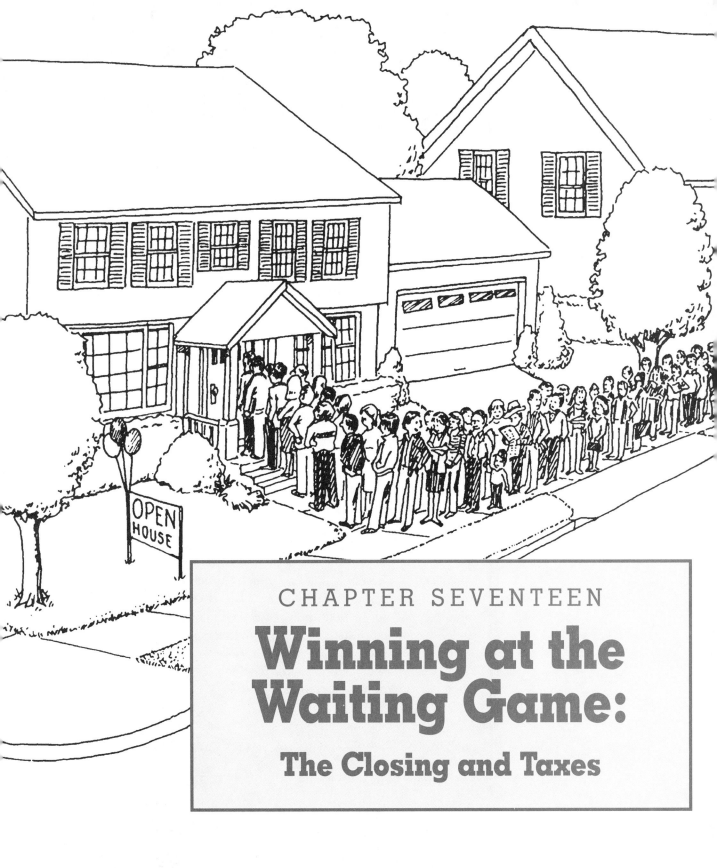

CHAPTER SEVENTEEN

Winning at the Waiting Game:

The Closing and Taxes

Once the contracts are signed and everyone has a copy, you still have some tense waiting time ahead. The inspectors usually come first. The termite man shouldn't take longer than fifteen or twenty minutes. The professional house inspector (or engineer) may spend as long as two hours—or more—poking around your place.

If it is not convenient for you to be at home to let the inspector in, the listing agent has the responsibility of meeting him or her and remaining on the property until the work is finished. It is *not* a good idea to go around with the inspector. It's too painful, for one thing. You don't *really* want to hear negative comments, do you? Also, the buyer might be there, which makes things a bit awkward. The agent can field any comments, saying, "I'm familiar with this house, what did you need to know?"

House inspectors usually submit a written report within two or three days of their on-site inspection. The report is given to the buyers; however, a copy or a brief summary of findings is usually also given to the agent. That agent should call you with the results as soon as they are in. If you do not hear within four days, call the agent and ask. You will breathe a little easier once that's over.

The big contingency is the mortgage. Your nail-biting and floor-pacing will depend a great deal on the type of mortgage your buyers are getting and the efficiency and volume of business of the particular lender they are using. (If your buyers have been *preapproved* for a loan, then your waiting time is cut and the process is simplified.)

Nothing can happen before the appraiser arrives, and most lenders try to have this done as soon as possible. The concern here is with *value*, not working systems. This visit takes fifteen or twenty minutes, and covers both the exterior and interior of the dwelling.

After the appraisal is made, a conventional mortgage can go quite quickly. There is no supervision by federal agencies or insurance companies. The decision to grant the mortgage rests with the lender alone.

Some lending institutions give loans with private mortgage insurance charged to the buyer. These are still conventional loans, however, and the process does not take much longer than noninsured loans.

Despite the potential quickness of conventional mortgages, it *is* possible for a mortgage commitment to take up to six weeks if the market is busy and the lender has a huge backlog. Your real-estate agent should be able to tell you the usual length of time for the lender your buyers are using.

The agent should keep checking on the lender to be certain that the folder containing your buyer's application hasn't fallen behind the file cabinet, and that everything is proceeding according to schedule.

Generally, FHA and VA loans take longer than conventional financing. The appraisals check not only the value of the property, but its condition as well, and there is considerably more paperwork. Figure maybe as long as eight weeks before you can breathe easier when that loan commitment comes in.

Is Your House Still on the Market?

Sellers worry a great deal about contract contingencies and about the fact that their house is off the market until all those conditions are met. So . . . should you leave up the For Sale sign and continue to allow your house to be shown? Or should you take down the sign and consider it sold?

To calm seller jitters, some realty agents put a notice through the MLS that the house is "on deposit," but they request that agents continue to show it until all contingencies are met. This practice is frowned on by some. For one thing, very few agents will actually show a property that is on deposit even when the owner requests the continue-to-show policy. It is just bad business. Put yourself in the sales agent's position: She shows the house, the buyers fall in love with it, they want it and nothing else, they wait three weeks, the mortgage for the first buyer goes through, and the house is sold to them. The second buyers are disappointed and resentful. Nine times out of ten, they start house hunting all over again—with another agent. Once having had this experience, no agent wants to lose customers this way again. So she stays clear of continue-to-show listings.

Second, from the seller's point of view, continuing to show is a bother. You must go on keeping your house and life in ready-to-show

TIP

If you are not satisfied with your agent's answers about the buyer's mortgage situation, call the lending institution and speak to a mortgage officer. Ask how that application is coming along.

DEFINITION PLEASE

Specific performance is a court order that the agreements of a contract must be enacted.

shape despite the fact that you think your house is sold. Better that you relax, let your hair down, stop worrying about the dishes in the sink, the vacuuming, or the laundry and have some fun, or start looking for another house while you await word on those contingencies.

But let's consider this from another angle. Why *should* you take your house off the market? What if the deal you think is so certain falls through? And you've lost four or six or eight weeks.

In a very good market for you, where the next buyer is likely to be just around the corner, you might want to go ahead and think of your house as sold. If something happens, well, there *is* that next buyer. In a down market for sellers, where you may not know where your next buyer is coming from, it would probably be best to continue showing the house, and even take a "back-up" buyer. You cannot afford to be out of the home-selling loop for two months.

Sold Is Sold, Right?

Once the contingencies are met, your house is SOLD. As mentioned, many contracts are written so that the 10 percent or so escrow money is turned over to the seller at this point. But whether you get the cash then or not, the money is yours. There is no backing out for the buyers. And if by chance they should make movements in that direction, a good agent will remind them that they will lose their escrow money and that they have signed a legal contract that can be brought to court to enforce specific performance.

We won't get into the intricacies of real-estate law here, but there have been occasions when buyers have walked away from a contract and sellers have sold the house under pressure to someone else. Most commonly, the sellers have won their suits for damages against the walk-away buyers. "Damages" usually include whatever difference there was between the agreed-on contract price with the original buyer and the price the sellers were forced to take because of pressure and the broken contract. There have also been instances in which the buyers have walked away from a contract and the sellers have gone on to sell the property for more than the original contract price. Needless to say, few of these cases get to court; the "damages" are hard to substantiate.

More commonly, however, walk-aways don't happen. Buyers who have put 10 percent of the price of the house, or at least several thousand dollars of their money, into escrow as good faith that they will buy the house, have gone through the trouble and expense of hunting down and applying for a mortgage, and have paid for termite and house inspections really want to buy that house.

Once the contingencies are met, even real-estate agents consider the property sold and start counting (and often spending) their commission money.

The Closing

All that is left now of the selling process is the settlement, or closing. This is a marvelous time for sellers! Essentially all they have to do is sign a few papers and collect their money.

In fact, some sellers do not even go to the closing. They sign the papers in advance and allow their lawyers to represent them and bring them back their checks. There is no real harm in doing this—it's sometimes done with a vacation property many miles from the seller's principal residence. However, unless it is very inconvenient or unless the sellers have already moved out of state, being present at the closing is preferable. There are always minor questions that come up; there is always something to be learned.

In some parts of the country, the transfer of title is handled by a closing agent, with no need for either buyer or seller to attend a closing. Since most sellers do have a settlement "ceremony," that transfer is being explained here.

The day before you go to the closing, run down the list of things you need to bring. You want to be certain there will be no snags at the table.

And please settle the sale of any personal items not named in the contract before the closing. A $200 portable dishwasher can do horrible things to the sale of a $198,000 house! Lawyers and sellers and buyers can come to blows over what, in retrospect, are the silliest things, like where are the keys to the toolshed, or whether the buyers paid the sellers for the dishwasher.

TIP

Be sure to bring to the closing:

- Any documents your lawyer or real-estate agent has told you you will need

- Keys to all entrances to your house, to the mailbox, and to any out-buildings, such as a shed

- Garage-door opener (often forgotten by the seller!)

- Combination to any alarm system

What to Expect at a Closing

Here is a listing of the typical documents buyers and sellers are asked to sign at a real-estate closing. There might be slight variations in your state or regional area.

This assumes that the buyers are taking out a conventional mortgage. Closings for loans backed by the Federal Housing Administration or the Department of Veterans Affairs may involve additional documents.

These documents are in no particular order. What comes first usually varies according to the closing officer's personal preference.

❏ Truth-in-Lending statement: Also known as Regulation Z document. Contains the full disclosure of the interest rate, annual percentage rate, amount financed and the total cost of the loan over its life. ***Signed by the buyer.***

❏ Itemization of amount financed: Summarizes and explains the prepaid finance costs—which are subtracted from the total loan amount—mentioned on the Truth-in-Lending statement. ***Signed by the buyer.***

❏ Consolidated buyer and seller settlement statement: Also known as the HUD [U.S. Department of Housing and Urban Development] statement. Itemizes the details of the financial transaction between the buyer and the seller. Contains all real-estate costs, plus costs to the borrower. ***Signed by the buyer and seller.***

❏ Monthly payment letter: Shows the total monthly payment, itemizing the portions for principal, interest, taxes, insurances, and other monthly escrows. ***Signed by the buyer.***

❏ Note: The actual agreement between the borrower and lender, explicitly stating the terms of borrowing. In effect, this is the IOU. ***Signed by the buyer.***

❏ Mortgage: An official document showing that a lien is being placed against the property. It allows the lender to foreclose the property in case the borrower defaults. ***Signed by the buyer.***

❏ Warranty deed: The document that transfers the title of the property from the seller to the buyer. It is ***signed by the seller,*** but contains the name of the buyer.

❏ Tax proration agreement: Buyer and seller agree to cooperate in re-prorating the property taxes in the following year once the actual bill is known. In theory, taxes should be re-prorated with every deal. In practice, this agreement is invoked only when there is a major change in the property tax bill. ***Signed by buyer and seller.***

❏ Homeowner's dues proration agreement: Same as the tax proration agreement, except that it addresses homeowner's dues. ***Signed by buyer and seller.***

❏ Name affidavit: Certifies that the parties at the closing are known by the names they are using in the transaction. If one of the parties has a former name or did business under another name, the affidavit makes that fact known. ***Signed by buyer and seller.***

❏ Acknowledgment of survey and termite reports: Assures that buyer has seen the survey and termite report. ***Signed by the buyer.***

❏ Notice to owner: Required by some states. Lets buyer know that the lender's title insurance policy protects only the lender. Also lets buyer know that an owner's title insurance policy can be purchased. ***Signed by the buyer.***

❏ Anti-coercion form: Required by some states. Lenders customarily require homeowners to buy insurance on the house and its contents. This document requires borrowers to state that the lender has not forced them to use any particular insurance company. ***Signed by the buyer***.

❏ Borrowers' affidavit: Requires borrowers to state that they have not altered the property in any way that might cloud the title. ***Signed by the buyer.***

❏ Sellers' affidavit: Requires sellers to state that they have not altered the property in any way that might cloud the title. ***Signed by the seller.***

❏ 1099 form: An Internal Revenue Service form that reports the gross proceeds from the transaction. ***Signed by the seller.***

❏ Confirmation of payoffs: A report of where money is being paid to redeem liens placed against the property. ***Signed by the seller.***

❏ Nonforeign owners notice: Notifies the buyer that if the seller is a foreigner and leaves the country without paying income taxes on the transaction, the buyer is liable for the taxes. Also known as the FIRPTA document. ***Signed by the buyer.***

❏ Compliance agreement: Requires buyer and seller to state that if there are unintentional typographical errors on any of the documents, they both will cooperate to correct changes in the documentation. ***Signed by the buyer and seller.***

Source: Gulf Atlantic Title Insurance Co.

The closing can be held at either party's lawyer's office, or at the real-estate agent's office, or at the title company, or even at the mortgage lender's office. One of those individuals will conduct the closing. The box on pages 196–197 will acquaint you (or reacquaint you if you sold a property some years earlier) with who signs what that day.

Your closing is not likely to be dramatic. Perhaps you won't have even a minor tale to tell in years to come, although sometimes a closing can be chilly because of a difference over price during negotiating that carries over to the settlement table. But enough activity is going on with whoever is in charge moving papers around, so there is usually no need for buyers and sellers to speak. Most closings are quiet, dignified, and even rather stuffy affairs that run about an hour. And the only noise is the shuffling of all those documents. Most likely, your closing will be like that. Go out afterward for lunch or dinner and celebrate!

And Then There's Uncle Sam

After the celebration comes the last part of the paperwork involved in selling your house: the taxes. There is good news here, though. The tax reforms of 1997 will benefit you instead of making things more difficult.

You will recall you signed a tax form at the closing that went to the Internal Revenue Service and that described the sale of your house. Sellers must also file a form along with their income tax return for the year of the sale.

Anyone who sells a principal residence, which is defined as a property owned and lived in for at least two of the previous five years, can exclude $250,000 of profit ($500,000 for married couples filing jointly) from the sale from federal income taxes. This exclusion may be used once every two years. Unlike the old rulings, the new law does not require you to reinvest in another house. You can buy a less costly place, or even rent if you choose. If you do sell a second time within that two-year period, or if you realize a profit greater than that exclusion, then you may have to pay tax on the profits from your sale.

Do you remember that one-time exemption for home owners over age fifty-five? That's been repealed by the new laws (they're still called the "new" laws, even though it's been a few years now since they were enacted).

There is other tax information that might apply to you.

- If you are widowed, you may claim up to $500,000 profit, tax free, on the sale of your house if you choose to sell within one year of the death of your spouse. (If you sell later than that, you may claim only a $250,000 profit exclusion, unless you have remarried and are filing jointly.)
- If you sell a property you inherited, you will be interested to know that $650,000 of property value on estate sales (although not necessarily real estate—your accountant will explain this to you) is exempted. The amount exempted from estate sales and farm sales, will increase by $25,000 each year beginning in 2000, to a total possible exemption of $1.3 million.
- If you sell at a loss, unfortunately that loss is still not deductible.

Naturally your accountant can explain all of this to you and help you with filing income taxes for the year of your sale.

TIP

Keep any receipts for repairs and replacements made to improve your property for sale. Some or all of them can help a bit when it comes to calculating taxes that you might owe.

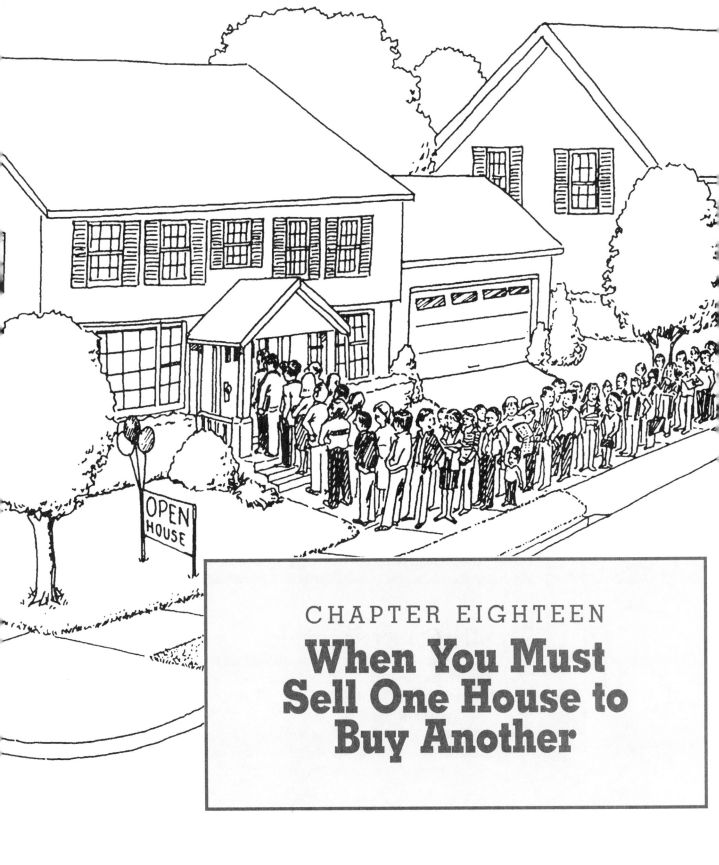

CHAPTER EIGHTEEN

When You Must Sell One House to Buy Another

T he young first-time buyer avoids this problem. And so do the elderly who are leaving home ownership. For those in-between, though, a change of house is a critical situation between tandem cycles of buying and selling, sometimes with dramatic emotional and financial consequences.

There are almost always problems with this type of selling. The essential concern is how to minimize them, and the essential step to accomplishing that is to recognize *why* the problems occur. For most people, they grow out of the two major activities required in changing one owner-occupied residence for another: liquefying assets (getting the money out of one property to put into another) and coordinating occupancy (the big switch of families and furniture). This process is often a chain reaction, with time and money as the activating forces.

Consider the stories that follow. Except for the transferred employee, all of these buyers depend on cash from *their* buyers in order to buy "up" or buy "new." In addition, all of them, including the transferee, depend on the ability of the sellers to move out. In the case of new construction, they depend on completion of work by the builder. A failure or a delay anywhere sends ripples in both directions through the chain.

Expect the ripples; rejoice if they do not occur. During the process, try to stay calm. The problems are always resolved somehow, and there will be fewer permanent consequences if everyone remains as rational and open to new ideas, options, and compromises as possible. Here are the most common sell/buy situations, along with insights for the sellers and buyers who must work their way through them.

The Corporate Transfer

This is the best of all possible worlds—financially, that is. Most companies offer to buy, at fair market value, the home of their transferred employee, or in some cases to lend him or her (without interest charge) the equity in that house, and then manage the property after the family moves out. Manage usually means maintain the house and pay mortgage installments, insurance, and taxes until it is actually sold. Most companies also have a specified period of time

My Biggest House-Related Worry Right Now

Well, your biggest worry is probably selling the house. But jot down other concerns that are causing some nail-biting. Will you be able to move before September, when the kids start at a new school? Will you find a buyer before the end of the year, an almost totally dead house-hunting season? Will everything blow up in your face if you buy that brand-new development house you want before you sell your present house? That kind of thing.

It will help you to refer to this list when considering a buyer's offer, thinking about reducing the price on your house, or making any other decision that might ease problem areas for you.

1. _____

_____

_____

2. _____

_____

_____

3. _____

_____

_____

4. _____

_____

_____

PAM'S MIGHTY MOVERS

If you are just beginning life as a corporate transferee, keep in mind what all transferees (and military families) know: When buying, it's smart to purchase a house that will sell quickly when you're on the move again. That means looking for a "typical" house in a "typical" neighborhood—nothing offbeat. You want something that is likely to interest the greatest number of buyers.

during which they will pay living expenses while the family house hunts or awaits closing.

If you are a selling transferee, therefore, you will know exactly what equity you have in your property as soon as the company finishes its fair-market-value appraisals. And you will know that the cash you need will be available for the closing date of the property you are about to buy. Your problems are not financial.

They are emotional. Most transfers are made over relatively long distances, and the uprooting process is even more painful when a family is housed in temporary quarters in a strange town. It is important, therefore, to consider the closing date in your choice of house.

Those properties most likely to be available exactly when you need them are vacant resales, new houses that are complete or on the verge of completion, houses of other corporate transferees, and, to a lesser extent, houses of people who have already purchased another property.

Avoid those properties where the owner wants to sell his or her house before seeking another or where the owner is having a new house built and the construction has just begun (even if the builder swears that she will have the job done on time). Also avoid the purchase of new construction that is anything less than virtually complete and only in need of finishing touches.

On the other hand, if you are buying the house of a transferee, you can be relatively certain that the property will close and be available for your occupancy on the date specified in the contract. Usually, you can also get reasonable delays of the closing date if you need extra time.

Changing Jobs

If a change of job and employer prompts your long-distance move, you will also have a financial cushion also, but as fine a one as the transferred employee. Few companies will buy a new employee's old residence; most, however, will pay moving expenses and provide some financial support for living expenses while awaiting a closing in the new location.

A long-distance job change often separates a family. Typically, the wife and children remain behind to sell the house while the husband goes on to his new job.

Free time at the new location is often spent house hunting, so selection of a new house usually follows hard on the heels of signing the sales contract on the old. Most change-of-job buyers want quick occupancy of the new house in order to get the family back together. If this is your situation, try to select from the same selling situations recommended to transferees, and avoid those situations in which delays are most likely.

If you are buying the house of a person who has changed jobs, you can usually expect an on-time closing. In fact, you should plan to close on time, for these sellers are usually both anxious about and in need of their equity. They will not take requests for delays of a month or two in good spirits.

Stepping Up

Stepping up—looking for a larger or more expensive house—usually occurs at least once in most home owners' lives. Move-ups are intent on finding their dream, or at least an acceptable substitute, before they put their present house on the market. Once they find such a property, they will sign a contract to buy. This contract almost always commits them to the purchase, whether or not their old house is sold before the closing date. In other words, they are in a "must-sell" position.

If you are selling because you are stepping up to the property you now want, try to get a closing date on that dream house several months in the future. It is much easier to wait out extra time in your old house than to make mortgage payments on two properties and a bridge loan. (There is a full explanation of bridge loans—temporary loans to allow home sellers to pull out their equity to put down on the next house—in the next chapter.)

It's wise here to price your old house close to its market value to stimulate a quick sale. If, however, no ready, willing, and able buyer appears before the closing date for your new house arrives, try to be patient and continue to live in that old house, at least until you have a signed purchase contract for it.

TIP

Home owners with particularly distinctive properties (a unique, not-for-everyone, architect designed house, or a house with five bedrooms or just two bedrooms) or in iffy locations (mixed-use neighborhood, or along a lake that floods occasionally) would especially be wise to wait until they have a contract of sale before going out to buy another house.

• • •

Remember, occupied houses generally sell more quickly than unfurnished ones—a good reason for staying in your old house as long as possible.

TIP

No matter what you are told, actual closing dates on new houses usually run one to six months, or even nine months, after the date that's in the sales contract.

You can also help to facilitate a sale by taking most bric-a-brac and all extra items of furniture to your new house. This tactic will give a look of spaciousness to your old property.

If you are buying a house from sellers who have already purchased another house, you have a strong negotiating hand. Your first offer should be at a low price with a distant closing date. If you follow with slight increases in the offering price and offers to close sooner and sooner, you may well save yourself several thousand dollars. Once the contract is signed, however, be prepared to close on time. Sellers carrying payments on two properties will not be happy about a request to delay an agreed-on closing date, especially if the sales price was keyed to a quick close. The sellers might then take steps that would force you to choose between closing on the appointed day and forfeiting an escrow deposit.

Building Your Dream House

Most site builders will tell you that they can construct a house in 90 to 120 days (depending on where you live and the climate during construction). But very rarely is a house ready for occupancy, no matter how fast the builder promises you it will be finished. Even more rarely can a buyer do *anything* to speed up the process.

If you are selling your old house while having another house built, allow plenty of time beyond the paper closing date on the new property for the closing on the old. You can calculate a rough estimate of how much extra time you will need by talking with people who have already had homes constructed by your builder. (This advice is especially appropriate if you are buying in a development. Patterns of both quality and completion time are amazingly consistent.)

The risk of setting too early a closing date on your old house is that you'll be forced to move out of it with nowhere to go. Such a situation could intensify the emotional stress of a move and cost you a bundle in extra living expenses and furniture storage.

In contrast, the risk of setting too late a closing date is small. Once you have a contract of sale on your old house, the process of getting a loan for your equity is a veritable breeze. With a bridge loan, you can close on your new house and begin to decorate it or move your personal belongings into it. If your two properties are not located too far apart, you might save more than the interest charge on that bridge loan in reduced moving expenses.

Before you decide to *buy* a house whose seller is having a house built, ask what the closing date is on the new construction. If you can, get the address of the property and drive by. Do not expect a closing within sixty days, unless the house being built is actually nearing completion.

Any selling/buying chain reaction with new construction as one of its elements is likely to have delays. Awareness of this situation, however, can work to your advantage. Negotiate and allow for extra time between the contract signing and the closing date.

The Safe Switch

Many conservative home sellers, and most of those not caught up in the fantasy of finding a dream house, contend that the best house-switching procedure is to sign a contract to sell before you sign a contract to buy. Usually these sellers are out looking at possible purchases while their homes are on the market, but they restrain themselves from making any firm commitment to buy. Once they accept an offer on their old house, however, they are in a must-buy position. Like the transferee, they must choose among the properties available at the moment.

If you choose to sell on a safe switch, be sure that you keep current with all the properties for sale in your price range. Once you receive an acceptable offer, you can in turn make an offer on one of the best available houses and adjust the closing dates on both properties as much to your advantage as possible. If you receive an excellent offer on your old house at a time when there is absolutely nothing on the market that you want to buy, you will need to decide

TIP

You can try to make the sale of your present house a contingency clause in the contract for a new one. Many sellers won't go along with it though, because a domino effect is created in which one deal that fails cancels out several others that depend on it.

TIP

More than one house seller has accepted a good offer on his or her property and, unable to find a suitable house to buy, has moved into a rental apartment. These days many complexes offer six- and seven-month leases, which free you to move into a house when you find the one you want. A few even offer three-month leases, although at a higher rent than for the longer terms.

between refusing that offer and accepting it with a request for a distant closing date (four to six months).

The safe switch is a gamble. You are betting your equity that an acceptable property will come on the market before your closing and you will not have to move into the Holiday Inn out on the interstate. Usually it's a good bet. Be aware, however, that a buyer can go to court to force a seller to close on his or her property in accordance with the contract even if the seller has no place to go.

If you are buying a property from sellers who are not certain of their future plans, realize that you may not be able to move in exactly when you choose. Even if you were to get a judgment of specific performance against them, the process could take many months. On the other hand, of course, the sellers might go out, find another house, close on it, and move out in plenty of time. This one is hard to predict.

The Empty Nest

The decision to sell is often difficult for the proverbial empty nesters; but once the decision is made, the sale itself usually follows quickly and with fewer problems than most. The children who once played soccer in the living room have left, often the house has been redecorated, and just as often its owners have some extra cash (perhaps for the first time in their lives). Usually these sellers are looking to step down to a smaller, easy-care residence, often a condominium.

In many instances, the question "Where are we going after we sell the house?" is already answered. An intended retirement condo may have been purchased years ago. Or perhaps a smaller house is being built. But these sellers expect to spend the summer (or winter) at their vacation home, so the completion date of the new house is not crucial. Even when another house has been purchased and closed on, the double payments are often easily within the income of the sellers. Moving-out problems, therefore, are rare.

If you are selling to move down in size and are especially flexible on your closing date, you can use that date as a point of negotiation in determining the sales price of the property. Find out whether your buyers want a quick or a distant closing. Start with an

Five Incentives to a Quick Sale

1. *Reduce the price.* An asking price at market value will bring you a selling price below market value. Not the best way to go, but definitely a way out of a problem situation.

2. *Offer a $2,000 cash decorating rebate to the buyer to be paid at the closing.* This incentive works better than a $2,000 price reduction because the buyers can spend it.

3. *Offer a $1,000 bonus to the selling real-estate agent.* Some brokers and Boards of Realtors prohibit such sales incentives, but others do not. Check to see where yours stands. This isn't a terribly good thing to do unless you are at wit's end (it screams desperation, which could translate into a lower sales price for you).

4. *Get FHA or VA preliminary approval for your property.* Your buyer will still have to apply and qualify for the loan, but you will know exactly how much financing each government agency will approve on your house. You can set the process into motion at the office of any lender who writes FHA-insured and VA-guaranteed loans. Besides attracting buyers, the approval will save time.

5. *Have your property professionally inspected.* The advantages of this were spelled out in chapter 6. Many inspection companies offer a maintenance and repair guarantee on all mechanical systems and major structural elements for a one-year term starting the day of the closing. A written inspection report and warranty policy quiet buyers' fears by assuring them that they are indeed getting a good house.

inclination in the opposite direction and negotiate toward their ideal date while keeping your price relatively firm.

Occasionally some empty-nest sellers get sentimental and just cannot bear to part with their home, even though they have signed a contract of sale. They consciously or subconsciously set up all kinds of impediments to the closing. Usually the threat of legal action to get a judgment of specific performance or pressure by the real-estate broker for payment of the commission will shake them up enough to precipitate a closing.

Divorce

The prospect of presenting an offer on a jointly owned property to a divorced or divorcing couple can make some realty agents break out in hives. Negotiating is difficult enough when a selling couple is working together; when each pulls in a different direction and also against each other, the negotiating task for the agent is like juggling eggs, and not hard-boiled eggs either.

If you're divorced or divorcing and selling your jointly owned property, try to set out some guidelines for a price that is mutually acceptable and the approximate time each of you needs between the contract signing and the closing. Do this when you list the property for sale. Then, when you find a buyer, try to stick to the guidelines. Meanwhile, make plans and take steps toward your future housing goals.

If you are *buying* a property involving a divorce, get everything in writing and signed by both selling parties. And be sure that you have a place to live beyond the closing date named in the contract. Given the emotional and financial variables of a divorce situation, delays and postponements are just about even-money bets.

Those are the most common sell/buy situations. In the next chapter we get down to more nitty-gritty problems, and ways to work around them in this nerve-wracking position.

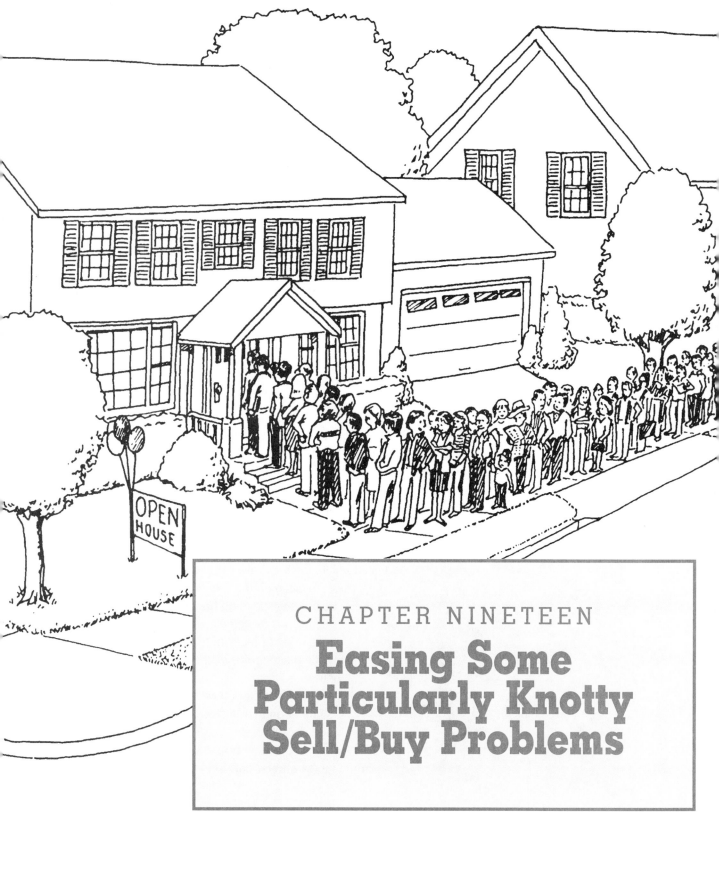

CHAPTER NINETEEN

Easing Some Particularly Knotty Sell/Buy Problems

Push comes to shove when, for example:

- The closing date on your new house is two weeks away and you have a mortgage commitment. You must also have the cash from the equity in your old house to close, but there is no buyer in sight.
- The closing date on your old house is one week away, scheduled for the same day as the closing on your new house. Your movers have reserved the date, your buyers have a mortgage commitment and are ready to move in, and you plan simply to carry your equity check from one closing to the other. Then the sellers in your new house inform you that they will not be able to move for two more months.
- You are carrying two mortgages (your present one and your new house) and the balance in your cash reserve fund has just dropped to two-digit numbers. You still do not have a buyer for your old house.

None of these nightmares—or the thousand other possible combinations of big trouble—will vanish if you wake up. But there are some things you can do that might help solve, or at least ease, your problems.

The Bridge Loan

What is usually called a bridge loan is really a loan of the equity you have accumulated in the property you are selling. Many experienced sellers routinely take out such a loan to make it easier to close on the property they are buying before they close on the property they are selling. This tactic helps them decorate and move in odd pieces of furniture, and it guarantees them a place to live after the closing on the old house.

When sellers have a qualified buyer and a signed contract, a bridge loan is easy to secure. Often the lender giving the mortgage loan on the new house will write the interim financing as a personal note due on the closing date of the property being sold. The closing agents do the paperwork and repay the interim lender. In fact, when the lender on the new house also holds the mortgage on the old house, a bridge loan is nothing but paperwork.

When sellers apply for a bridge loan without a buyer for the property they are selling, most lenders place a lien on that property, which makes that bridge loan a kind of second mortgage. When the amount of the loan is large, or when the lender has some doubt as to whether the eventual sales price of the house will actually repay the amount borrowed, the loan may be written as liens on *both* the old house and the new.

Points and origination fees on interim financing are not uncommon. They make the loans more profitable for the lender.

Some lenders require monthly payments on interim financing, whereas others allow the interest to accrue until the borrower repays the loan. Of the two methods of payment, the second is preferable, since cash is likely to be scarce for a borrower who has no buyer in sight.

Many different types of lenders write equity loans: banks, finance companies, mortgage brokers, even some large real-estate firms. The availability, the interest rates, and the particular terms of these loans vary with the lender, the financial marketplace at the time, and the area of the country. If you are having trouble finding interim financing, talk with the sales agent who sold you the new property. Usually, that agent and her broker cannot collect their commission until the closing actually takes place. That fact will stimulate considerable effort on their part to secure financing for you.

"Time Is of the Essence"

This legal term is abused and ignored more often than it is used effectively. When written into a contract, as it is in some states, or when served as a special notice to either party, the phrase means that a specific date is an essential part of the contractual obligation and that failure to act upon that date is therefore a breach of contract.

When served to buyers, it can result in the loss of deposit moneys if they do not close on the appointed day. It can even result in a court judgment for damages that could include the amount of

DEFINITION PLEASE

Another expression for a bridge loan is *interim financing.*

If you and your real-estate agent are tossing about terms like *time is of the essence* and *specific performance,* you need a lawyer, no matter what the conventional real-estate closing practices in your area are.

the difference between their contractual purchase price and the price at which the seller must sell in order to move the property quickly.

When sellers default after they have been notified that time is of the essence, their failure to close and vacate the property can free the buyers from their obligation to purchase the property without loss of their escrow funds. Or the buyers can go to court for a "judgment of specific performance," which will force the sellers to sell their property according to the terms of the contract in question. This process, however, can take several months.

These possibilities and penalties have the sound of major weapons, but often "time is of the essence" as a legal tool is just saber rattling. Think about these examples:

1. *Time is of the essence served to a builder who has not completed the house he promised to have ready a month ago.* "I can't make the date," he says. "If you want your deposit money back, you can have it." (He is now signing contracts to build the same model for $8,000 more and would *love* to be able to sell your house to someone else at the new price.)

2. *Time is of the essence served to a buyer whose mortgage commitment has not yet come through.* "I can't close on that date because I won't have the money," she says. "But you're not entitled to keep my deposit money if I can't buy." (She's right. When you allowed the contract cutoff date for the mortgage commitment to pass without notifying the buyer and putting your property back on the market, you gave mute consent to an extension. You must now wait for the lender's reply.)

3. *Time is of the essence served to sellers who won't move out on time.* "All right, take back your deposit," they say. "We'll just put our house back on the market since we have no place to go anyway." (You, the buyer, don't want your money back, you want that particular house.)

Variations of these vignettes could fill several more pages, but by now you get the drift, don't you? It is usually not only better but often essential to work out compromises rather than rely on "time is of the essence." However, if no compromise can be reached, you

can go to court (or threaten to do so) to enforce specific performance of the terms of the contract or to file suit for damages.

Occupancy before Closing

For the moment let's assume that your buyers want to move into your old house as soon as possible, but you can't move out because the vacant house *you* are buying is tied up in legal and financial paperwork. You might consider applying to your sellers for occupancy before closing.

Or, on the flip side, you are financially strapped by carrying two houses. You now have a buyer for your old house and he is anxious to take possession, but the closing will be held up at least six more weeks to process his mortgage application. You might consider arranging for his occupancy before closing if he pays you per diem rent.

In situations like these, an addendum is usually attached to the contract of sale stating that the buyers accept the property in the condition that it is in on the day of occupancy and that all maintenance responsibility for the property is theirs as of that date. Be sure everyone involved in the sale signs this addendum.

Since you still own the property until then, the buyers usually pay you a per diem rent for their time in your house.

Occupancy after Closing

One method of getting sellers to move out more quickly is to insist on a closing near the date specified in the contract and then allow them to remain in the house if they pay rent to you, the new owner. (The per diem rate is usually quite high.)

The risk in this situation is to the buyer (you): Will the property be turned over to you in the same condition as on the day of closing? To protect against the possibility of damages, a part of the sales price of the house (say $10,000 or so) is not paid to the seller at the closing, but held in escrow by an attorney or other fiduciary agent. The per diem rent is deducted from this fund, along with the cost for repair of any damages that might occur between the closing and the former owner's vacating of the premises.

Sometimes occupancy for a few days after closing is granted to a seller who is having difficulty coordinating a move. Some cash is still held in escrow, however, and there is still a per diem rental fee.

Be sure to maintain your home owners insurance policy on your house until the property transfer is satisfactorily completed.

The more silent, invisible, but very real problem in choosing to rent is that you may have to pay taxes on a profit as a landlord—a profit that you saw only on paper! Before renting, be sure to talk with your accountant or tax attorney.

Generally it is preferable to pass title and occupancy together. But if the closing cannot take place without some adjustments, the adjustments should be made.

Month-to-Month Tenants

When you're at the end of your money, where do you go? You might try talking with the lender who holds the mortgage on the house you are selling. Sometimes a suspension of payments can be arranged until the property is sold.

Or you might try renting on a month-to-month basis to tenants who will allow real-estate agents to continue to show the property. The obvious advantage of the rental is income; at least part of the mortgage payments and other expenses are being met with money other than yours. A secondary advantage is occupancy and mainte-nance. Even if the furniture is not lovely, a lived-in house shows better (as long as the tenants keep it neat and relatively uncluttered, that is). And if you can get the tenants to do the yard work (even if it means agreeing on a slightly lower rent), you will come out ahead financially. You might even call it preventive medicine, because you'll have fewer headaches and horrid moods.

But—and of course there is going to be a *but*—renting on a month-to-month basis has its disadvantages. What if the tenants are not cooperative with real-estate agents who want to show or are showing the property? What if the tenants turn out to be untidy, or downright dirty? What if they do not want the house to be sold because they like living in it and therefore bad-mouth the property to prospective buyers? What if occupancy becomes a problem? Will you really be able to get the tenants to move out on closing day?

If you do rent, remember that you cannot give month-to-month tenants an option to buy and still keep your house on the market. When any party holds an option on a property, no one else can buy that property until the option expires. (There is a discussion of renting with an option to buy in chapter 14.)

You should also avoid, if possible, a right of first refusal. Under this agreement your tenants would have the right to match an agreed-on purchase price from another buyer and buy the property. This situation is a negative one for the seller, because most sales

Should You Become a Landlord?

The old maxim Know Thyself certainly applies to being a landlord. If you are thinking about renting your house, ask yourself the following questions. If you can answer yes to all or almost all of them, you are likely to be a good landlord.

- Do you have the time to maintain that house—raking leaves, shoveling snow, and so on? (You might offer tenants a rent break in exchange for keeping up the exterior.)
- Are you well organized? Sloppy recordkeeping and owning an investment property do not go together.
- Do you know, or are you willing to find out, what, if any, rent controls are in effect in your community?
- Can you afford to make necessary repairs to the house so it is in good condition when your tenants move in?
- In a like vein, will you have the money for repairs if an emergency crops up while the tenants are living there?
- Can you be firm if the rent is more than a couple of days late?
- Do you realize you might be called at 11:30 P.M. with a complaint? Sometimes it is a legitimate one (even though it *could* have waited until morning), but there is more than one property owner who has been awakened at that hour by tenants telling him a light bulb has burned out! Or that their telephone doesn't work!
- Would you be up to getting rid of problem tenants if it should come to that?

agents avoid showing properties that have a right of first refusal specified in the listing contract. (And if you have one, it must be stated clearly on the listing sheet.) Why avoid this option? Sales agents know that they will lose their customers, who are likely to stomp off in a hissy fit, if they go through the hassle of negotiating a sale only to have another party take the property at their price!

The Guaranteed Sale

Some of the nation's large real-estate firms offer guaranteed sales plans. The advertising for these proposals goes something like this: "List with us and we will guarantee that your house will be sold in ninety days, or we will buy it!"

Is this as good a deal as it sounds?

The price at which the real-estate firm will buy your property is usually 10 to 20 percent less than its market value, and those are conservative percentages. (One or two outside appraisers are hired to determine the fair-market-value figure, from which the 10 to 20 percent discount will be made.) Worse yet, you will probably have to pay a commission to the broker, even though she is also the new buyer.

To say such an arrangement is costly is a kindness. Before you enter it in desperation, try reducing the asking price on your property below its market value by 2 percent. If this doesn't bring an offer in a month, reduce another 5 percent. Even allowing for negotiating space, you should still do better than a fixed discount of 10, 15, or 20 percent.

Meanwhile, if your listing expires, you can offer the same or better discount at a for-sale-by-owner price, which will be at less expense to you because you won't have to pay the commission. (Unless, that is, you should happen to sell to someone who originally saw the house with a sales agent and your listing contract has a hold-over clause, which means the agent can earn a commission from that sale.)

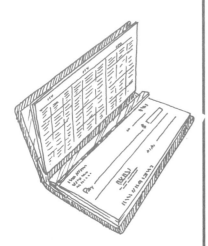

Selling the Vacant House

Sellers are human, and so they often find it difficult to resist moving into their newly purchased house even though they have not yet found a buyer for the one they are selling. It is not until the movers pick up the last few pieces of furniture that these sellers notice how very shopworn their old house looks when empty. Suddenly the nail holes in the drywall behind the sofa, where they tried to hang an arrangement of pictures and needed a few tries at each, look like so many bullet holes. The worn places in the wall-to-wall carpet create a trail of indentation from one room to the next. Other indentations are reminders of where the furniture stood, and every room echoes, yes, echoes like an empty house.

Inevitably the same thought strikes virtually every one of these sellers: "Good God! No one is ever going to buy this place!" Then come the palpitations.

But wait a second. If you plan to move out before selling, check the following points carefully.

Decorating

While you were still living in the house, a thorough and meticulous cleaning was all that was necessary for marketing. With an empty house, you will probably need to do some redecorating. Take heart, however. Repair and fix-up costs, as you will learn from your accountant, can be a downward adjustment on the selling price of the house. Not a *great* deduction, but still a deduction.

Your very cheapest decorating tool is paint, and it effectively covers much wear and tear around your place. If you decide to wallpaper, keep your choice of patterns quiet and neutral. Pick a style that will appeal to the largest possible number of people. Tear up very worn carpeting and have the floors beneath it refinished or, if you have only subfloors beneath your carpets, install new wall-to-wall. (Choose neutral colors, no matter how cheap the bright colors are.) Leave curtains and draperies on the windows throughout the house in order to cut down echoes and give the illusion of occupancy from the outside. Window coverings give the house "warmth" inside too. Besides, they probably won't fit in your new house anyway.

If you have some spare furniture (chairs, a couch, tables, lamps, even beds), leave them in the house. When prospective buyers look at an empty house, they always imagine that their furniture takes up much more space than it actually does. A few visible pieces left behind help put furniture in perspective with room size. Also, lamps are essential if the house is to be shown in the evening.

INFORMATION

Yes, a furnished house shows better than an empty one. But a clean, freshly painted empty house will look better to house hunters than a dirty, cluttered, furnished one.

Dried flowers, or arrangements of eucalyptus, also lend warmth to a room and add to a "decorated" look. In lieu of a piece of furniture, try for a large ficus tree in one part of a room, but only if you can easily stop back at the house to water it periodically (dead or dying plants will hurt your cause). Similarly, hanging plants and other small live greenery work well if you can pay attention to them.

The kitchen and bathrooms are worth some extra time and money since they are among the primary selling points of the house. You've read about sprucing them up, either simply or with some time and cash, in chapter 7.

An investment of $1,500 or so is not out of line in an effort to sell a vacant house. Borrow the money if you must. If you don't and the house does not sell, that amount and more will be gobbled up by mortgage payments, taxes, and insurance, not to mention the cost of maintenance. Remember, once you move out, your goal is to sell the house quickly.

Maintenance

You will have to return periodically to dust and vacuum (and water those plants) or hire someone to do so. And you will have to keep the lawn mowed, the hedgers trimmed, the walks and driveway shoveled in winter, and the leaves raked in fall. If you have moved a long distance, and if you don't have a friend or neighbor who will do it for you, you probably should hire a maintenance firm to do this work. Your realty agent can help you find such a manager.

If your house is for sale through the winter, you can save some money by shutting down the heating system and draining the water from the pipes to prevent their freezing and bursting. Do not, however, turn off the electricity. Lights are needed to show the house in the evening, and to inspect the basement.

Although few people would believe it, a vacant house for sale over the summer is a more difficult problem than in winter. Since windows are usually kept closed and locked and since no one wants to air-condition an empty house, the property shows as hot and stuffy. You or someone in charge must also look out for mice, squirrels, bats, ants, and other pests. Any sign of such infestation will turn many buyers away. And put up No Smoking signs in obvious places; stale tobacco odors are nauseating.

Showings

When selling an empty house it is essential that you allow the broker to use a lockbox. Many sales agents will not make two out-of-the-way trips to a listing broker's office to pick up and return keys, and you want every possible showing to take place.

In some areas, listing agents find a showing book effective in a vacant house. This is nothing more than a guest book that can be purchased in stationery stores or some gift shops. Each showing agent is asked to fill in his or her name, the agency name, the date, and the time of showing. The listing agent can then phone the showing agents to gather customer opinions or comments or to try to stimulate an offer by giving advance notice of price reductions or special terms.

Business cards are a problem everywhere. Usually agents will leave their cards on kitchen counters, foyer tables, shelves, or even on living room windowsills. Dozens of such cards scattered about the house do not impress a potential buyer with the desirability of the property. They particularly stand out in a vacant, or nearly vacant, house. You can somewhat alleviate, if not eliminate, the problem by having a wicker basket, or a box, on the kitchen counter with a small note reading "Cards, please." Leave two or three in the basket so that those who come in will add theirs to the pile, but don't let the basket get too full. Have the listing agent collect the cards at regular intervals, or collect them yourself, if you can. These cards will provide you with information on who is showing the property and how often. This is information you might want to consider if your listing contract is approaching its expiration date and you are considering signing with a new agent.

Confusing, Isn't It?

In reading this chapter, did you feel rather Janus-like, facing two directions at once? Filling the role of both seller and buyer at the same time *can* be complicated. But take heart, it will end. You will say goodbye to the seller part you are playing, and can concentrate on being the buyer in your new place, enjoying all that *that* role has to offer.

TIP

Why not contact a local pet sitter? Many also offer to check empty houses. Their rates are likely to be less than a real estate's management office, and most are reliable. After all, they're responsible enough to care for pets in an owner's absence. However, be sure the sitter knows what you expect (to go into the house, for example, and not just walk around the exterior). Look in the Yellow Pages under "Pet Sitters" or ask around your neighborhood.

CHAPTER TWENTY

Getting a Move On

While planning for the closing on your old house, you are probably also gearing up for The Move. As if things haven't been hectic enough for you, now you must transport your four, seven, or ten rooms of furnishings across town or across the country! Now that you are this close to owning your new property, the fidgets set in about the whole business. Will I miss my family and friends? you wonder. How will the new neighbors be? Will I be able to find a good job there?

All of those concerns are natural. Moving is a major upheaval. Still, keep in mind that you *are* going to a dwelling you have chosen and presumably like a good deal, if not downright love. And moving can be made a little easier with a bit of knowledge and planning.

Three Steps to a Successful Move

You have to organize moving the way you orchestrate a wedding. It is dangerous to leave anything to chance. So when a closing date on your new house is announced, appoint someone in the household (you?) as "wedding director" to take charge of the move. It's not that everyone else won't help, but you need one person in command, with his or her notepad and pencil.

The three steps to be explained here, in the order they should be attacked, are (1) looking into the new community, (2) taking an inventory of what's to go and what's to be left behind, and (3) selecting a mover.

Your New Community

You obviously know something about your new town, thanks at least to all the driving around you did while house hunting. But you also need to do some homework, even if your new town is just minutes away from the old one. Each community has its own distinctive character and "voice."

Subscribe to the Newspaper.
You'd be wise to get at least a Sunday subscription to the newspaper in the new town. This is one of the best steps

you can take to help familiarize yourself with Pleasantville before you arrive to stay. The paper can acquaint you with stores, especially national chains that have shops in your community; with local social events, including groups you might eventually like to join; school news if you have kids who will be attending; and service directories.

But even more important, as you read through the news pages, you will find a sense of how the community functions. That will help you hit the ground running when you arrive. You'll have up-to-the-minute news on the latest zoning battle, on local election issues, and on what the local movers and shakers have been up to lately.

Check for the name and address, and subscription information, of the paper in the *Gale Directory of Publications and Broadcast Media*. You can find it in the reference department at most public libraries.

Tool Around. The move shouldn't be all work. You can write or call or visit the Web site for the local Chamber of Commerce or Convention and Visitors Bureau in Pleasantville. Ask for the "new-comer's package." You can also query them about anything of special interest to you and your family. Is there a symphony orchestra, for example, or a place nearby for fly-fishing?

Heading out of state? Then contact the Department of Tourism, located in the state capital. Ask for material on your favorite sport or outdoor activity. It will be nice to know what leisure activities await you after the fatigue of the move.

Actually, it's not a bad idea to write to that office even if you are moving to another part of your present state. There may be activities in the new spot that will surprise you.

Take Inventory

The thought may seem overwhelming, but it must be done sooner or later. Take stock of all your belongings, from what is in the hall closet to (if you are in a house now) what has been stashed in the corner of the basement for ten years. And we won't even get into all those cartons in the garage. Do you have an attic too? Egad! Decide what will go with you and what will stay behind, either to be given away or sold.

TIP

If you are cleaning out the house and you need boxes, you can get them from a local supermarket. Try to be there on days when the shelves are being restocked, so you can take the boxes before they are broken down. (Be sure to ask first, although no one is likely to mind.) You can also purchase cardboard boxes from self-storage warehouses.

TIP

For packing up long-stemmed artificial flowers, get those long, narrow boxes that are used to deliver fresh flowers to florists. You might ask an area flower shop to save you a box or two.

There are a number of ways you can get rid of "stuff" these days. Here are some choices for where to send what you don't want to take with you.

Charities. You can give unwanted items to Goodwill Industries, veterans' associations, Parents Anonymous, and any number of other nonprofit groups in your area. Many groups will pick up at your door, saving you drop-off time. Be sure to allow plenty of time before you move for these associations to call for your boxes. You want all that stuff, and those phone calls, out of the way before you begin packing what you want to take.

Consignment Shops. Here you can bring unwanted clothing—including shoes, purses, belts, and jewelry—and furniture (clothing usually has its own stores, as does furniture). You will usually get around 40 percent of what those items eventually sell for. Clothing must be in perfect condition—this is not the same as a thrift shop—as well as clean and ironed. Although you will make some money using consignment shops, you'll have to follow up with them to see what they have sold of yours. So it's wise to take things over there at least two months before your move.

Classified Ads. Sell unwanted items through classified advertisements in your local paper, or through notices tacked up at supermarkets, the office, social centers, and so forth. You can also advertise, usually free, in your community association's newsletter.

Garage Sales (*Lobby Sales, Gate Sales, and Block Sales*). The ever-present garage sale proves the adage that one man's poison is another man's meat. You can hold one of these sales by yourself, or ask some neighbors to join you, making an event likely to bring out more shoppers.

Organization is the key here. That means giving yourself plenty of time before deciding to have a sale and actually putting up a sign. You need to prepare the items for sale—washing, polishing, deciding how to display, and so on. Keep in mind you can get more money for the item you are selling if it looks good, so apply a little elbow grease if you have the time. A higher price will be your reward.

Naturally, you will pick a date, and a season for that matter, when sales are commonly held in your part of the country. As for weekends, some holidays attract buyers (Memorial Day, Independence Day, Labor Day), while others do not (Mother's Day,

Father's Day). Many moving companies offer free booklets on how to stage a garage sale, providing information on publicizing the event, security precautions to take, and so forth. Ask your mover.

Tag Sale. If you have a lot to sell, or if you are selling the contents of a house you inherited, you may want to take the tag sale route to getting rid of unwanted furnishings. You can hire an individual or company to run a tag sale for you. This takes the work out of your hands entirely and can be useful if you are particularly attached to your things and hate the thought of selling them yourself and seeing them hauled down the driveway to someone else's car. It can also be a good idea if you are not sure of the value of your things.

Not every community or region has an individual who conducts tag sales, so this may not be an option where you are. Still, if such a person does exist, her (it is usually a woman) fame is usually spread by word of mouth. A tag sale operator will inventory your furnishings, price them (calling in an appraiser if necessary), arrange them in the most attractive setting, publicize the sale, and run the operation on sale day, bringing in assistants. The charge to you can range from the operator's flat fee to a percentage—usually 25 percent—of the sale's income.

Auction. You can also call in an auctioneer. Here, too, as with a tag sale, the work is taken out of your hands. The auctioneer can be particularly helpful if you have objects that need appraising or if you have expensive collections that you do not want to keep. The fee can be a flat rate or a percentage of the day's sales. You might want to use an auctioneer if you have valuable art, china, or collectibles and want his or her services only for that collection. Check the Yellow Pages under both "Auction" and "Auctioneers."

Storage. Self-storage is another option. This may be the best choice if you want to get rid of goods for the moment, perhaps until you decide what you really need in the new place.

You have seen one-story self-storage complexes along major highways; the number of these facilities has grown over the last couple of decades. They appear to have replaced, in number and in popularity, the old, several-story-high warehouses in inner cities.

If you have not heard of self-storage, it works like this: You rent space on a month-to-month basis in structures like those one-story

INFORMATION

Did you know some people have *lived* in their self-storage unit? Storage-facility management frowns on that use for a cubicle, though. Others use their space as an office or practice studio. That's pretty much okay, if renters adhere to facility rules and regulations.

complexes or, in a city, multistory buildings. Space is broken down to a few dozen or a few hundred cubicles. Rates vary according to the section of the country and the size of the unit you choose to rent. Broadly speaking, you can lease a small five-by-five-foot cubicle for around $40 a month, a ten-by-ten foot for around $75 a month. Some units are quite large—twenty-four by twenty-six feet, for example—and rent for several hundred dollars a month. Check the insurance the facilities offer, and look to see if what you are placing there is covered by your home owners or renter's insurance policy.

In some buildings you will have twenty-four-hour access to your belongings; in other facilities there are set hours when you can visit. Just about anything except hazardous and combustible materials can be stored, and most facilities understandably frown on food kept in cubicles.

Besides furniture, you can store seasonal sports gear, holiday decorations, luggage, porch and patio furniture, and those cartons of miscellany we all acquire. Boats, recreation vehicles (RVs), and extra cars can be stored as well. Newer units are climate controlled, so there is no need to worry about dampness or mold.

Modern self-storage space in the suburbs offers the bonus of being able to drive right up to your cubicle for easy loading and unloading. In cities self-storage is still likely to be in those old multistory warehouse buildings. Old-fashioned warehouses are still around, used principally by people storing estate furnishings or by those going abroad and needing to store a whole household.

Select a Mover

Since you are selling a house (or a condo or co-op), you will be moving at least four rooms of furniture. That's more than a studio apartment, and will probably call for professional movers. You may also be long past the days of asking a few friends for help, renting a truck, and treating them to pizza and beer afterward. You have a couple of choices here.

- You can still rent a truck, but this time one that comes with two or three or more workers. They may charge $50 to $100 an hour, depending on where you live. This can be quite a

TIP

One national relocation specialist suggests using professionals if you are moving more than six rooms of furniture and more than two appliances (refrigerator, washing machine, etc.), or if your household goods are worth more than $50,000.

bargain if you are not moving an eight-room house across three states. But note that the fellows are not likely to supply you with cartons or bubble wrap or any other niceties.

- You can rent a van and drive it with some friends. Here you can expect to pay, again depending on a number of factors, about $100 a day; add maybe another $75 to $100 for insurance. These trucks come in a variety of sizes and are rented by national companies such as U-Haul, Ryder, and Budget. Check your Yellow Pages under "Movers."
- If you are moving a sizable household, you will probably call a moving company. Before you pick up the phone, understand that (1) moving can be *very* expensive and (2) the field has its share of charlatans. You want to be careful you do not end up with an overinflated estimate, or that your movers don't drop every box marked "fragile," or that you experience the worst moving nightmare—the company that just never shows up!

Which Company? You have quite a choice. There are local movers and large nationwide companies. Of course you will want to check any mover you seriously consider with your local consumer protection agency.

Try to get estimates from three movers. When you call, a representative from that carrier will come to your house to look over what you plan to take with you and give you an estimate. For short, intrastate (within the state) moves of under forty miles or so, the estimate can be an hourly rate or one based on cubic footage of the goods. The charge for interstate moves (from one state to another) is based on the weight of the goods and the distance the movers will travel. To be really smart, have all your goods inventoried before the estimators pull up.

The Estimate. Some companies will offer you a binding estimate, which means that "estimate" is really the cost you will be charged. With others the estimate is just that, and the final charge can—and probably will—be higher. If you are given three binding estimates, the choice then is a personal one, unless one mover offers more auxiliary services than another—some free cartons, for example, or packing paper.

It's important to give each mover exactly the same information about what is going and what is staying behind, so you can accurately evaluate the estimates you are given. Change your mind from Mover A to Mover B, with a totally different story for Mover C, and you will only confuse yourself and add more expense to the move.

TIP

If you can, try to move in the off-season for this business. Most movers offer a better price then, so be sure to ask for that consideration. Also, midweek is slower for them than weekends.

But what if you get two binding estimates and one nonbinding one? Sometimes the binding estimates are higher, just because they *are* binding. The nonbinding one may be a better deal for you if it is lower and if you are sure you have told the mover everything that will be going along. Keep in mind, if on moving day you add a few more items, especially heavy ones, to a binding estimate, that may throw the movers for a loop, causing delays, more paperwork, and additional charges. In that case a nonbinding quote becomes the better deal.

The Importance of Timing. Moving companies are busiest from April through October, with business peaking between June and September. You guessed right if you think that is because so many families move after their children have finished the school year and before they enroll in a new school.

Movers do overbook during their peak season to make up for slow time during the remainder of the year. That can leave you cooling your heels and waiting for a van at one end or the other some nice, humid July afternoon. When you look over and sign the company's documents, remember that *oral promises on pickup and delivery dates mean nothing.* Get everything in writing. A growing number of carriers, especially the larger ones, offer payments for every day their trucks are late. If you must move during the peak season, try to give the carrier as much notice as possible; sixty days is not too much. And check back with the company a few weeks, and then again several days, before they are due, to reconfirm.

Liability. Moving companies are required to assume liability for the value of the goods they transport. However, there are different levels of liability. Make sure you know how much protection you are purchasing from the carrier you choose.

If you plan to transport valuables such as antiques and art, call those items to the attention of the mover to be sure of adequate coverage. Check your home owners insurance policy, too, to see if it, or any special endorsements to it, mentions coverage during a move.

If a dispute arises that cannot be settled between you and the mover, most companies require that you both submit to binding arbitration. That means you and the mover must go along with whatever decision the arbitrator reaches about your problem. The arbitrator's word is final. The mover will provide you with a booklet describing the arbitration procedure.

The Corporate Move

If your company is relocating you, they are likely to help you every step of the way, monetarily and with service. At the very least, they will pay for the move. By all means, ask. Relocating is expensive and is likely to cost you *something*, no matter how much of the tab the corporation picks up. But if you are worth transferring (and it is assumed that the company is asking you to move), then they should be willing to pick up the bulk of your expenses and contribute in any other way to an easy transition. That certainly includes paying a moving tab.

The Role of Relocation Companies

Relocation agencies can be as small as a one-person shop, or a fairly large private concern, or the arm of a real-estate agency. In fact, most large realty firms have a relocation office, although the size of that unit varies.

The relocation company's representative first talks to the transferee, at the request of his or her corporation, to learn about family needs in the new community—neighborhood, size and style of house, nearness to schools. Then, he or she will put the transferee in touch with real-estate agents in the new town. The relocation person spells out company benefits and policies regarding moves. He or she introduces the employee to the community—its cultural attractions, educational facilities, shops, and the like—and in general helps make the whole experience for the transferee run as smoothly as possible. The employee's corporation pays for all of this hand-holding.

Some companies immediately turn over the transferee to one of these concerns. In other cases, the services are provided in-house.

If your employer makes no mention of relocation services, ask if they are provided. If the answer is no and you are left to fend for yourself in a move (although maybe the company is paying for the expense of relocating), you should know that the larger relocation outfits work only through corporations. You cannot call them and

INFORMATION

If you are moving from one state to another, your moving company must have Federal Highway Administration authority for interstate moves. You can call that agency at (703) 280-4001 to confirm.

• • •

A new trend seen in relocation offices these days is the transferee who brings along an elderly parent or parent-in-law. More than one relocation specialist has been asked to find a house for the transferring family, plus an apartment for his mother, and another one for hers!

What Goes Along with You on Moving Day

There are some items you will need immediately after the move, with no time to wait for the moving van to deliver them. Pack them in a carton and take them with you in your car.

- ❏ Plastic bags
- ❏ Facial tissues
- ❏ Change of clothing
- ❏ Sleepwear
- ❏ Personal items (toothbrush, razor, etc.)
- ❏ Bed linens
- ❏ Towels
- ❏ A lamp or two
- ❏ Extension cords
- ❏ A few light bulbs
- ❏ Portable radio (optional)

Here are items you will need for your first few meals. These go in a separate carton, labeled so you can get to it easily.

- ❏ Disposable plates, cups, utensils
- ❏ Plastic or aluminum wrap
- ❏ Can opener
- ❏ Soap, sponges, detergent
- ❏ Pots and pans
- ❏ Paper towels

Don't forget food and water bowls for your pet, plus pet food, cat litter, a litter pan, and a few favorite toys. You might also want to bring some floppy disks for a computer project, a special plant, or any other items you would feel better having with you rather than with the movers.

Make Yourself at Home

Here are some tips to help you settle in as quickly as possible.

- Unpack the family records and arrange for automobile license and registration, if that is necessary. Get the kids registered in school, line up the doctor, dentist, hairdresser, health club, and so on. All of that will help you hit the ground running in your new community.

- National retail chains are almost everywhere. Stake out your favorites in your new locale, whether they're fast-food eateries, book or clothing stores, or record shops. You'll feel at home in those familiar surroundings.

- There might be a newcomer's club where you are. Check the daily newspaper for notices of their meetings. Join it for a quick way to meet people as new to town as you are. In the same vein, look into religious, sports, and professional groups you might join. Make an effort and join *something*. It's the only way not to feel lonely in a new town.

- If you are moving to a single-family development with an owners' association, or to a condominium, go to association meetings. Neighbors are potential good friends.

- Entertainment books are published for many cities and regions around the country. They are filled with coupons offering discounted restaurant meals and local attractions. The coupons will get you out and about. The books cost between $25 and $45, depending on locale. Call Entertainment Publications at (800) 445-4137 to see if there is one for your community.

Keeping Tabs on Your Mover

You can call the American Moving and Storage Association's membership department at (703) 683-7410 to see if the mover you are considering is a member, or if you want to confirm that a particular local company is an agent for a van line.

ask them to take you on as a client. That may not be true of small outfits, though. Check the Yellow Pages under "Relocation Services." By all means investigate through your local consumer protection agency any company you are thinking of engaging to help you. Ask the company or individual for references, and then call those people.

If you are picking up the tab, realize that costs will vary. A specialist may charge you a flat fee for one day's or two days' work, or an hourly fee or a package charge for however long it takes to see you settled in. Most spend ten to fourteen hours with a client.

One day soon you *will* be settled in. Your new neighborhood will be familiar to you. You will have switched back to thinking of your new place as a "home" and not a "house." Your job of selling will be over—and well done, too! Congratulations, and very best of luck in your new home!

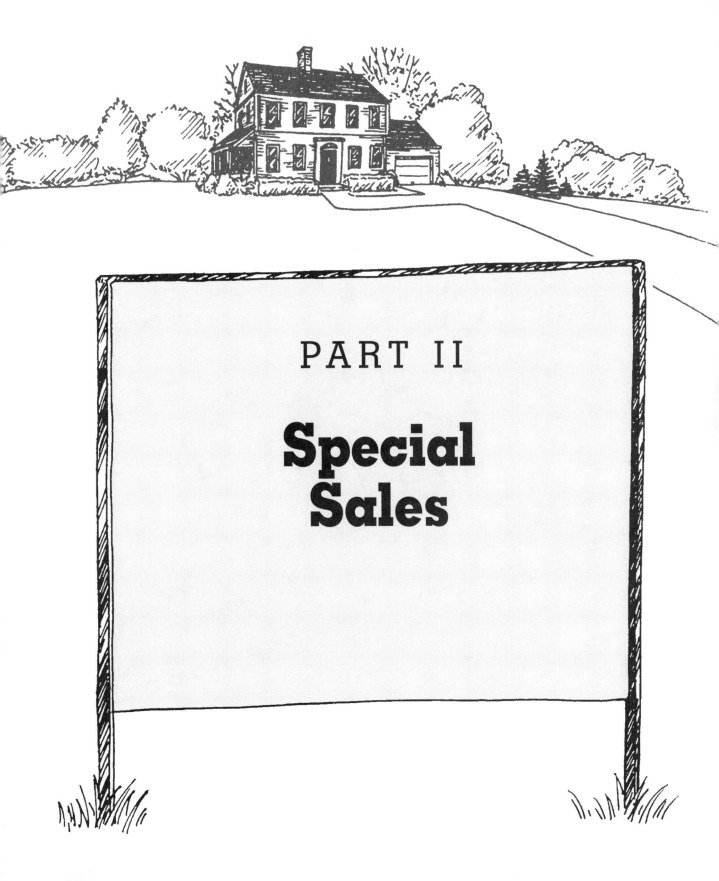

PART II

Special Sales

CHAPTER TWENTY-ONE

Selling a Condominium or Cooperative

If Your Condo Is Brand-New

If you are in a brand-new complex, with some apartments still unsold, you may be asked the following questions:

- *Does the developer still own any of these apartments?* The buyer is trying to determine how much influence the developer has on the running of the community. If he owns too many units, he may still be in charge. Even if he is just on the condo's board of directors, he may have too much influence.

- *How many condos have been sold, and at what point is the community turned over to the owners?* The smart shopper will want at least 75 percent of the apartments sold before she buys into that complex. If there are fewer than that, the community could turn out to be an unsuccessful project for the developer, perhaps leading to bankruptcy.

All of the preceding chapters can help you, if not every part of each chapter. But, as you well know, you do have special concerns when *you* decide to sell. First, let's look at a few areas where condo and co-op owners have something in common before we reach the fork in the road.

All Together Now . . .

Yes, it's still house, house, house instead of home, even though you are selling an apartment. "House" implies ownership, and space, to the apartment buyer. No doubt you have used the word yourself occasionally. Indeed, more than one apartment renter has referred to his or her place as "my house."

Actually, if you slip and say "home" when selling, you will be forgiven here. You want to convey that feel-good word too. It's "home" even in a condo complex of 300 almost exactly alike apartments.

The word you must avoid, however, when talking about your place is *unit*. That is a term used by lenders ("We don't issue loans in buildings of fewer than 12 units") and developers ("I'm putting up a 250-unit complex over on Route 42") and real-estate writers. It does not convey the impression you want to make on your would-be buyer. It's cold and impersonal and belongs to finance and construction, not to Sally and Joe Truehart selling the "home" that has meant so much to them to someone who will equally care for and enjoy it.

You Tell 'Em

If you have some time before taking the first steps to selling—and almost everyone has at least a few months—then take a look around your building or complex to see if anything needs to be done to the common areas that could make a more favorable impression on buyers. For example, has the board been planning to take down that dead tree just inside the entrance? Or repaper the lobby? Now is the time to begin campaigning—all right, *nagging*—to have that job done. Does your building have a doorman? Is he friendly? Is his uniform clean? Will he make a good first impression on a would-be buyer?

Questions Condo Buyers Are Likely to Ask

You'd be wise to have answers ready for these queries:

- *How old is this complex?*
- *What is the percentage of owners and renters?* If there are more than 25 percent who are renters, your buyer might have a problem securing a mortgage. Lenders think that a rental figure over 25 percent could have a negative effect on the appearance, and therefore value, of the community.
- *How is this property managed?* Most condo communities have professional property managers who supervise the handling of the common areas.
- *What are the monthly mainte- nance fees? Will they be going up soon?* Tell buyers. They may go on to talk with a board member or delve into the com- munity's financial documents and read for themselves.
- *Are there any unusual by-laws or CC&Rs (covenants, conditions, and restrictions)?* Your real-estate

agent should have copies of these to give to buyers. If you are asked this question, hand the prospect one of your copies. Don't apologize for a laundry list of restrictions. That can be evi- dence of a well-run complex.
- *Is there a reserve fund?* Buyers will want to feel that there are some savings in the event of an emergency repair or replace- ment, or perhaps the need to pay a lawyer's fee. They don't want to be hit up for money right away if something goes wrong.
- *What's the noise level around here?* Noise is the condo owner's number-one com- plaint. Inside your apartment, he may ask you to help him check the soundproofing between rooms.
- *Do I have to pay extra for using the pool and the clubhouse?* You need to explain whether use of amenities comes with your maintenance fee or is a sepa- rate charge.

You want your house to look good, and in a communal situation, that means the common areas too. Remember, your buyer is also purchasing the grounds and the lobby, and although you do not have control over them, it's important that you do your best to see that those spaces look as good as they can.

Why Not Rent?

Here is a thought. Apartments are often easier to rent than houses and bring special benefits to the owner-landlord. Have you considered renting your condo or co-op after you move on? You might be able to take out a loan against the equity in your place for the down-payment on the new house. You will enjoy the tax advantages that go with having an investment property, and can watch its continuing appreciation with pleasure, too.

Perhaps you are selling in a bad market. Maybe you are in a condominium complex where eleven apartments are for sale; yours makes twelve. *And* a brand-new community of who-knows-how-many units is going up right next door to you. The competition for buyers is fierce. Renting might buy you time until you can sell at, or close to, the price you want. Maybe even after the market improves, you will elect to keep that apartment as an investment.

Naturally, you will want to talk to your financial adviser about the wisdom of this move in your particular situation. Also, renting a condo, and especially a co-op, depends on whether your by-laws allow long-term tenants. Some boards will forbid extended renting, some may say yes and charge a special fee, while others will just up your monthly maintenance fee. If you are moving some distance away, you can hire a management company to look after the place for you.

Disclosure

You read all about this topic in chapter 11. Here's a poser for you: If you know your building or complex is going to be hit with a large assessment to pay for a much-needed repair or replacement, and you want to bail out before you have to pay your share of that assessment or higher maintenance fee, do you have to tell prospective buyers about what's down the road?

Most contracts of sale contain a clause addressing the status of maintenance charges, assessments, and taxes. (Maybe you purchased your present home some years ago and this comes as news to you.) The clause reads to the effect that the seller has not been notified of any upcoming increases in charges. So if a seller knew that maintenance fees were going up and did not inform the buyer, the buyer would have a legal claim against the seller for failure to disclose that important fact.

On the other hand, most contracts of sale have a clause that says the purchaser has examined all by-laws and financial statements and does not rely on any representations made by any broker or by the seller as to those matters. The buyer has seen for himself or herself. Also, most boards allow serious would-be buyers access to all financial statements and even to minutes of the board meeting.

These facts still might not let you off the hook in the situation where you've heard through the grapevine that a change is on the way, but have not been officially notified. Ask your real-estate agent and attorney about any disclosure questions you have. Some should-you-tell points fall squarely in that huge gray area of "maybe." You will no doubt want a lawyer when selling a property with the mountain of paperwork condos and co-ops bring.

Inspection: More than Meets the Eye

Whether you go with a house inspection of your apartment or not—and you might want to, especially in the older building, which is usually the co-op—you ought to ask a house inspector to look at the common areas where you live. That means checking out the major heating, plumbing, and electrical facilities and the roof in a high-rise building.

Your buyer might still have his or her inspector do that, but you will want to know ahead of time if there are any serious problems. That can mean maintenance fees will be rising, which could affect your asking price and the amount you finally accept for that apartment.

TIP

Make sure the inspector you hire is familiar with this type of work. You don't want someone whose experience is strictly with single-family houses.

S-P-A-C-E

If sellers of eleven-room center-hall colonials must straighten up their houses to give the illusion of space, condo and co-op dwellers must be doubly diligent in doing so. Even the teeniest hint that your apartment is too small will send a prospect running to another community.

Be sure that the entry into your apartment is as clear and as roomy as possible. That will be the first impression prospects have of your apartment. That means putting the bicycles you keep just inside the door somewhere else, and maybe even getting rid of the hall table that you've been using until you find something better, but which is really too large for the space.

If you can't get rid of extras and no-longer-needed furnishings and clothing in the usual way—charities or a gate or lobby sale—then consider renting a self-storage unit (see chapter 20). Jammed, packed closets in an apartment shriek, "This place is *small;* all your stuff will never fit in here."

Don't consider cramming the spillover from your apartment into your storage locker in the basement or elsewhere on the premises while your place is on the market. Buyers are entitled to see that, too. Your locker should be clean, neatly organized, and only about three-quarters full. You want buyers to see that there's plenty of space—in fact, you aren't even using all that's available!

Little Things Mean a Lot

You may wash your windows frequently if you live in a garden-complex condo community. But if you are in a multistory building, and you live above the ground floor, you very likely do not, or may never have. And it doesn't bother you either. But it will bother a buyer, so spend the money to have the windows washed professionally.

In a small space, which is what your apartment might be when compared to a typical house, everything must be especially neat. Leave a tissue on the floor and it stands out. So make sure your place always looks good—beds made, carpets vacuumed, and clutter put away.

If your apartment has poor natural light, turn on the lamps when you leave for work in the morning, in case an agent brings a buyer through during the day. To lighten up a dark space while your place is on the market, replace heavy draperies at the windows with inexpensive sheers.

Advertising

This can be difficult for both the condo and the co-op seller. It's hard to put a For Sale sign in front of your co-op apartment on the eighth floor!

Most co-op sales are handled through real-estate agents because they are more complex than condos, which are just like single-family houses in terms of ownership. Selling shares in a corporation, which is what the co-op apartment owner is doing, takes even more paperwork than the condo, so the knowledge of professionals is welcome. There is also the co-op board of directors (more about them on pages 245). And since virtually all co-ops are in multifamily buildings, with no opportunity for drive-by house hunters to notice an apartment for sale, it takes a pro to get the word out.

If you are in a condo garden-apartment complex, you may find that signs in front of apartments for sale must conform to a certain size and look. That size is very small indeed—maybe seven-by-ten inches or so compared to a regular For Sale sign of about

Some "lookers" will be moving down from a house to an apartment, and are likely to be *very* concerned about space in a condo or co-op home. That's another reason for showing closets and a locker that appear roomy.

twenty-by-thirty inches. It is more difficult for a buyer driving by to see these signs than it would be to see the usual For Sale signs. However, small signs are better than no signs.

For Condo Sellers

Don't forget to note for buyers any fees that go with amenities at your complex, such as clubhouse dues or golfing fees.

If you live in a complex with quite a few apartments for sale, or if you are in an area that is overbuilt with condos, you may have a tough time selling, or at least at the price you want. Gather together as much ammunition as you can. Chapters 14 and 18 offer tips about extras you can offer buyers, whether selling on your own or with a broker.

Here are a couple of suggestions especially for those in communal living situations.

- To give prospects an idea of what life will be like for them at Whispering Hills, you might pick up a few copies of the community's newsletter to pass out to serious lookers. (Try to pick issues that do not mention complaints or problems!) If you have a clubhouse and some pictures of pool parties there, get some copies made. Maybe there is a newspaper clipping you've filed away about a charity golf tournament on the course that's part of your community. Copy that, too. You can put together a little packet for buyers that contains the newsletter and photos and anything else that will help a prospective resident imagine living in your place, which looks so friendly and lively.
- If you are in an older building or complex, or one with no amenities, you are likely to attract a single person with just one income to contribute to home owning, or a couple buying their first home. Here you stress the affordability of your apartment, and how home ownership is within easy reach of that prospective buyer.

For Co-op Sellers

Buyers here will want to see documents that also include a mortgage, if there is one on the building. Or maybe there is more than one. How about a lawsuit? Is the building undergoing that?

As you recall when you first moved into your apartment, you had to be approved for residency by the cooperative board of directors. (Perhaps this never happened to you because you bought your apartment when the building was converted from rental status. Good for you! You probably bought at a reduced price and stand to make a nice profit, all things being equal.) A nerve-wracking experience, wasn't it? Now your buyer must be approved as well. That approval will be one of the contingencies in the sales contract. If approval is denied, the contract is canceled and the earnest money is returned to the would-be buyer.

These days it is hard to gauge who will and will not be accepted by the board. Some boards will refuse all applicants who need financing for their apartment. Some will find a prospect's finances too meager, and worry that he or she will not be able to afford an assessment should one come along soon or somewhere in the future. Discrimination is still present in cooperative buildings. Because the co-op is a private corporation, it can pretty much decide who it wants to belong. If your would-be buyer is a rock star or an ex-president, you'd better forget about selling. Members of other groups often do not make the cut either.

Discrimination seems to be easing just a bit, at least in some buildings and in some areas. A good deal depends on where you are selling your apartment. The fanciest addresses are still the most "discriminating." Other buildings and boards care only about money and whether the buyer has fairly deep pockets and is not likely to make noise. These considerations are beginning to override social prejudice.

If the owner of a house needs to do a good bit of preparatory work in getting his or her place ready for sale, the condo or co-op seller must do even more. Communal living adds just that much more paperwork—and, for you, homework—to this project. Do your homework well, however, and your gold star will be the successful sale of your apartment!

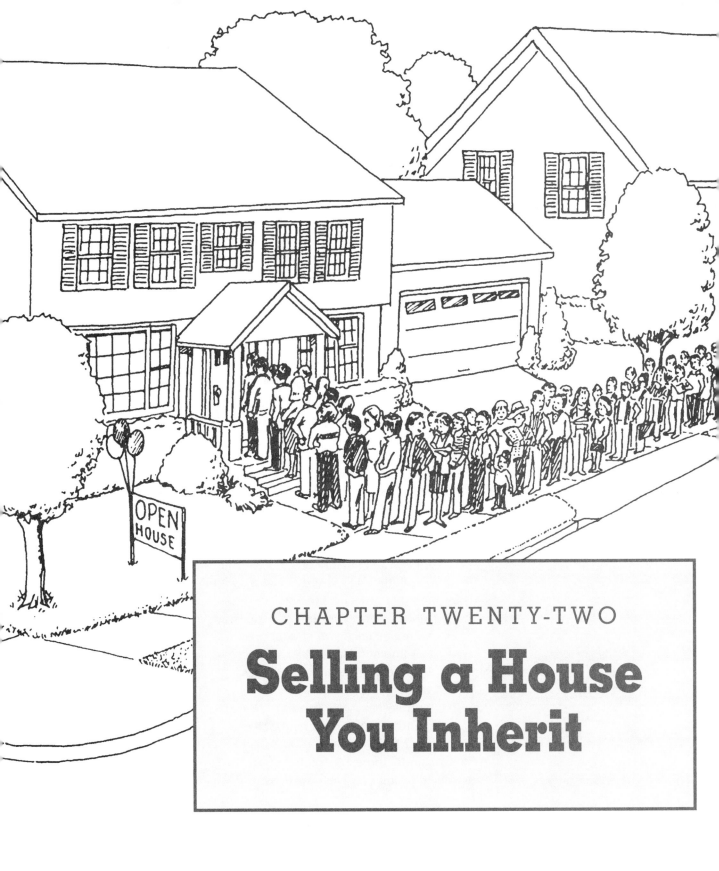

CHAPTER TWENTY-TWO

Selling a House You Inherit

INFORMATION

A person who inherits a co-op apartment may not be allowed to live there! That individual may have to be interviewed by the co-op board as someone seeking to purchase. If the board does not think that the beneficiary can afford maintenance fees and special assessments that might arise, there is no acceptance.

• • •

You must have a power of attorney, or guardianship, to sell an ailing relative's or friend's house, and the document must be worded so there is no question of your legal ability to sell that property.

Mrs. Elder died at the age of seventy-nine in her house in Peaceful Valley where she had lived for forty-one years. She had been alone since the death of her husband some fourteen years earlier. The couple had raised three children there—Rosemary, Kate, and Steve. Friends and neighbors looked in on Mrs. Elder frequently. Although she suffered from a variety of ailments, she had been determined to remain on her own as long as she could. Her children lived not too far from "home" and visited often. The three inherited their mother's house on her death and, not surprisingly, decided to sell it.

The "How" of Estate Sales

Houses that are small estate sales and that belonged to seniors can be very difficult to sell. For any number of reasons they are often not kept up, from the mailbox at the curb to the front lawn to the rooms inside. Furnishings are old and do not, in real-estate parlance, "show well." Appliances are outdated. Paint or wallpaper has faded. Because the elderly are often cold, windows are rarely thrown open and the houses retain a musty odor. Most of all, they are crowded, jammed with mementos of years past, items their owners treasured. To buyers it can be disconcerting to walk into these houses, knowing that the owner has died, and everything is just as he or she left it two weeks or two months ago. Too often the property is not at all appealing.

So it was with Mrs. Elder's house. Although her children came over to visit, their lives were also busy, with their families and their jobs, and there was little time for redecorating Mom's place. Besides, every time they mentioned taking on one renovation project or another, Mrs. Elder would say "Oh, don't bother. I don't want the fuss and the muss." Kate cleaned each week, and Rosemary shopped for her mother and took her on errands. Steve helped her with her finances and paid for a man to come and cut the grass during the summer. There were bare

patches in the lawn, though, and the shrubbery needed pruning. It wasn't terrible looking, just not as spiffy as it would have been had Mrs. Elder been a typical seller who spent time fixing up her place before putting it on the market.

Mrs. Elder's house was neither overpriced nor undesirable, but it didn't sell. After three months the listing expired. Rosemary, Kate, and Steve talked together over the phone, and then Rosemary spoke in person to the real-estate agent. They were despondent. They did not want to rent the property and they did not want to sell below market value, but they were worried about the furniture and belongings that had been left in the house so that it would not appear empty.

It is true, as you have read, that generally houses sell better when they are being lived in. But that was the problem here. Mrs. Elder's house wasn't being lived in!

The real-estate agent made some radical suggestions. Remove all the furniture and invest some money in remodeling and redecorating. Then list the house again at a higher price.

Mrs. Elder's children, their spouses, and their children rolled up their sleeves. They put new self-stick floor tiles in the kitchen. They pulled out the old metal cabinets and replaced them with wooden units ordered from a major catalog house at a sale price. They had new countertops installed, and they replaced the old stove with a new double-oven model. They cut back the hedges that were blocking light from the living room windows, and then washed all the windows in the house. They repainted the ceilings and trim. The yellowed surfaces took on a new brightness and the whole atmosphere seemed lighter.

But they didn't stop there. They discovered a paint store that carried discontinued wallpaper patterns at prices that were one-half to one-third of the original list price, and they repapered with patterns and colors that were widely acceptable. Finally, they pulled up the worn carpet and had the hardwood floors sanded and stained.

All of that work took them two months. Then they relisted the house at $7,000 higher than previously. Within three weeks the property was sold at a negotiated figure just $1,500 below the new asking price.

Getting a Loved One's Papers Together

To sell successfully you will need some papers from your relative's files. Some of these documents—proof of special insurance coverage, for example—can also be a selling point for buyers. Here is what you want.

- The deed to the property
- If there is a mortgage, those papers and the payment coupon book
- A copy of the property tax bill
- A year of utility bills
- Home-owners insurance statement and proof of payment
- Proof of any other special coverage, such as flood insurance or windstorm protection
- Any warranties—home owners, appliance, or mechanical systems

TIP

If you can, look through your loved one's files or checkbook to see what service people he or she used. They can help you with any needed repairs. This can be particularly helpful if you don't live in the area.

• • •

Save the receipts for whatever you have purchased to fix up the house, especially if there is more than one person involved in inheriting the house and you all plan to divide the expenses.

Not every estate sale needs this kind of makeover, but if a house that you have inherited, or that you are handling for a hospitalized loved one who is not going to return home, is not selling, consider removing the furniture and giving it a face-lift.

If it is a house you have visited often, or which is frozen in your memory in a certain state, perhaps when you were a child or even an adult, then you may not see it as it really is: a problem property. To give it a face-lift, you should take the house *off* the market. When a house sits too long with a For Sale sign out front, it becomes bogged down. The listing has been around the real-estate office too much, and it gets a reputation as a "dog." Once this idea takes hold, it's very hard to arouse any enthusiasm among buyers or agents.

When the house has been redecorated and all the improvements have been completed, relist at a higher price and note in prominent print on the listing sheet that the property has been modernized, redecorated, refurbished, or whatever appropriate descriptive terms you can come up with to denote *new and improved*. This will stimulate new interest among agents, and it is the agents whom you must interest in order to have the property shown more often and with more enthusiasm.

You do have a choice here. You can leave the house as you found it and save yourself the trouble, selling it more or less "as is." But if you employ the more detailed strategy, then in exchange for your effort you are likely to make a profit—and sell it faster.

Negotiating

After the Elder heirs refurbished the house, they listed it at $123,500. The opening bid of the buyers came by phone.

"Rosemary," said the agent, "This is Ann Jones of Helpful Realty. We have an offer on your property on Oak Street for $111,000."

"That's much too low," Rosemary said. "it's below market value and we have to cover the costs of remodeling, you know."

"Will you make a counteroffer?" asked Mrs. Jones.

"I don't think so at that price. Those buyers can't really be serious. It isn't even worth discussing with my brother and sister."

When a first offer is very low, some agents present it by phone. This is generally considered poor real-estate practice, but it is done more often than most professionals would like to admit. When a phone offer is made, the agent is supposed to have a signed offer form and an earnest money check in his or her possession. You can ask to see these if you wish; you can simply refuse to counter until the bid is more "realistic"; or you can counter with a figure very close to your original asking price.

Ann Jones called back within the hour to make an appointment to see the three Elder heirs together that evening. She presented an earnest money check for $1,000 and a signed offer form for $117,500.

The house had been back on the market for less than three weeks and the Elder heirs felt that they could get their full asking price. They told Ann Jones they would wait until they could get $123,500.

Ann returned the following evening. She explained that her buyers were from out of state. The husband had been transferred into the area on a three- to five-year assignment and would be returning to the Northeast at the end of that term. They did not want to go higher on the price of a house, because they wanted to have the cash to do some traveling in this part of the country.

The Elders repeated that they felt they could get $123,500 for the house. The agent agreed with them, but she had a suggestion. Since none of the Elder heirs needed the cash from the equity in Mrs. Elder's house to buy another house, why not consider taking back a second mortgage for the $6,000 difference in price? The loan to the buyers could be written at an interest rate of 8.5 percent, with the entire principal due in five years or whenever the property was sold.

This suggestion seemed to solve everyone's problem. The Elder heirs guaranteed themselves a small extra income in annual interest payments (they opted for payments just once a year, but seller and buyer could have agreed on monthly or quarterly checks). The buyers postponed paying that $6,000 extra for the house until it was sold, three to five years' worth of inflation later. It was a deal that made everyone happy.

If the house you are selling still has a mortgage, don't forget to keep up those payments. It could take several months to sell the property and you don't want to flirt with foreclosure!

TIP

If you are a sole heir, you *can* sell a house from a distance. It's wise, though, to make at least one trip to see the house so you can decide what needs to be done, work out a sale price, and sign with a real-estate agent. The rest of the transaction can be handled by phone, mail, fax, e-mail, and a proxy for you at the closing.

Do You Have the Authority to Sell?

Can the Elder siblings simply walk into a real-estate office and tell an agent they want to sell the house of their late mother? No. Usually the executor for the estate passes along the authority for the heirs to sell a house, acknowledging that they are now its legitimate owners. If you inherit real estate, you will want to check this with your loved one's attorney to see how you actually take over ownership of that property.

Fortunately, Mrs. Elder died *testate*, or with a valid will, naming Rosemary, Kate, and Steve her beneficiaries. There was no question who would inherit the house. If she had died *intestate*, or with no valid will, the situation would have been more complicated. No doubt her three children still would have inherited, but Mrs. Elder's estate would have had to pass through probate court to determine her legitimate heirs. (Legally, the term *heir* is used when inheriting an intestate estate, *beneficiary* when inheriting from a legitimate will. However, both words are often used interchangeably in common usage.)

There are ways to avoid probate. For instance, an estate can be held in a trust. A life insurance policy naming a beneficiary also skirts probate. Once you become embroiled in the ABCs of your relative's will and the house you inherited, you will learn a good deal about probate and estate law!

An Auction

Sometimes if an inherited property is located far away from the heirs and they cannot spare the time to oversee its sale through regular channels, an auction becomes a viable choice. Let's get this property sold in a day! they say. And that's indeed what can happen with an auction.

These days, auctioning a house is not necessarily a measure of desperation. A voluntary auction is not the same as a foreclosure auction. The auctioneer invites bids but is not required to accept them. There is usually a floor bid for starters, and the sellers usually reserve the right to accept or reject the top bid.

Since an auction audience is almost invariably seeking a bargain, few top bids approach fair market value, and sometimes there are

DEFINITION PLEASE

no bids at all. For the house seller, an auction probably will not bring a good selling price, and indeed may not get the house sold at all. Still, there is always the chance that several buyers will find the house especially attractive, and will bid up the price to a respectable figure.

If you are interested in this route to a sale, and just want to get an unexpected property off your hands, contact an auctioneer. Check the Yellow Pages for "Auction" or "Auctioneer." Look for someone who is a member of the National Auctioneers Association, the professional organization for this specialty. Here are some questions to ask of the man or woman you are considering engaging.

- *Have you auctioned houses before?* Naturally you do not want to sign with someone whose specialty is antiques or cattle.
- *What is your fee?* Is it a percentage of the sale price or a flat fee? How does this compare with a real-estate agent's fee? It is up to you to decide whether you will be paying too much to try to sell quickly. And what if the house doesn't sell? Is the auctioneer's fee the same?
- *Will you explain the auction procedure to me?* You want to know about the type of auction that will be held. Will buyers raise a paddle to enter a bid, or raise their hands or what? At what point do you pay the auctioneer? After the sale? After you have received the money for your house?
- *How will you publicize the auction?* Naturally, you want as many people to attend as possible, so look for newspaper advertising by the auctioneer, plus other draws, including a brochure or "kit" showing the place.
- *Will there be a preview showing of the house before the auction?* You'll likely be told there will be, probably a few days during the week before the sale. Buyers will want to know what exactly they are bidding on, and some even bring a house inspector with them to the preview so they know how to gauge their bid.
- *How is financing handled?* Buyers are often told in the auction instructions, in the brochure or kit, that if they want to bid they must bring a money order or cashier's check in a

Probate is defined as a state court procedure that administers the estate of a deceased resident, whether that individual died with a will or without one. This administration is conducted in **probate court**.

certain amount They are then given a certain amount of time to secure a mortgage. Back-up bidders' names are taken in the event the winning bidder cannot secure satisfactory financing.

Ask any questions that pertain to your own particular situation and your part of the country. Auctioneers have their own style for conducting house auctions.

Renting the House

Perhaps you do not want to sell the house you inherit, or cannot sell it (some suggestions in chapter 14 might help you there). You opt instead to go with renting, maybe just until the real-estate market picks up where you are, or maybe with no particular deadline in mind.

If you find your house in the same condition as Mrs. Elder's, you will certainly want to make some improvements before you start looking for tenants. Here are some other points you'll want to give thought to if becoming a landlord will be new to you.

- If you live quite a few miles away from the house and town, can you be a good long-distance landlord? Is there anyone in that community you know, or your loved one knew, who can look in on the place if a problem develops?
- You will have to acquaint yourself with rental laws in that town—if and when you can increase the rent, what your rights and responsibilities are, and so on. Check this with city hall.
- Reading the classified advertisements in the local paper should give you an idea of what rents are being charged in your particular part of town and for what type of

property. Interestingly, it is sometimes more profitable for the landlord to rent an apartment than a house. A house will only rent for so much, given the part of town, amenities, and so forth. That does not always bring a rent high enough to cover mortgage payments, property taxes, lawn care, and repairs. A two-family house that could be practically the same size as the one-family can net an owner more.

- Speaking of two-family, would the house you inherited lend itself easily and attractively to conversion to two full living units (a living unit contains a kitchen and full bath)? Would you be allowed to undertake a conversion according to zoning regulations for that neighborhood? If you're game and the town says okay, and the house is in an area with a shortage of rental housing—a university town maybe—you could do very well indeed, between rents and tax advantages, with what would then become a real-estate investment.

- You can try to rent it yourself, or let a real-estate agency do it for you. (Some agencies do not bother with rentals; others do, but only as a sideline, hoping eventually to get that house listed for sale by their office.) If you go with a realty office, because you live too far away or you just don't want to select tenants yourself, be sure that the agent checks that prospect's references—*all of them*. That includes current job and salary, credit report, and previous landlord. (Realize, though, that a landlord may give a problem tenant a wonderful reference, just to get rid of him or her.)

- Keep in mind anti-discrimination laws. You could face a lawsuit by a would-be tenant who is the recipient of that bias.

Ownership Styles for the House You Want To Keep

Whatever you plan for the house you inherited, you will need to give some thought to the style of ownership you want, just as you would if you went out and purchased any other property. You have some choices. A "fee simple" title means that you own a particular piece

> ## DEFINITION PLEASE
>
> ***Tenants,*** as used in the ownership styles discussed in these paragraphs, means owners, not renters. More commonly, of course, the term "tenants" refers to those who lease real property.

TIP

If you are married and want to keep inherited property rather than sell it, you would be wise to check with your accountant. There are also tax issues that in some cases make ownership as "tenants in common" the better way for married couples who own real estate, even when there are no children from a former union involved.

of property. This title can be held by one person or more than one. There are three basic ways for more than one person to hold title.

1. With "joint tenants with right of survivorship," each owner owns the entire property. When one of those joint owners dies, the deceased owner's interest in the house is automatically transferred to the surviving owner or owners. It does not require any mention in a will, and does not go through probate. Married couples often own property this way.

2. "Tenancy by the entirety" is just for husbands and wives and is only for a primary residence. It is a form of joint tenancy with right of survivorship.

3. Then there is "tenants in common." This is how friends or relatives buying a house together, or unmarried individuals in a relationship usually buy property. This means each owner owns a specific percentage of the property, sometimes in equal shares with the other(s) and sometimes not. Owners can leave their share to anyone they choose. A beneficiary does not have to be one or all of the other owners. Some married couples own real estate this way when they want to leave property to children from a former union.

Mrs. Elder's heirs will probably own their mother's house as "tenants in common." That way each can leave his or her share to a spouse and/or children. On the other hand, they could choose to own this particular property as "joint tenants." As such, at death each person's share reverts automatically to the other sibling(s). A house is a sizable inheritance and you will want to seek advice on how to retain as many financial benefits as possible from that good fortune.

Next comes selling a second home, a happier transaction. Or did you inherit a vacation house? Then this chapter and the next one will come in handy.

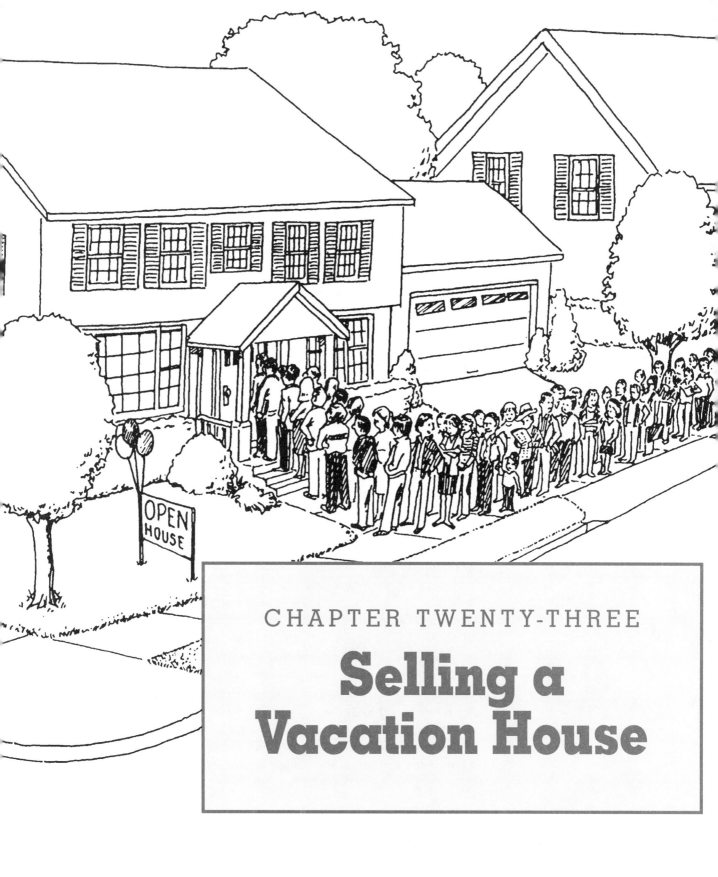

CHAPTER TWENTY-THREE

Selling a Vacation House

Yes, you are thinking "house" rather than "home" during the selling process. But "second home" (and to a lesser degree "vacation home") is common usage for this type of realty transaction. So "second home" will be used often in this chapter.

Y ou and your spouse bought that little lakeside bungalow just after you had Billy. Billy is now six and was followed by Melanie, four and Jason, now six months. The bungalow is too small, so you are looking for something else in that resort community, a house that will give all of you room to stretch. *Or* . . .

You are tired of the lake. Your tastes have changed. You are all skiers now. You want to head for the mountains and a tidy little chalet that can become your *new* second home base. *Or* . . .

You are single and seem to be working harder than ever. Your getaway cabin near that charming historic village is empty most of the time. Allowing family and friends to use it has become a scheduling nightmare, although you generously continue to hand over the keys as often as you can. Enough of this, you sigh with fatigue.

Whatever your reason, you want to sell the vacation house that was once the getaway of your dreams. Oh well, the next one, either now or a few years down the road, will be the *new* second home of your dreams!

How does this work, anyway? How do you sell a house that might be 75 miles away—or 2,000 miles from "home."

You do it very carefully. Just because the house is out of sight does not make it any less important and less deserving of as much time as you can spare for it as your primary house. Selling well, remember, translates into money in your pocket.

Get Going, and Sell!

It is interesting that financial planners say many folks hold on to their vacation properties long after they stop using them. One reason is "status." It sounds nice to be able to say, "Well, when we were at our beach house . . ." or "Yeah, we take a few weeks in the winter to ski. We have a little place at Park City." Others fail to sell because they think it will look to those who know them as if they have fallen on hard times, and the vacation home is the first step in cutting back. Some don't sell simply because of inertia. If they do not use the house much, or at all, well, it's still there, isn't it? You don't have to actually *do* anything about it. At least not right now. And some second-home owners hang in there long after it is practical to do so because the house has such happy memories for them.

All of these owners are making a mistake. By selling when you no longer use or want your second home, you free up some money for other uses, perhaps more pertinent to your current lifestyle. You may want the money to start a business, educate a child, buy a larger primary home or, yes, buy another second home, this time in a more inviting community or housing style, one that you will use and enjoy often.

You might want to consider this as well: It would be smart to sell if you see prices in your vacation community dropping by more than a routine fluctuation. Maybe storms in the area have caused growing beach erosion that is threatening your community. City fathers have held meetings on the issue and are uncertain of a solution. Whatever it is likely to be, it will cost home owners money, probably lots of it. Too, would-be buyers are likely to wonder at the wisdom of an investment there.

If you see a slew of condominium communities either already under construction or on the drawing board, you might want to sell your condo before the new ones are built, glutting the market and making yours more difficult to sell alongside the shiny new models those developments have to offer. If overbuilding in general is looming, and is likely to put a strain on existing facilities—sewers, schools, police department, etc.—and lead to higher taxes for that expansion, you might want to beat it out of that resort before the new tax bills are handed out.

How will you know if bad news is coming up, or has already arrived? You'd be wise to protect your investment by reading the local paper in your vacation community. That might mean a subscription sent to your year-round house in the months you are not holidaying. That way you will know what's happening and be able to plan your selling strategy, rather than arrive in town one day for vacation and hear the bad news.

INFORMATION

A bit of trivia: The first house built for summer use only in this country was in New Hampshire. It was constructed in 1769 for John Wentworth, the last royal governor of that state. It stood on 4,000 acres in Wolfeboro, on the shores of Lake Wentworth. (*Source: The Old Farmer's Almanac.*)

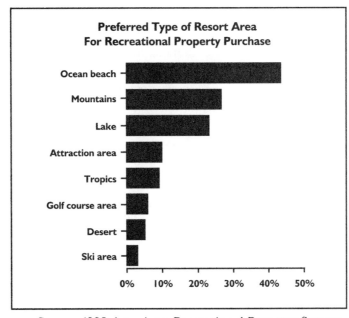

**Preferred Type of Resort Area
For Recreational Property Purchase**

Source: 1999 American Recreational Property Survey,
American Resort Development Association.

Selling by the Season

You read in chapter 3 how seasons and specific months can affect a house sale. They can affect a vacation home as well, just in different seasons and different months.

Do you think right now that you would like to have one last stay at your second home during the "high" season there? Try not to if you are serious about selling. The best time to sell a vacation property is a couple of months before the high season. If you live in a beach community, for example, would-be buyers will be looking in March, April, and May in order to buy and close on their new home in time to enjoy summer there. That is the best time to have your home spruced up and ready to sell.

The next best time to sell is the high season itself, when you will have a sizable pool of potential buyers, between other owners like yourself and the horde of tourists likely to visit. If you do not want to sell then because you will be there and do not want the nuisance of showing buyers through, you might want to rethink that stand. Folks living in, and obviously enjoying, a house make an attractive setting for buyers, one that is far more appealing than a dark, cold, deserted house shown off-season.

If you put your house on the market very much beyond the end of the season, you will likely have to settle for a lower price. If your beach house remains unsold through the winter months, it becomes a little dog-eared at your realty agent's office, or even in your own marketing if you're selling it yourself. By the time the next season rolls around, it looks downright tired to real-estate agents *and* to prospective buyers.

But let's say your house is in a ski community, at the foot of a mountain. As you know, winter resorts can be very appealing in the summer, too, even though that is technically the off-season there. What is lacking there, though, in the downtime is that large pool of possible buyers that hits town in the high season. To some extent, then, the foregoing in-season and out-of-season suggestions apply to you skiers, too, although not as much as to folks in beach communities.

Do you have a country house? Like the beach people, you probably consider summer the high season, with fall very attractive too. Unless there are resorts and winter sports or some major sightseeing attractions nearby, winter is off-season (selling a rural home buried under a foot of snow is certainly a challenge one would just as soon skip).

In your own community you probably know exactly which weeks are "hot" and which are dead as the proverbial doornail.

As you read all of this about seasons, you may find it seems vaguely familiar to you. You're right! You are being told to sell at the exact opposite time you were supposed to buy. Remember the admonition "Buy in the off-season, you'll get a better deal"? Well, that's why now you don't want to *sell* in the off-season.

Some Paperwork

You've heard the saying that preparation is 90 percent of the success of many jobs? That is true in selling a second home too. You are the only one who knows exactly how much your house has to offer any buyer, so it is up to you to call attention to its many pluses and those of the resort town as well.

INFORMATION

Florida is a case by itself in the high- and low-season definition. If you live in an area where the "snowbirds" come down for the winter months—that's likely to be roughly south of the line from Tampa east to Orlando and continuing east to around Melbourne—that's your high season. Some snowbirds do winter in other parts of the state, however. You will know about your community's strictly seasonal population, if indeed there is one.

Most Attractive and Realistic Price for Recreational Property Purchase

Product	1995*	1999 Non-Owners Only*	1999 All Respondents**
$10,000 or less	10.3%	9.5%	9.6%
$10,001 to $25,000	20.8%	17.0%	16.5%
$25,001 to $50,000	29.2%	28.4%	26.8%
$50,001 to $100,000	27.0%	27.6%	28.6%
$100,001 to $150,000	8.7%	9.0%	9.8%
$151,000 to $200,000	2.7%	5.2%	5.0%
More than $200,000	1.4%	3.4%	3.7%
TOTAL	100.0%	100.0%	100.0%

Source: 1999 American Recreational Property Survey,
American Resort Development Association.

 * Excludes households who already own recreational property.
** Includes both households who already own and those who do not
  own recreational property.

Note: For those who cite a price of $25,000 or less, the primary recreational property types available in this price range are timeshares, campground memberships, and perhaps a few homesites or small acreages in less expensive areas.

Here are some papers you will need to put together before plunking down that For Sale sign. If some of them sound familiar, it is because they are also needed when selling a primary residence. They're included here so you will have a complete picture of a vacation-home sale.

- If you live in a community with an owners association, check the by-laws to see if there are any restrictions on your sale. Look through them, too, to inform yourself about the number of pets allowed, and whether an apartment can be rented and for how long. Many condos, for example, do not allow short-term rentals.

  Be sure to give a copy of your association's covenants to your real-estate agent so she can apprise prospects about what they can and cannot do there. Buyers should read those documents carefully before making an offer to buy.

- You will also want to read those documents for points that are likely to be of interest to a second-home buyer and that could advance your sale. For instance, does a dock slip at a nearby marina come with the sale? Do you have access to a free beach, where others are charged a daily or seasonal fee? Does your condo unit come with discounted ski lift tickets? Are they for prime winter weeks, or for secondary ones? Is there a lively social program in-season at your condo's clubhouse?

  Remember, anything happening socially in your community or in the entire town is going to be of interest to buyers who may not know your region well at all. Seeking out places of interest and looking to make friends can sometimes be difficult in a vacation community, since new residents may not know exactly what is going on, or what is happening that would be of particular interest to them.

- Do you plan to sell your place furnished or unfurnished? Country houses are usually sold unfurnished, while ski houses usually come with furnishings. Beach houses and condo apartments anywhere can go either way, furnished or not.

- Be sure to save any receipts for repairs or replacements you make while preparing the house to go on the market. You

might need them come tax time. In fact, to keep things straight, keep a separate "vacation-home" file, if you have not already done so, apart from the receipts, and so on, you keep for your primary residence.

Clever Marketing

Here is an idea that should help with selling your property, whether you do it yourself or engage a real-estate agent. (For complete information, see chapters 8 and 9 for the FSBO route and chapter 10 for the agent route.) Draw up a simple flier describing your house. You can do it either by hand or on a typewriter or computer. Use 8 1/2-by-11-inch paper or fold the paper in thirds to make it a brochure. You can add a copy of a photo of the place (photocopied) and call the brochure something like "What We've Particularly Enjoyed about Dune Beach."

The flier or brochure should give the address of the house, a map directing a house hunter to it if necessary, and a description of the house in terms of lot size, exterior, square footage, number of rooms and baths, and any other features likely to interest a buyer—a fireplace, perhaps, certainly a skylight, porch, garage, parking spaces, and the like. Add property taxes, too.

So far it sounds like the flier suggested in chapter 9 for selling your primary residence. But here is where it becomes different, and adds an element that is perhaps more important for this type of property. List any amenities that go with the house, like free admission to a nearby golf course, seasonal beach passes, and the like.

Then add a couple of paragraphs about the fun you have had in that house. Fun is, after all, what a vacation property is all about. You might write, "We're only ten minutes away from the Grand Island Hotel, which has concerts open to the public every Friday evening during the summer." And, "We've often taken guests to the River Run Inn for lunch or dinner. There are canoes for rent right at the inn. It's a casual restaurant, so you can stop there *after* canoeing if you like."

One or two paragraphs is enough. You just want to convey to prospective buyers that you have had good times while living in this

Before You Put Your Place on the Market

1. Make sure there is no damage to the exterior of your house due to wind, rain, sun, or storms. Repaint, or at least retouch, if needed.
2. Get papers together showing not just your home-owners insurance policy but also special coverages, such as flood, windstorm, hurricane, and so on. These will interest buyers *a lot*.
3. If you're selling your home furnished, replace worn or faded upholstery, toss pillows, and the like with fresher fabrics. Get rid of chipped dishes and burnt pots, too. Buyers *will* notice, and will base their offer accordingly.
4. If you are selling in-season while you are staying there, try to keep the place from looking like a horde of vacationers is staying there. Take drying bath towels off balcony railings and the tops of bushes, remove ski gear from the hallway, and try to hide any other evidence of your holiday that will get in the way of prospective buyers' getting a clean look at the house. (Yes, buyers will soon clutter up the place with their own things, but they don't want to see *your* clutter.)
5. When prospective buyers come to call, be sure cots and sleeping bags have been taken up. It's nice that your tiny condominium will sleep twelve, but you can *tell* that to buyers, not have them tripping over themselves and thinking how crowded the place is.
6. You really ought to read chapters 6 and 7, which offer suggestions for fixing up a principal residence for sale. Much of the same advice applies. And you thought you could get away with just this brief list of things to do!

house and are sure the new owners will, too—there is *so much* to do in the region!

Put your name and main home phone number on the back of the brochure. Make photocopies or run it off on your printer, leaving a batch on the kitchen counter when you leave to return to your primary home. Take some back with you, too. You can use them to do some marketing when you're back home (more about that later).

Do It Yourself or Use an Agent?

This is the question many primary-residence sellers must answer, and as a second-home owner you have that choice, too.

On Your Own

This can work if you live within a two-hour drive of your vacation home, and can show the property. It can also work if you live a greater distance away, but are able to leave the showing of the house in the hands of a capable friend, who will have answers ready for prospects and in general act as your "agent," although you will no doubt talk by phone with the eventual buyer. You will probably want to pay your friend a percentage of the sale price of the house, or perhaps a flat fee. Whatever that amount is, though, it is likely to be far less than a 6 percent commission. Do you know someone in your resort community who can act in that capacity for you?

You can advertise in the local newspaper there, referring prospects to you in your year-round home. You can also advertise in the newspaper of the largest city or cities near your principal residence. Advertise, too, in newsletters of organizations to which you belong, which can be as varied as religious groups, local charities, environmental clubs, alumni associations, and the like. Don't forget your office bulletin board (and any other bulletin board in an office you can gain access to). You can take your house sale online, too (see chapter 12). Keep photocopying your brochure as you run out of copies. Offer to send one to anyone who shows interest in your place.

If your home is especially distinctive and in a place virtually anyone would like (such as Hawaii, or Orlando, Florida), you might want to advertise in national publications such as *USA Today, The New York Times,* or *The Wall Street Journal.*

Don't spend too much time trying to sell the property yourself, however. You could waste an entire high season. Give it a six-week preseason and early high-season trial, and if you have no luck, and are eager to sell, then head for a real-estate office.

With an Agent

Working long distance with a real-estate agent is not that difficult in these days of telephone, pager, fax, and e-mail. The agent can contact you virtually anywhere in your year-round house area. You can expect to pay the usual residential commission of 6 percent, although, as you read in chapter 10, commissions are totally negotiable.

If you have been happy with a particular agency's renting your place for you over the years, that's a good segue into having them represent you for the house sale. If you have no realty contacts in the resort community, take a walk along the main street, where most agencies are likely to be located. Look in the windows, which usually carry photographs of properties for sale, with pertinent information, such as location, number of rooms, and price. Do you see any that look like your house? Pick up the local newspaper and check the real-estate display advertisements (the large ads with a box around them), as opposed to the classifieds. Who advertises? Interview a few of those agents following the suggestions given in chapter 10.

If you also want to do some advertising on your own in your primary home community, try for a clause in your contract that states that if you send a buyer to the agent because of your advertising or talking about the property, you pay a commission of less than 6 percent.

It would be wise not to dicker too much over this point, though, if you are in a hurry to sell. Human nature being what it is, agents are likely to work harder to sell properties bringing them as much commission as possible. You don't want your house to take a back seat to others.

You are in luck selling this type of property. Vacation homes have become very popular in recent years, as baby boomers move into and through their fifties, one of the most popular ages for buying these homes. You may have no trouble at all finding the right buyer for your getaway!

INFORMATION

You can sign over power of attorney to your real-estate agent to act in your stead at the closing of the sale. You usually do not need a lawyer here. Selling is less complex than buying, and you do not really have to go to your vacation-home locale for that transfer of property if you are not able to or do not choose to do so. A transfer of funds to your account at home can be done electronically.

CHAPTER TWENTY-FOUR

Selling a Resort Time-Share

INFORMATION

Florida has the most time-share resorts in this country: the Sunshine State boasts more than 230 of them. California comes in second with under 100, quite a drop from the first-place winner.

Sally and Howard Moore want to sell their time-share apartment because they are tired of going to Lake Serene every year. Or not going and feeling guilty about it.

David Russell inherited a time-share week, and said to himself, without even investigating his inheritance, "What do I want with this? I'll sell it."

Maybe you have a different reason. In any event, like Sally, Howard, and David, you have decided to become a former time-share owner.

How do you go about that?

That's a tough one. Let's start at the beginning. You need to follow the trail here to see why selling your time-share apartment is not the same as selling other recreation property. It's a lot harder.

What Time-Sharing Is—and Is Not

Here is what a time-share is not: It is not a real-estate investment. You are not building equity, and you are not very likely to make any money at all holding on to your purchase over the years. What you *are* doing is buying a week or two, or a month or even a season, of guaranteed vacation time in a particular spot for twenty-five or thirty years or the life of that resort.

There are two ways to buy a time-share: (1) fee simple ownership, which gives you a deed to your apartment or (2) a right-to-use lease, which is just that—the right to use Apartment 50 at Sunny Shores Resort and Golf Club for the first week in July for the length of that lease or for the duration of that resort.

There are some variations on that theme. Disney Vacation Clubs, for example, offers buyers purchase points rather than blocks of time. The points can be used at other Disney resorts or in trading around the world.

A vacation week can cost a buyer as little as $2,000 or less to as much as $25,000 in some glossy five-star resorts.

The Olden Days

Time-sharing as a vacation concept can be traced to Switzerland in the 1960s. It did *not* get off to a solid start in this country. By the 1970s, time-sharing, which is also known as interval ownership, had unfortunately developed a reputation for fly-by-night salespeople and shady practices. Naturally, not all developers were sleazy. Still, there were enough to cause would-be consumers to cringe at the word time-share. Shall we say, sales did not exactly soar.

By the late 1980s, however, there were signs of a change. Most states had laws regulating time-share sales more strictly. Then came the greatest seal of approval: big names in the hospitality industry and other well-known companies that were to become giants in the field, entered time-sharing. Complexes carrying the names of Marriott, Disney, Hyatt, and Hilton appeared on the scene. Now things were different. Consumer reservations were in great measure lifted. After all, if these folks were getting into time-sharing, well . . .

Today resorts run the gamut from those plush five-star complexes with hundreds of apartments to former motels of maybe fifty units or so that have been converted to time-shares.

The Difficulty in Selling

Time-share units can be hard to sell. In part, this is because there are always newer, flashier resorts being built to attract the time-share shopper. The competition is truly incredible.

Think of it this way. In 300-unit Sunny Shores Resort and Golf Club, for example, there can be not just 300 owners but *15,000*. That's if each apartment has 50 one-week owners (two weeks each year are usually kept open for repairs and remodeling). And if just one-quarter of those owners wants to sell, that's over 3,700 time-share units on the market *in just one resort in one town*. Where are the buyers going to come from for that many units? Many of those apartments will remain unsold for years and years.

Now consider that a builder decides to construct a new time-share resort just two miles from Sunny Shores. He's putting up 250 apartments in a resort he'll call The Captain's Club. That's several thousand more potential owners. Add that to Sunny Shores' would-be

INFORMATION

Marriott Vacation Club International is the world's largest time-share owner-ship company, with 41 resorts in 27 locations around the world.

sellers and you could have a flood of apartments for sale within two miles of each other. If Sunny Shores is eight years old, and The Captain's Club is brand-new, guess where most buyers will likely head? And guess who will have the power to do a mass-marketing campaign to get those apartments sold? If you said The Captain's Club's developer and not the individual Sunny Shores owners, you would be right.

Another reason some folks run into problems selling is that many sellers, because of competition and because of their wish to unload their apartments, sell their week at incredibly low prices, sometimes well under $2,000.

Reasons for Holding on to Your Time-Share

You have probably guessed the first reason to stay an owner: difficulty in selling. You might want to hang on to your apartment and save yourself time and effort and aggravation, especially since you may not get your dollar investment back. But there are other reasons you could decide to stay a time-share owner.

Trading

The Moores want to sell because they are tired of vacationing in the same place year after year, but they might not have to keep going back to Lake Serene. For those of you who feel the way they do, try trading. It might be possible to swap your annual week for one week every year in other resorts around the country and around the world.

To trade successfully, you need to own a week in a resort area that will interest the most time-share owners. For example, if your week is just outside the hamlet of Upper Succotash, and there is nothing much to do for miles around, you are likely to find it hard to swap. Similarly, you can only trade your time (high season, mid season or off season in that resort) for a similar season. So if you have a week in April in the mountains, you cannot trade that for the week between Christmas and New Year's in Hawaii. However, a week at Vail in February *could* swap for that week in Hawaii.

Joining an Exchange Company. It can pay you to look into trading. It is easier than selling, and can lead to some spiffy holidays. The largest company handling exchanges, arranging 1.8 million or so trades a year, is RCI, 3502 Woodview Trace, Indianapolis, IN 46268. To reach RCI, call (317) 876-1692 or visit www.rci.com.

RCI's fee is $84, which entitles you to place your property in their huge pool of time-shares belonging to RCI members. It also brings you their bimonthly glossy magazine, *Endless Vacation.* If RCI finds a spot for you in this country or in Canada, their fee is $118. International trades are $155.

If you think your week is not particularly desirable, you could be wrong. Many owners prefer to drive to their vacations these days, so you could be in luck. Also, some might want to visit family and friends in a hometown near your time-share resort, making your apartment a perfect base for them.

Once you join RCI, tell them where you would like to vacation and they can engineer a "search" for you to find what you want. You will have to pay the swap fee; but if the search doesn't generate the vacation you requested, your money will be refunded.

Successful swaps depend not only on the location of your resort and the time of year you own there, but also on your own flexibility and vacation habits. For example, if you live in the Midwest and wouldn't mind driving to Gatlinburg, Tennessee, for a May vacation, you will find a trade easier than if you want a week in the Caribbean in January.

Interval International (II) is another company that arranges swaps. While smaller than RCI, II has some 850,000 members (yes, some time-share owners belong to both companies). Interval International is located at 6262 Sunset Drive, Miami, FL 33143. Call (305) 666-1861, or visit www.intervalworld.com.

David Russell, who inherited his time-share, might enjoy different vacations, too. He could find swapping opens up new holiday opportunities.

Doing It Yourself. If you don't want to go through RCI or II, you can try to swap on your own. Running advertisements in newspapers where you live year-round could bring a nibble. So could advertising on office bulletin boards, in professional journals, and in local newsletters. You can also try the Internet.

You do not have to trade with a fellow time-share owner. Perhaps someone owning a house in a resort community will trade you one week in that house for a week at your time-share resort.

TIP

If you want to sell, and you are not in a particularly distinctive area, look around—dig around—for all the possible tourist and entertainment options within a fifty-mile radius. Collect brochures to show would-be buyers how they can enjoy a holiday at your community. You can get material from a regional Convention and Visitors Bureau or the state Department of Tourism.

In negotiating with a potential buyer who seems to prefer a brand-new complex to your "old" time-share, point out that if in July that buyer were to purchase one week in June at the new resort, there would likely be about fifty families who'd stayed there before him. So it's really like a resale by the time he gets there!

Renting

Here is another option for getting the most from your time-share. Your resort's administrative office *might* handle rentals, although you cannot rely on them to find you a vacationer. Usually there are too many owners who want to rent for the resort to keep everyone happy. Here, too, take the advice offered and work on your own.

Inquire at your resort's office what they are asking for a one-week rental. Either use that as a rate for renting it yourself, or come down a few dollars, explaining to prospects exactly how much lower your fee is than the resort's.

Your Estate File

Your time-share is part of your estate. You can leave it in your will to anyone you choose (unless you bought as joint tenants with right of survivorship, which means upon your death your share automatically reverts to the other joint tenant[s]). You might want to hold on to that resort week, and consider it one of your financial assets.

"No, No, I Really Want to Sell"

Okay, then let's concentrate on selling. You should know, however, that you are likely to get nowhere near what you paid for your unit. As you have been reading, some time-shares are sold for a song, and they may have been bought for $5,000, $7,000, or more. Your chances of getting at least a refund of your initial investment are best at top resorts, and in high season too, but even there you will usually be hoping for a figure that is at least close to what you paid—forget about a profit.

In a 1995 *New York Times* article, the director of resales for Marriott said that owners in Marriott time-share resorts "can probably expect to get 70 percent to 110 percent of what they paid for [their units.]" Overall, on average, sellers recoup 50 to 75 percent of their purchase price. That slight profit at Marriott and other five-star resorts comes, of course, with the very "hottest" vacation weeks.

You have several options for selling:

- You can ask if your time-share complex will sell your week for you. Some of the tonier resorts will. Keep in mind, if there are any units still unsold in that complex, they will try to sell them first. You will likely have to pay the resale office a fee as well.
- You can ask a real-estate agency in your resort town to handle a sale for you. Some do. Anyone who sells time-share weeks in any agency must hold a salesperson's or broker's real-estate license.

    You have read in other parts of this book that real-estate brokers' commissions can be negotiated. In a time-share sale, you might be charged a typical residential realty fee of 6 percent, but you could have to pay a good deal more. An agency may also charge you a flat fee, which could be as high as 50 percent of the price of your apartment when it sells!
- You can try to sell your unit by yourself, using the suggestions in this chapter for trading and renting. Try newspapers in large cities near you, and papers in that resort community, *advertising there in high season, no matter what week of the year you own.* That will bring you the highest number of potential buyers. Look into magazine advertising, too, especially city and regional publications. *Yankee* magazine, for example, which covers New England, runs classified advertisements for time-shares being sold by individual owners.
- The Web can help, too. There is a spot called Timeshare Users Group, or TUG. You can check them out at *www.time-shareusers-group.com.* TUG's members are time-share owners like you. The site offers an exchange of information, tips, and classified ads, such as time-share weeks for sale by member owners. TUG has some links to RCI, to Interval International, and to some of the major time-share resorts. There is a modest $15 membership fee, which can make selling your time-share particularly cost-effective.

TIP

You might tell an interested buyer looking at your resale that you can afford to sell cheaper than the developers of new resorts because you do not have the markup they do to cover their huge marketing expenses.

• • •

Most states offer a cooling-off period to allow time-share buyers to change their minds, even if they have signed a contract. That time can be three days or maybe as many as fifteen. Call the state's attorney general's office for information about this and any other information you should know about time-shares in your resort's state.

- The American Resort Development Association, the industry trade group, offers selling tips on its Web pages too. They are at www.arda.com. You can also reach the Washington, D.C.–based group at (202) 371-6700.
- *TimeSharing Today* is a bimonthly magazine ($18 for a two-year subscription; [888]TS-TODAY) that provides tips on selling, industry news, and reviews of new resorts. Its classified ads are also posted free on www.tstoday.com.

Is Financing Available?

Perhaps you have a buyer who can pay you $5,500 in cash for your one-week time-share apartment. Even if you are selling a $25,000 week, you might have a buyer who whips out a checkbook.

Financing is not that common. Time-share purchases that are leased time, rather than fee simple, are usually financed with a personal loan if the buyer does not hand over cash.

If your apartment is financed, you might ask your lender if the buyer can assume your loan. Some banks would rather do that than have sellers abandon their financial responsibility. Again, your competition here might be brand-new resorts, where developers are still selling vacation weeks and have probably arranged financing for individual buyers with their lender.

It is likely to take a little work on your part (maybe more than just a little). But if you explore all avenues of a sale, you are likely to find a buyer. Keep in mind, it may not be at the price you would like. But your time-share week or two will be sold!

Glossary

Abstract of title. A synopsis of the history of a title, indicating changes in ownership and including liens, mortgages, charges, encumbrances, encroachments, or any other matter that might affect the title.

Access. The means of approaching a property.

Acre. A measure of land. One acre equals 43,560 square feet or 208.71 feet on each side. A builder's acre is generally 200-by-200 feet.

Addendum. Something added. In real-estate contracts, a page added to the sales contract. It should be initialed by all parties concerned.

Agreement of sale. A written agreement by which a buyer agrees to buy and a seller agrees to sell a certain piece of property under the terms and conditions stated therein.

Amenities. Features of a property—pool, clubhouse, tennis courts, and the like—that make it more attractive to a buyer or renter.

Amortization. Prorated repayment of a debt. Most mortgages are being amortized every month that you make a payment to the lender.

Appraisal. Procedure employed by a disinterested professional to estimate the value of a piece of property.

Appurtenances. Whatever is annexed to land or used with it that will pass to the buyer with conveyance of title, for example, a garage.

As is. A term used in a contract to mean that the buyer is buying what he or she sees as he or she sees it. There is no representation as to quality and no promise to make any repairs.

Assessed valuation. An evaluation of property by an agency of the government for taxation purposes.

Assessment. Tax or charge levied on property by a taxing authority to pay for improvements such as sidewalks, streets, and sewers. Can also be a charge by an ownership community, such as a cooperative, to member residents.

Balloon mortgage. Short-term loan (five to seven years or so) where principal falls due at the end of that time. The home owner must pay in full or refinance.

Boilerplate. A standard contract form with blanks to be filled in by the party or parties signing.

Bona fide. In good faith, without deceit or deception.

Bridge loan. A loan of the equity you have accumulated in property you are selling. Many experienced sellers take out a bridge loan to facilitate a closing on a property they are buying before they close on the property they are selling.

Broom-clean condition. Everything must be removed from the premises and the dirt swept out; it does not mean washing the windows and walls.

Capital appreciation. The increase in market value for a property beyond the price you paid for it.

Capital gain. The portion of your taxable profit realized on the sale of real estate that is *not* taxed at your ordinary income tax rate.

Caravan. When four or five real-estate salespeople from one agency go in one car to see several open houses that have been scheduled for new listings.

Cash flow. The dollar income generated by a rental property after all expenses are met. Negative cash flow occurs when expenses generated by a property exceed its income.

Caveat emptor. A Latin phrase meaning "Let the buyer beware." Becoming out-of-date since the introduction of seller disclosure laws in most states.

Certified check. Payment that is guaranteed by the bank upon which it is drawn. A certified check is usually brought by a buyer to a closing to pay those costs.

Chattel. Items of personal property, such as furniture, appliances, and lighting fixtures that are not permanently affixed to the property being sold.

Closing. The meeting of all concerned parties in order to transfer title to a property.

Closing costs. Expenses over and above the price of the property that must be paid before title is transferred. Also known as *settlement costs.*

Cloud on the title. A defect in the title that may affect the owner's ability to market his or her property. That could be a lien, a claim, or a judgment.

Commission. Payment given by the seller of a property to a real-estate agent for his or her services. Usually paid at the closing.

Common facilities. Areas in a condominium, cooperative, mobile home park, apartment complex, or private home association shared by all residents. Examples include hallways, grounds, parking facilities, laundry room, swimming pool, and golf course.

Condominium. Housing style where the buyers own their apartment units outright, plus an undivided share in the common areas of the community.

Consideration. Anything of value but usually a sum of money. A contract to buy property must have a consideration in order to be binding.

Contingency. A provision in a contract that keeps it from becoming binding until certain activities are accomplished. The buyer's securing a satisfactory mortgage is often a contingency to a sale.

Contract. An agreement between two parties. To be valid, a real-estate contract must be dated, must be in writing, and must include a consideration, a description of the property, the place and date of delivery of the deed, and all terms and conditions that were mutually agreed on. It must also be executed (signed) by all concerned parties.

Convey. To transfer property from one person to another.

Conveyances. The document by which title is transferred. A deed is a conveyance.

Cooperative. A housing style where buyers purchase shares in the corporation that owns the building. The number of shares varies according to the size of the apartment being bought or sometimes its purchase price. Tenant-shareholders have a proprietary lease that gives them the right to their units.

Curb appeal. Used by real-estate agents to mean that the exterior of a house for sale (its facade, front lawn, and driveway) is so neat and attractive that would-be buyers who drive past want to make an appointment to see the inside.

Deed. A written instrument that conveys title to real property.

Depreciation. Gradual loss on paper in market value of real estate, especially because of age, obsolescence, wear and tear, or economic conditions.

Discount. See *Points*.

Discount broker. One who works for the seller at a fee lower than the traditional 6 percent, usually offering fewer services than the full-commission broker.

Down payment. An initial cash investment in purchasing real estate, usually a small percentage of the sale price.

Earnest money. Sum of money, as evidence of good faith, that accompanies a signed offer to purchase.

Easement. A right of way or access. The right of one party to cross or use for some specified purpose the property of another. Water, sewage, and utility suppliers frequently hold an easement across private property.

Eminent domain. The right by which a government may acquire private property for public use without the consent of the owner but upon payment of reasonable compensation.

Encroachment. A building or part of a building that extends beyond its boundary and therefore intrudes upon the property of another party.

Encumbrance. A right or restriction on a property that reduces its value. That might be a claim, lien, liability, or zoning restriction. The report of the title search usually shows all encumbrances.

Equity. The value an owner has in a piece of property exclusive of its mortgage and other liens.

Escrow. Money or documents held by a third party until specific conditions of an agreement or contract are fulfilled.

Escrow account. A trust into which escrow moneys are deposited and from which they are disbursed. Both lawyers and real-estate brokers can maintain escrow accounts.

Exclusive agent. A real-estate salesperson with the sole right to sell a property within a specified period of time. The property becomes an exclusive listing.

Fair market value. Generally accepted as the highest price that a ready, willing, and able buyer will pay and the lowest price a ready, willing, and able seller will accept for the property in question.

FHA. Federal Housing Administration, an agency within the U.S. Department of Housing and Urban Development that insures mortgages on residential property, with down-payment requirements usually lower than the prevailing ones on the open market.

Fixtures. Items of personal property that have been permanently attached to the real property and are therefore included in the transfer of real estate. For example, the kitchen sink is a fixture.

Floor time. The time that realty offices require their salespersons to be physically present in the office each week to answer phones and talk with walk-ins while other agents are out.

Foreclosure. Legal proceedings instigated by a lender to deprive a person of ownership rights when mortgage payments have not been held up.

FSBO. Pronounced "fizz-bo," it stands for for-sale-by-owner properties.

GI loan. See *VA loan*.

Home. As defined in *Merriam Webster's Collegiate Dictionary,* (1) one's place of residence; (2) the social unit formed by a family living together; (3) a familiar or usual setting; congenial environment; also the focus of one's domestic attention.

HUD. U.S. Department of Housing and Urban Development, from which almost all of the federal government's housing programs flow.

Interim financing. Another name for a *bridge loan.*

Joint tenancy (with right of survivorship). Property ownership by two or more persons with an undivided interest. If one owner dies, the property automatically passes to the other(s).

Key boxes. Another name for a lockbox.

Lease/purchase option. Opportunity to purchase a piece of property by renting it for a specified period, usually one year, with the provision that you may choose to buy after or during the leasing period at a predetermined sales price.

Leverage. The effective use of money to buy property by using the smallest amount of one's own capital that is permitted and borrowing as much as possible in order to obtain the maximum percentage of return on the original investment.

Liquidity. The speed at which an investment can be converted to cash. For example, there is little liquidity in a house, but shares of stock can ordinarily be sold quickly for cash.

Listing agent. The person who signs up the house to be marketed by his or her agency.

Lockbox. A metal device attached to a seller's door, containing a key to the house. Real-estate agents have keys to the lockbox so they can show the house if the seller is not home.

Market value. Generally accepted as the highest price that a ready, willing, and able buyer will pay and the lowest price a ready, willing, and able seller will accept for the property in question.

Maturity date. The date on which principal and interest on a mortgage or other loan must be paid in full.

Mortgage. A legal document that creates a lien upon a piece of property.

Mortgagee. The party or institution that lends the money.

Mortgagor. The party or person that borrows the money.

Multiple listing. An agreement that allows real-estate brokers to distribute information on the properties that they have listed for sale to other members of a local real-estate organization in order to provide the widest possible marketing of those properties. Commissions are split by mutual agreement between the listing broker and the selling broker.

Multiple listing service (MLS). The office that supervises the printing and distribution of listings shared by members of the local Board of Realtors.

Option. The exclusive right to purchase or lease a property at a stipulated price or rent within a specified period of time.

Plat book. Planning volume that shows location, size, and name(s) of owner(s) of every piece of land within a specific development or for an entire neighborhood or town.

Points. Sometimes called *discount*. A fee that a lending institution charges for granting a mortgage. One point is 1 percent of the face value of the loan.

Power of attorney. Instrument in writing that gives one person the right to act as agent for another in signing papers, deeds, and so on.

Preapproved. Being preapproved for a loan means the house hunter has gone through the mortgage application process, and the lender guarantees to lend that buyer X amount of dollars for a home loan within a certain time frame. All that is needed to complete the granting of the mortgage is the address of the house and an appraisal by the lender.

Preinspection. A real-estate agent's personal look at your house, before he or she brings around prospective buyers.

Prepayment. Paying back of a loan before it has reached its maturity date.

Prequalified. Being prequalified for a loan means that a mortgage lender has told you, based on the information you give him or her about your finances, how much house you can afford to buy.

Principal. The amount of money borrowed; the amount of money still owed.

Private mortgage insurance (PMI). A premium charged some home buyers who make a down payment of less than 10 percent. It is offered by a number of insurance companies around the country and costs a few hundred dollars a year.

Probate. A state court procedure that administers the estate of a deceased resident, whether that individual died with a will or without one.

Probate court. The state court in which probate is administered.

Real-estate broker. A man or woman who has passed a state broker's test and represents others in realty transactions. Anyone having his or her own office must be a broker.

Real-estate salesperson. A man or woman who has passed a state examination for that position and who must work under the supervision of a broker. Often called an *agent*.

Real property. Land and buildings and anything permanently attached to them. Houses and condominiums are real property; cooperative apartments are personal property.

Realtor. A real-estate broker who is a member of the National Association of Realtors, a professional group. Not everyone who sells real estate is a Realtor. The word is a registered trademark and is capitalized.

Redlining. Alleged practice of some lending institutions involving their refusal to make loans on properties they deem to be bad risks, sometimes entire blocks or neighborhoods.

Refinance. To pay off one loan by taking out another on the same property.

Rent control. Regulation by a local government agency of rental charges, usually according to set formulas for increase.

Right of survivorship. Granted to two joint owners who purchase property under that buying style. Stipulates that one gets full rights and becomes sole owner of the property on the death of the other. Right of survivorship is the basic difference between buying property as joint tenants and as tenants in common.

Riparian rights. The right of a property owner whose land abuts a body of water to swim in that water, build a wharf, and so on.

Second mortgage. A lien on a property that is subordinate to a first mortgage. In the event of default, the second mortgage is repaid after the first. Some second mortgages are home equity loans.

Selling agent. The agent who actually brings a buyer for the house.

Settlement costs. See *Closing costs*.

Specific performance. A court order that states that the agreements of a contract must be enacted.

Square foot. Used to measure buildings in realty transactions. For example, if a two-story house has dimensions of 30 feet by 30 feet, the area is 900 square feet on each floor, for a total of 1,800 square feet.

Subletting. A leasing of property by one tenant from another tenant, the one who holds the lease.

Sump pump. An automatic water pump set into the basement floor to prevent groundwater from seeping into the basement.

Tax shelter. A realty investment that produces income tax deductions.

Tenancy in common. Style of ownership in which two or more persons purchase a property jointly but with no right of survivorship. Owners are free to will their share to anyone they choose, a principal difference between that form of ownership and joint tenancy.

Tenants. As used in the ownership styles discussed in inheriting a property, the term means owners, not renters. More commonly, *tenants* refer to those who lease real property.

Title. Actual ownership; the right of possession; evidence of ownership.

Title insurance. An insurance policy that protects against any losses incurred because of defective title.

Title search. A professional examination of public records to determine the chain of ownership of a particular piece of property, noting any liens, mortgages, encumbrances, easements, restrictions, or other factors that might affect the title.

Townhome. A (usually) two-story living unit often operating under the condominium form of ownership.

Trust deed. An instrument used in place of a mortgage in certain states; a third party trustee, not the lender, holds the title to the property until the loan is paid out or defaulted.

Usury. Charging a higher rate of interest on a loan than is legally allowed.

VA loan. Mortgage backed by the Veterans Administration. Sometimes referred to as a *GI loan*.

Variance. An exception to a zoning ordinance granted to meet certain specified needs.

Void. Canceled; not legally enforceable.

Waiver. Renunciation, disclaiming, or surrender of some claim, right, or prerogative.

Zoning. Procedure that classifies real property for a number of different uses—residential, commercial, industrial, and so forth—in accordance with a land-use plan. Ordinances are enforced by a governing body or locality.

Index

A

abstract, 52, 53
addendum, 182, 183
advertising, 98–100, 243–44, 273, 274
    writing the ad, 99–100
agents, real-estate, 7–10, 83–87, 105,
    108–24, 110–11.
appraisal, 44, 192
asbestos, 128–29
assessments, 41–42, 53
attorney, 182, 184, 185, 189, 190
attorney fees, 50, 54
auctions, 160, 252–54
authority to sell, 252

B

best time to sell, 26–35
    home-selling calendar, 27–32
    local economy, 33–35
    national economy, 32–33
    time factors, 26–27
binder, 182, 184, 190
boilerplate contract, 179
bridge loan, 212–13
brokers, 110
    discount, 114
    real-estate, 110
broom-clean condition, 186
building a house, 206–7
buyer information, 165
buyer statistics, 109
buyer turnoffs, 64
buyers and sellers, 8

C

calendar, home-selling, 27–32
CC&Rs, 124
clauses, 187–90
    disclosure, 189
    professional house-inspection, 188
    termite inspection, 187–88
    walk-through, 189–90
    withdrawal, 121–22
closing, 192–99
    appraisal, 192
    contract contingencies, 193
    costs, 50–55
    documents to sign, 196–97
    escrow, 194–95
    occupancy, 215–16
    taking house off market, 193–94
    taxes after the sale, 199
    time required, 206
    tips, 195
    transfer of title, 195

walk-aways, 194–95
commission, 55, 114, 120, 167, 187
comparing home sales, 47
condominium sale, 238–45
    advertising, 243–44
    board of directors, 238, 243, 245
    buyer approval, 245
    disclosure, 240–41
    discrimination, 245
    dues, 244
    improvements, 238, 239, 243
    inspection, 241
    preparing for market, 241–42
    questions from buyers, 239
    renting to tenants, 240
    for sale sign, 243–44
contracts, 182–90
    addendum, 182, 183
    attorney, 182, 184, 185, 189, 190
    binder, 182, 184, 190
    boilerplate, 179
    canceling, 121
    choosing, 119
    clauses, 187–90
    contingencies, 185–86, 193
    disclosure clause, 189
    escrow, 182, 184
    exclusive agency, 119
    exclusive right to sell, 119
    expiration date, 120
    legal description, 184
    listing, 118–20
    mortgage contingency clause, 185–86
    open listing, 119
    points covered, 184–87
    professional house-inspection clause, 188
    reading, 190
    repairs, 188–89
    sales, 122, 182–90.
    termite inspection clause, 187–88
    walk-through clause, 189–90
    withdrawal clause, 121–22
curb appeal, 58–63. *See also* home
    improvements; repairs
    garage, 61
    improvements, 58–63
    landscaping, 60–61

D

Department of Veterans Affairs, 53
disclosure, 126–32, 240–41
    clause, 189
    concerns, 129–32
    fixer-uppers, 132

forms, 126–27
Disclosure of Property Condition form,
    126–27
documents, 123, 196–97
    at closing, 196–97
    for estate sales, 249
    to show buyers, 123
    for vacation home, 261–64

E

earnest money, 120, 182
economy, 32–35
empty nest, 208, 210
escrow, 182, 184, 194–95
estate sales, 248–56
    auctions, 252–54
    authority to sell, 252
    beneficiary, 252
    documents, 249
    executor for estate, 252
    fee-simple title, 255
    heirs, 250, 252
    intestate, 252
    joint tenants, 256
    keeping the home, 255–56
    negotiating, 250–51
    probate, 252, 253
    probate court, 253
    renting to tenants, 254–55
    tenancy by the entirety, 256
    tenants in common, 256
    testate, 252
    tips, 250, 252
    wills, 252
exclusive-agency contract, 119
exclusive-right-to-sell contract, 119
executor for estate, 252
expenses when selling, 50–55

F

fair housing law, 118
Federal Housing Administration, 53
    loan approval, 209
    loans, 193
fee-simple title, 255
fees, 50–56
    abstract, 52
    assessments, 41–42, 53
    attorney, 50
    house inspection, 65–66
    liens, 53
    mortgage cancellation, 53
    points, 52–53
    prepayment penalty, 53, 56
    property taxes, 53

real-estate broker's commission, 55
recording, 50
survey, 52
and taxes, 50
title search and insurance, 52
transfer tax, 50
utility, 54
financing, 158, 213, 276
fix-up house, 71–79. *See also* home
improvements; repairs
checklist, 72–73
tips, 70–79
for sale by owner (FSBO), 82–87
advertising, 98–100
assistance, 87
community services, 94–95
contacting real-estate agents, 105
guidelines, 83–87
listing sheet, 90–92
negotiating, 104–5
offers, 98
phone calls, 100–102
prequalifying buyers, 95–96, 98
real-estate agents, 83–87
showing the property, 102–4
ten must-dos, 90–105
through the Internet, 134–35
tips, 92–94, 98–101
transaction duties, 97
for sale sign, 140–41, 243–44

G, H
guaranteed sale, 218
heirs, 250, 252
home, defined, 8
home improvements, 58–68. *See also*
curb appeal; repairs
basement, 61–62
garage, 61
landscaping, 60–61
minor repairs, 70–79
termites, 62–63
Home Owners Warranty, 68
house inspection, 65–68, 192–93
clause, 188
fees, 65–66
repairs, 188–89
house inspectors, 65–66, 192
American Society of Home
Inspectors (ASHI), 66
house, not selling
auctions, 160
buyers' comments, 152–54
lease/purchase option, 156–57

local marketplace, 155
priced too high, 154–55
seller financing, 158
suggestions, 155–60
tactics, 159
tight money market, 155

I, J
inheriting a home, 248–56. *See also*
estate sales
interim financing, 213
intestate, 252
joint tenants/right of survivorship, 256
judgment of specific performance, 214

K, L
keybox. *See* lockbox
keys, 124. *See also* lockbox
kids, preparing for sale, 148–50
laws
fair housing, 118
real-estate, 94
lead, 126–28
Lead-Based Paint Disclosure form, 126–27
lease/purchase option, 131, 156–57
legal costs, 50–52
legal counsel, 54
legal description, 184
liens, 53
listing agent, 111
listing contract, 118–20
listing sheet, 90–92
items included, 90–92, 122–24
photos, 124
preparing, 122–24
loans, 193, 209
bridge, 212–13
mortgage, 192–93
prequalifying buyers, 95–96, 98
lockbox, 124, 139–40

M
market knowledge (quiz), 5
marketplace, 32–35, 44–46, 155, 259
memorandum of sale, 182
Model Home Sales Contract, 99
months for selling, 27–32
mortgage, balance due, 53
mortgage cancellation fee, 53
mortgage contingency clause, 185–86
mortgage insurance, 185
mortgage loan, 192–93
motivation for selling, 12–24
company transfer, 13–14

death, 24
divorce, 19–20
house purchase, 15–19
protection of investment, 20–24
worksheet, 21
movers, 230, 234
liability, 230
regulations, 231
moving. *See* successful move
moving expenses, 55
multiple listing service (MLS), 112, 119

N, O
negotiating estate sales, 250–51
negotiating failures, 169
negotiating scenarios, 162–79
net profit, 55, 167
occupancy after closing, 215–16
occupancy before closing, 215
offers, 98, 163, 182, 184
being prepared for, 98
on-the-market time, 138–50
last-minute preparations, 146
lockbox, 139–40
no-shows, 145, 147
open house, 141–43
pets during showings, 148–50
preparing kids, 148–50
for sale sign, 140–41
telephone calls, 144–45
valuables, 143
open house, 141–43
protecting property, 143
public open house, 142–43
Realtors' open house, 141–42
open-listing contract, 119
owner financing, 158

P
packing tips, 226.
pets during showings, 148–50
points, 52–53
preapproval, 192
preinspection, 31
prepayment penalty, 53, 56
prequalified, 96
prequalifying buyers, 95–96, 98
prices. *See* sales price, setting
private mortgage insurance (PMI), 185
probate, 252, 253
probate court, 253
profit, 50–56
after sale, 55–56
calculating worksheet, 51

expenses, 50–55
selling price, 55–56
property taxes, 53

R
radon, 128
real-estate agencies, 111–13
choosing, 111
franchises, 112
real-estate agents, 7–10
finding, 115
interviewing, 116–18
and real-estate brokers, 110–11
working with, 83–87, 108–24
real-estate brokers, 110
discount brokers, 114
real-estate law, 194
real-estate transfer tax, 50
Realtor, defined, 110
Realtor.com, 134
realty transaction, 97
reasons for selling, 12–24
recording fee, 50
relocating, 202–4, 231
relocation companies, 231, 234
renting to tenants, 216–18
repairs, 70–79, 188–89

S
safe switch, 207–8
sale, quick, 209
sales, affected by seasons, 27–32
sales contracts, 182–90
additions, 187–90
sales price, setting, 38–48
comparative market analysis, 44–46
comparison shopping, 43–44
competing real-estate agencies, 46–48
professional appraisal, 44
replacement cost, 42–43
sales comparisons (worksheet), 47
tax assessments, 41–42
sell/buy difficulties, 202–10.
divorce, 210
empty nest, 208, 209
quick sale, 209
safe switch, 207–8
when building a house, 206–7
when changing jobs, 204–5
when stepping up, 205–6
when transferring, 202–4
worksheets, 203
sell/buy solutions, 212–21.
bridge loan, 212–13

decorating, 219–20
guaranteed sale, 218
interim financing, 213
judgment of performance, 214
occupancy after closing, 215–16
occupancy before closing, 215
renting to tenants, 216–18
seller defaulting, 214
suspension of payments, 216
time is of the essence, 213–15
vacant house, 218–21
seller defaulting, 214
seller financing, 158
selling, 7–10
best time for, 26–35
motivation for, 12–24
by owner, 82–87.
selling a condominium, 238–45.
selling a second home, 258–67.
selling a time-share, 270–76.
selling a vacation home, 258–67.
selling an estate, 248–56.
sellingand the Internet, 136
for sale by owner, 134–35
tips, 136
working with an agent, 135
specific performance, 194
successful move, 202–4, 224–34
to new community, 224–25
organizing, 224–28
packing tips, 226, 232
relocating, 231
relocation companies, 231, 234
selecting a mover, 228–31
settling in, 233
steps to take, 224–31
timing, 230
truck rental costs, 228–29
survey, 52

T
taxes, 50, 187
after the sale, 199
assessments, 41–42
property, 53
transfer, 50
telephone calls, 144–45
tenancy by the entirety, 256
tenants, defined, 255
tenants in common, 256
termite inspection, 187–88
clause, 187–88
termites, 62–63
testate, 252

time is of the essence, 213–15
time-share, renting, 274
time-share, selling, 270–76
advertising, 273, 275
American Resort Dev. Assn, 276
difficulty in selling, 271–72
estate, 274
exchange companies, 272–73
fee-simple ownership, 270
financing, 276
negotiating, 274
options, 274–76
real-estate agency, 275
renting, 274
right-to-use lease, 270
Timeshare Users Group, 275
trading, 271–74
title search and insurance, 52
title, transfer of, 50, 195
transfers, job, 202–4, 231

U, V
utility fees, 54
vacant house, 218–21
maintenance, 220–21
showings, 221
vacation homes, selling, 258–67
affected by seasons, 260–61
amenities, 263, 264
best time to sell, 260–61
documents needed, 261–64
marketing, 264–66
preferred resort areas, 260–61
preparing for market, 265
prices, 262
restrictions, 263
staying current with marketplace, 259
using an agent, 267
on your own, 266–67
Veterans Administration (VA)
loans, 193, 209

W
walk-through clause, 189–90
wills, 252
withdrawal clause, 121–22
worksheets
buyers' comments, 153
calculating net profit, 51
fix-up checklist, 72–73
motivation for selling, 21
sales comparisons, 47
sell/buy difficulties, 203

THE EVERYTHING. HOMEBUYING BOOK 2ND EDITION

By Ruth Rejnis

Finding and buying a home you'll love can be easy This fully updated edition of *The Everything® Homebuying Book, 2nd Edition* walks prospective buyers completely through the process, from open house to closing the deal. This book details the exact steps you need to follow, including qualifying for a mortgage, dealing with brokers, negotiating the best deal possible, and much more!

Trade paperback,
$14.95 ($22.95 CAN)
1-58062-809-5, 352 pages

OTHER *EVERYTHING®* BOOKS BY ADAMS MEDIA CORPORATION

BUSINESS

Everything® **Business Planning Book**
Everything® **Coaching & Mentoring Book**
Everything® **Home-Based Business Book**
Everything® **Leadership Book**
Everything® **Managing People Book**
Everything® **Network Marketing Book**
Everything® **Online Business Book**
Everything® **Project Management Book**
Everything® **Selling Book**
Everything® **Start Your Own Business Book**
Everything® **Time Management Book**

COMPUTERS

Everything® **Build Your Own Home Page Book**
Everything® **Computer Book**

Everything® **Internet Book**
Everything® **Microsoft® Word 2000 Book**

COOKING

Everything® **Bartender's Book, $9.95**
Everything® **Barbecue Cookbook**
Everything® **Chocolate Cookbook**
Everything® **Cookbook**
Everything® **Dessert Cookbook**
Everything® **Diabetes Cookbook**
Everything® **Low-Carb Cookbook**
Everything® **Low-Fat High-Flavor Cookbook**
Everything® **Mediterranean Cookbook**
Everything® **One-Pot Cookbook**
Everything® **Pasta Book**
Everything® **Quick Meals Cookbook**
Everything® **Slow Cooker Cookbook**

Everything® **Soup Cookbook**
Everything® **Thai Cookbook**
Everything® **Vegetarian Cookbook**
Everything® **Wine Book**

HEALTH

Everything® **Anti-Aging Book**
Everything® **Dieting Book**
Everything® **Herbal Remedies Book**
Everything® **Hypnosis Book**
Everything® **Menopause Book**
Everything® **Stress Management Book**
Everything® **Vitamins, Minerals, and Nutritional Supplements Book**
Everything® **Nutrition Book**

HISTORY

Everything® **American History Book**

All Everything® books are priced at $12.95 or $14.95, unless otherwise stated. Prices subject to change without notice.
Canadian prices range from $11.95–$22.95 and are subject to change without notice.

Everything® **Civil War Book**
Everything® **World War II Book**

HOBBIES

Everything® **Bridge Book**
Everything® **Candlemaking Book**
Everything® **Casino Gambling Book**
Everything® **Chess Basics Book**
Everything® **Collectibles Book**
Everything® **Crossword and Puzzle Book**
Everything® **Digital Photography Book**
Everything® **Drums Book (with CD),**
    $19.95, ($31.95 CAN)
Everything® **Family Tree Book**
Everything® **Games Book**
Everything® **Guitar Book**
Everything® **Knitting Book**
Everything® **Magic Book**
Everything® **Motorcycle Book**
Everything® **Online Genealogy Book**
Everything® **Playing Piano and**
    Keyboards Book
Everything® **Rock & Blues Guitar**
    Book (with CD), $19.95,
    ($31.95 CAN)
Everything® **Scrapbooking Book**

HOME IMPROVEMENT

Everything® **Feng Shui Book**
Everything® **Gardening Book**
Everything® **Home Decorating Book**
Everything® **Landscaping Book**
Everything® **Lawn Care Book**
Everything® **Organize Your Home Book**

KIDS' STORY BOOKS

Everything® **Bedtime Story Book**
Everything® **Bible Stories Book**
Everything® **Fairy Tales Book**
Everything® **Mother Goose Book**

NEW AGE

Everything® **Astrology Book**

Everything® **Divining the Future Book**
Everything® **Dreams Book**
Everything® **Ghost Book**
Everything® **Meditation Book**
Everything® **Numerology Book**
Everything® **Palmistry Book**
Everything® **Spells and Charms Book**
Everything® **Tarot Book**
Everything® **Wicca and Witchcraft Book**

PARENTING

Everything® **Baby Names Book**
Everything® **Baby Shower Book**
Everything® **Baby's First Food Book**
Everything® **Baby's First Year Book**
Everything® **Breastfeeding Book**
Everything® **Get Ready for Baby Book**
Everything® **Homeschooling Book**
Everything® **Potty Training Book,**
    $9.95, ($15.95 CAN)
Everything® **Pregnancy Book**
Everything® **Pregnancy Organizer,**
    $15.00, ($22.95 CAN)
Everything® **Toddler Book**
Everything® **Tween Book**

PERSONAL FINANCE

Everything® **Budgeting Book**
Everything® **Get Out of Debt Book**
Everything® **Get Rich Book**
Everything® **Investing Book**
Everything® **Homebuying Book, 2nd Ed.**
Everything® **Homeselling Book**
Everything® **Money Book**
Everything® **Mutual Funds Book**
Everything® **Online Investing Book**
Everything® **Personal Finance Book**

PETS

Everything® **Cat Book**
Everything® **Dog Book**
Everything® **Dog Training and Tricks**
Everything® **Horse Book**
Everything® **Puppy Book**
Everything® **Tropical Fish Book**

REFERENCE

Everything® **Astronomy Book**
Everything® **Car Care Book**
Everything® **Christmas Book, $15.00,**
    ($21.95 CAN)
Everything® **Classical Mythology Book**
Everything® **Divorce Book**
Everything® **Etiquette Book**
Everything® **Great Thinkers Book**
Everything® **Learning French Book**
Everything® **Learning German Book**
Everything® **Learning Italian Book**
Everything® **Learning Latin Book**
Everything® **Learning Spanish Book**
Everything® **Mafia Book**
Everything® **Philosophy Book**
Everything® **Shakespeare Book**
Everything® **Tall Tales, Legends, &**
    Other Outrageous Lies Book
Everything® **Toasts Book**
Everything® **Trivia Book**
Everything® **Weather Book**
Everything® **Wills & Estate Planning**
    Book

RELIGION

Everything® **Angels Book**
Everything® **Buddhism Book**
Everything® **Catholicism Book**
Everything® **Judaism Book**
Everything® **Saints Book**
Everything® **World's Religions Book**
Everything® **Understanding Islam Book**

SCHOOL & CAREERS

Everything® **After College Book**
Everything® **College Survival Book**
Everything® **Cover Letter Book**
Everything® **Get-a-Job Book**
Everything® **Hot Careers Book**
Everything® **Job Interview Book**
Everything® **Online Job Search Book**
Everything® **Resume Book, 2nd Ed.**
Everything® **Study Book**

All Everything® books are priced at $12.95 or $14.95, unless otherwise stated. Prices subject to change without notice.
Canadian prices range from $11.95–$22.95 and are subject to change without notice.

WE HAVE EVERYTHING . . . .

SPORTS/FITNESS

Everything® **Bicycle Book**
Everything® **Fishing Book**
Everything® **Fly-Fishing Book**
Everything® **Golf Book**
Everything® **Golf Instruction Book**
Everything® **Pilates Book**
Everything® **Running Book**
Everything® **Sailing Book, 2nd Ed.**
Everything® **T'ai Chi and QiGong Book**
Everything® **Total Fitness Book**
Everything® **Weight Training Book**
Everything® **Yoga Book**

TRAVEL

Everything® **Guide to Las Vegas**
Everything® **Guide to New England**
Everything® **Guide to New York City**
Everything® **Guide to Washington D.C.**

Everything® **Travel Guide to The Disneyland Resort®, California Adventure®, Universal Studios®, and the Anaheim Area**
Everything® **Travel Guide to the Walt Disney World® Resort, Universal Studios®, and Greater Orlando, 3rd Ed.**

WEDDINGS & ROMANCE

Everything® **Creative Wedding Ideas Book**
Everything® **Dating Book**
Everything® **Jewish Wedding Book**
Everything® **Romance Book**
Everything® **Wedding Book, 2nd Ed.**
Everything® **Wedding Organizer, $15.00 ($22.95 CAN)**

Everything® **Wedding Checklist, $7.95 ($11.95 CAN)**
Everything® **Wedding Etiquette Book, $7.95 ($11.95 CAN)**
Everything® **Wedding Shower Book, $7.95 ($12.95 CAN)**
Everything® **Wedding Vows Book, $7.95 ($11.95 CAN)**
Everything® **Weddings on a Budget Book, $9.95 ($15.95 CAN)**

WRITING

Everything® **Creative Writing Book**
Everything® **Get Published Book**
Everything® **Grammar and Style Book**
Everything® **Grant Writing Book**
Everything® **Guide to Writing Children's Books**
Everything® **Writing Well Book**

ALSO AVAILABLE:

THE EVERYTHING®  KIDS' SERIES!

Each book is 8" x 91/4", 144 pages, and two-color throughout.

Everything® **Kids' Baseball Book, 2nd Edition, $6.95** ($11.95 CAN)
Everything® **Kids' Bugs Book, $6.95** ($10.95 CAN)
Everything® **Kids' Cookbook, $6.95** ($10.95 CAN)
Everything® **Kids' Joke Book, $6.95** ($10.95 CAN)
Everything® **Kids' Math Puzzles Book, $6.95** ($10.95 CAN)
Everything® **Kids' Mazes Book, $6.95** ($10.95 CAN)
Everything® **Kids' Money Book, $6.95** ($11.95 CAN)

Everything® **Kids' Monsters Book, $6.95** ($10.95 CAN)
Everything® **Kids' Nature Book, $6.95** ($11.95 CAN)
Everything® **Kids' Puzzle Book $6.95,** ($10.95 CAN)
Everything® **Kids' Science Experiments Book, $6.95** ($10.95 CAN)
Everything® **Kids' Soccer Book, $6.95** ($11.95 CAN)
Everything® **Kids' Travel Activity Book, $6.95** ($10.95 CAN)

Available wherever books are sold!
To order, call 800-872-5627, or visit us at everything.com

Everything® is a registered trademark of Adams Media Corporation.